'Epic, from lights out to chequered flag.'

Steve Jones, Channel 4 F1 presenter

'*Grid to Glory* is an engaging and absorbing behind-the-scenes pass to the key moments in the sport's illustrious history.'

Lawrence Barretto, Channel 4 F1 commentator

'Taking you behind the scenes of F1's rich history – a must-read.'

Lee McKenzie, Channel 4 F1 presenter

'With the same flair he brings to the commentary box, Alex Jacques turns F1's history into a fast-flowing, edge-of-your-seat read. *Grid to Glory* doesn't just tell the story – it races through it. Every racing fan needs this on their shelf.'

Nate Saunders, journalist for ESPN

'One of the most dynamic and lively characters of the motorsport paddocks and a true Formula One fan. Alex dedicates his life to the sport and the job and that not only comes across in his commentary but also in this wonderful book.'

Alice Powell, British racing driver

'If you like what Alex Jacques does with a microphone, you're going to absolutely love what he does with a pen. Using his trademark eloquence and humour, Alex has managed to boil down 75 years of the rich history of Formula One into these key moments. From personalities to technologies, politicians to playboys, he tells nearly every must-know story for any F1 fan with enough depth that even seasoned fans will learn plenty.'

James Hinchcliffe, racing driver and commentator for FOX Sports

'Who better than Alex Jacques, the voice of F1, to guide you through the most sensational, controversial, tragic and significant moments of our beloved sport. From the creation of the World Championship to *Drive to Survive* and Abu Dhabi 2021, his passion, commitment and knowledge makes his brilliant debut book a joy to read. Enjoy this magnificent journey through 75 years of Formula One.'

Laura Winter, F1TV broadcaster

'In his inimitable style, Alex delves into the rich history of Formula One to explore carefully and expertly the championship's 75 best races, as F1 commemorates the landmark anniversary – a must-read for connoisseurs of a well-loved sport.'

Phillip Horton, journalist for *Autoweek* and *The New York Times*

GRID TO GLORY

75 MILESTONE FORMULA ONE MOMENTS

Alex Jacques

Michael O'Mara Books Limited

First published in Great Britain in 2025 by
Michael O'Mara Books Limited
9 Lion Yard
Tremadoc Road
London SW4 7NQ

EU representative:
Authorised Rep Compliance Ltd
Ground Floor
71 Baggot Street Lower
Dublin D02 P593, Ireland

Copyright © Alex Jacques 2025

All rights reserved. You may not copy, store, distribute, transmit, reproduce or otherwise make available this publication (or any part of it) in any form, or by any means (electronic, digital, optical, mechanical, photocopying, recording, machine readable, text/data mining or otherwise), without the prior written permission of the publisher. Any person who does any unauthorized act in relation to this publication may be liable to criminal prosecution and civil claims for damages.

A CIP catalogue record for this book is available from the British Library.

This product is made of material from well-managed, FSC®-certified forests and other controlled sources. The manufacturing processes conform to the environmental regulations of the country of origin.

For further information see www.mombooks.com/about/sustainability-climate-focus
Report any safety issues to product.safety@mombooks.com and see www.mombooks.com/contact/product-safety

UK editions:
ISBN: 978-1-78929-768-3 in hardback print format
ISBN: 978-1-78929-781-2 in trade paperback print format
ISBN: 978-1-78929-769-0 in ebook format

US editions:
ISBN: 978-1-78929-802-4 in paperback print format
ISBN: 978-1-78929-815-4 in ebook format

1 2 3 4 5 6 7 8 9 10

Cover design: Ana Bjezancevic
Front cover photographs: Top: David Phipps/Sutton Images/Getty Images (Niki Lauda); bottom: Giuseppe Cacace/AFP via Getty Images (Lando Norris)
Back cover photographs: Top left: Sutton Motorsports/ZUMA Press/Alamy Stock Photo (Damon Hill); top right: Song Haiyuan/Paddocker/Alamy Stock Photo (Max Verstappen); bottom: Steven Tee/LAT Images/Getty Images (Ferrari)

Designed and typeset by Claire Cater and Natasha Le Coultre

Printed and bound by CPI Group (UK) Ltd, Croydon, CR0 4YY

www.mombooks.com

Contents

Foreword by David Coulthard — 9
Preface: The Start of My Fascination with Formula One — 11

1. The Creation of the World Championship — 12
2. Jack Brabham – the Australian Legend Who Almost Missed Out — 15
3. Bernie Ecclestone – The Journey to Control F1 — 18
4. Murray Walker Defines Modern Sports Commentary — 22
5. Enzo Ferrari Sends Stirling Moss Home — 26
6. The Creation of the Constructors' Championship — 29
7. Stirling and Alf Change the Game — 34
8. Stirling Moss, the Gentleman Racer — 37
9. The Great Fangio Gets Kidnapped — 39
10. Jackie Stewart Stares at Death — 41
11. The Original Hollywood Fight to Take Racing to the Big Screen — 44
12. Cosworth DFV Engine – A British Engineering Achievement Worth Celebrating — 48
13. The Making of Colin Chapman — 52
14. Jim Clark's Death – It Could Happen to Anybody — 56
15. Colin Chapman – After Jim — 60
16. The Ad Men Arrive — 64
17. March Burst on to the Scene and Win — 67
18. Ron Dennis Crashes Through his Windscreen — 71
19. The Used-Car Deal that Gave Hunt a Shot — 76
20. Slowing Down F1 – Introducing the Safety Car — 81
21. Project 34 – The Legendary Six-Wheeler — 84
22. Lella Lombardi Makes Her Point — 88
23. Niki Lauda Chooses to Drive — 91
24. Niki Lauda Chooses to Stop — 97

25	The Yellow Teapot – Renault Build a Turbo Engine	102
26	Sid Watkins – Bringing Safety to Formula One	106
27	The Brabham Fan Car	111
28	John Barnard's Carbon-Fibre Car	115
29	Ferrari's Villeneuve and Pironi – A Racing Tragedy	119
30	The Strike	125
31	Adrian Newey Makes His First Mark in F1	129
32	Ginny Williams Refuses to Let Her Husband Die	134
33	Mansell's Tyre Bursts to Break a Generation's Heart	140
34	Prost vs Senna, Part One – Japan 1989	145
35	Prost vs Senna, Part Two – Japan 1990	150
36	Jean Alesi's Sliding Door	153
37	Bertrand Gachot Is Late for Dinner	157
38	The Battle for Schumacher's First Full-Time F1 Contract	160
39	Senna's Lap of the Gods	163
40	The Death of Ayrton Senna	167
41	Schumacher's Dark Arts	173
42	Awards and Rewards – Three Defining Days in the Career of Lewis Hamilton	180
43	Hill Gets Fired in the Press	184
44	Hill vs the World and the Washer	188
45	Schumacher Wins in the Pit Lane	192
46	European Grand Prix 1999 – What Happens When the Lights Don't Go Out	196
47	The Real Rules of the Game	200
48	The Shootout that Made Jenson Button's Career	203
49	Mercedes' Disgruntled Employee Changes the Race	206
50	The Greatest Overtake of All Time	210
51	Ferrari's Team Order Farce in Austria	213
52	Rossi and Surtees – From Two to Four Wheels	218
53	Kimi Rips the Tyre Off and Everyone Ignores It	222

54	Politics in Indianapolis Overwhelm the Sport, Setting Up Years of Change	225
55	The Rebirth of the Second Tier	231
56	Adrian Newey Goes for Dinner on the King's Road	234
57	Budapest – McLaren at War	237
58	Kubica – The Man Who Could Have Challenged Alonso and Hamilton	241
59	Vettel Becomes the Youngest Winner … With the B Team	245
60	Brawn's Two Titles – Won in Translation	248
61	A Crazy Bridgestone Race Defines an Entire Era	253
62	Lewis and Niki Chat in Singapore	257
63	'Multi 21, Seb … Multi 21'	261
64	Claire Takes Over Williams	265
65	The Battle that Saved Mercedes' Engine Advantage	269
66	Marko Promotes Max Straight into F1 at Seventeen	273
67	Verstappen and Son – The Road to Becoming F1's Youngest Winner	278
68	Rosberg Retires at Thirty-One	283
69	*Drive to Survive*	286
70	The Cost Cap and the Pandemic	289
71	Grosjean Cheats Death	293
72	Silverstone Ignites a Battle for the Ages	297
73	Abu Dhabi – Hamilton vs Verstappen	302
74	Charles, Herve and Jules	308
75	Hamilton Moves to Ferrari	312
Picture Credits		316
Index		317

Foreword by David Coulthard

Alex Jacques is my third partner, which may sound a little promiscuous, but to be clear, since I retired from Grand Prix racing at the end of 2008 and immediately started working as a pundit for the BBC's coverage of Formula One, I have had the pleasure of sharing the commentary box with ex-Formula One driver Martin Brundle, followed by the vastly experienced broadcaster Ben Edwards, and now AJ.

And what a Number Three he is. Where to start? Alex is knowledgeable, entertaining, generous, giving me the space to add my views. And he has the voice. A voice that welcomes you in, sets the scene and takes you on a journey. Never over-hyped, never undersold, just the right balance of light and shade to make it a pleasure to watch him work, while remembering I am not there to be entertained by him but to support his commentary as an ex-racer. To say I love working with Alex may seem a little gushy for a Scotsman, for anybody asked to write a foreword, but it's true. I love working with Alex as it doesn't seem like work; it feels like two people sharing a passion and knowledge with the audience who choose to tune in to our coverage.

In *Grid to Glory*, Alex's passion and knowledge shine through once again. Enjoy his standout moments from the past 75 years of Grand Prix Racing – which embarrassingly starts with me causing one of the largest first-lap crashes in F1 history!

Preface: The Start of My Fascination with Formula One

I'm nine years old, sitting in the living room and flicking through the *four* TV channels available to a UK free-to-air audience at the time. After two clicks of the remote, I find something unusual: a wet road littered with cars. Two men called Murray and Martin are talking about a huge crash. On the ever-repeated replay, it emerges that some chap called David had caused the pile-up.

What eventually unfolded was a classic race in conditions we'd never run in today. Damon Hill won; Eddie Jordan danced. Wide-eyed, I watched the incredible spectacle. Vividly painted cars racing on an epic circuit in near monsoon conditions, with overtakes, spins, crashes and even one driver trying to fight another. I knew, I had found my sport.

The next 75 short chapters give you a whistle-stop run through the championship's history, celebrating my favourite sport. This is not an exhaustive list. There are key moments I've had to omit due a variety of dull reasons, like ongoing action or conflict of interest, but in the following chapters you will find moments that altered the course of F1 or were remarkable because of the characters who featured in them.

On that August day in 1998, I could not believe sport could be so exciting, and I still feel that way a full 11 years into commentating on motor racing. I hope my excitement comes across, both on air and in the following pages.

Alex Jacques
London, 2025

1

The Creation of the World Championship

And still the argument continued ... What to call motor racing's intended highest category?

A meeting in Paris had agreed on the 'Formula' part, but what should follow? Around the table, suggestions flew. Some wanted the letter A, while others preferred 'International' to reflect the journey they would embark on around the globe. In the end, only one name seemed to fit and so it was forever decided: Formula A would be the title known the world over for excellence in motor racing ... and at the very next meeting, they changed their minds. Formula One was born, and this time it stuck for 75 years.

Many top-level races had been contested long before the name was chosen. The very first race was organized by France's then biggest newspaper, *Le Petit Journal*. The paper previously had great success holding a cycling contest for charity three years earlier. Then 1894 saw a new idea: a self-powered 'carriage race' with 'the use of horses unnecessary'. The primitive vehicles would be raced from Paris to Rouen.

In typical motor racing fashion, a row broke out about the rules. Entrants disagreed whether the cars should accommodate two or four passengers. Atypically for motorsport, there was a speed limit: 7 mph in urban areas and 12 mph in the countryside. The first race was won by Albert Lemaître in his Peugeot 'Type Five' which boasted a whopping 3 whole horsepower.

In the following years, the idea caught on and the ingredients were created for what would come to comprise the sport we know today. James Gordon Bennett established the Gordon Bennett Cup with funding from his father's newspaper, *The New York Herald*. Six international races were held between 1900 and 1905, with entries from Europe and the USA via their national automobile clubs.

The first race to be named a 'Grand Prix' was run by the Automobile Club of France in June 1906 at a mammoth circuit at Le Mans. The 'big prize' event was created to allow countries to enter more than three cars: 32 participants from 12 different manufacturers raced on the 65-mile circuit. The race was won by Ferenc Szisz from Hungary in a Renault, having raced for an epic 783 miles. During the race, every car had not only its driver but also a mechanic on board, the only two people allowed to work on or repair the car. The tyre company, Michelin, had developed detachable wheels, which meant the car didn't have to be disassembled for them to be changed – a significant part of how Renault ended up winning the race!

Grand Prix racing had begun, but in the pre-World War I years, without a formal championship to tie everything together, the rules varied considerably between each country's national club.

A key development towards a unified championship was the creation of permanent circuits, which started with Brooklands in the UK in 1907. While the circuit was permanent, the route was not, its path dictated by straw bales – a world away from today's advanced barriers. Brooklands circuit was the first to hold Grand Prix racing in the UK, in 1926 and 1927, with the first permanent layout introduced in 1937. The circuit closed during World War II and sadly never reopened.

Forty years after the *Journal*'s first race, 18 events around the world now proclaimed their races to be 'Grand Prix'. This meant a governing body was required to provide a vague sense of organization. Preceding World War II there was a championship for the world's best drivers, who piloted glamorous sleek machines from the dominant manufacturers, Alfa Romeo and Mercedes. Crucially, it was called the European Championship and it was not a global event. After World War II, the organizers dreamt of something bigger.

In February 1950, podium-scoring driver and former bobsleigh gold medallist, Italian Antonio Brivio Sforza, argued for the creation of a World Championship a year after motorcycle racing had started its own. The announcement was made. The Fédération Internationale de l'Automobil (FIA) Formula One World Championship would begin in May with the calendar comprising races in Britain, Monaco, America, Switzerland, Belgium and France, and culminating in Italy. The race in the USA was not a Grand Prix but in fact the legendary Indianapolis 500, which would be included up until 1960. This was done to create the ruse of a full worldwide championship, but the IndyCar and F1 grids did not attempt to compete in each other's races in the 1950s – that only came later once the race had fallen off the F1 calendar.

The first World Championship was only for drivers. The winner took home just eight points for a win (they did award a fastest lap point, though): 13 May 1950 became a landmark day with the first official World Championship Grand Prix to be held at Silverstone. A total of 21 drivers took to the start, which began with the waving of the Union Flag. King George VI and Queen Elizabeth watched on as Giuseppe 'Nino' Farina won the first World Championship race in a pre-war Alfa Romeo. Whether the royals enjoyed it is debatable, as no reigning British monarch has attended the race since. Perhaps they got caught in the traffic when trying to leave.

A few months later, Farina won the very first title in Monza after future Formula One world champion Juan Manuel Fangio broke down in the last race of the season. Only 33 other names have ever joined Farina as a world champion driver in the 75 seasons since. From a slow, disparate beginning taking many decades to solidify into a full championship, this is an account of the motor racing that came next, the key moments and the people that shaped Formula One into the sport we know today.

2

Jack Brabham – the Australian Legend Who Almost Missed Out

In 1946, Jack Brabham was adjusting to life outside the Australian Air Force when he saw his first motor race in Brisbane.

The competition was interstate midget car racing – a widespread, affordable, hugely popular and exciting contest. The best way to describe what Brabham was watching – first from the wooden grandstands and then soon after as an operator within the racing paddock – is a motorbike speedway with cars.

The cars were basic: small, thin single-seaters with two-speed gearboxes and engines that competed on oval tracks and needed to be more reliable than powerful. The roughhouse tactics of dirt oval racing immediately caught Brabham's attention, fearful as he initially was of the aggressive driving and beaten-up machinery. At the end of a race, the cars would appear littered with puncture holes from the grit surface, but it was undeniably thrilling and Brabham was hooked.

Brabham started travelling to all the dirt races as an engineer to his friend and driver Johnny Schonberg. It was intense behind the wheel. Such was the dust and gravel thrown into a competitor's path, drivers would start the race with six pairs of goggles on – discarding each pair as the race progressed and they became too dirty to peer through. Jack initially dismissed the drivers competing as mad, but with every event his reaction mellowed and his interest grew.

In their second season on the dirt oval championship together, Brabham continued to improve the car for Johnny, but Johnny Schonberg's wife (whose name wasn't recorded) was fearful of the risks her husband was taking. Motor racing was still in its infancy and even with the restricted speeds of a dirt oval, the danger was sizeable, with next to no safety measures in place – the drivers competed without full-face helmets, despite the flying gravel. Reluctantly, Schonberg agreed his driving career was finished.

So began the driving career of a giant. 'We were left with a motor car without a driver. So, I thought I better have a go myself,' remarked Brabham years later. He struck up an instant reputation as a methodical, knowledgeable driver with a pure racing instinct. But remarkably, despite his speed, he still viewed his time behind the wheel as a mere hobby and began to give full consideration to getting a 'proper job' and leaving the racing to someone else. After much discussion, Brabham and his father, Tom, resolved to move into the haulage business together – swapping racetracks for trucking across the country and moving goods on the prosperous South Australia to Sydney route.

Local newspaper adverts had been surveyed and a shortlist drawn up. In Adelaide, the search was now on for the beginnings of a new life. Excited about the prospect of the adventure, Jack Brabham and his father enthusiastically journeyed around Adelaide seeking the perfect vehicle for their new business. Unknowingly, a racing family dynasty and great Australian sporting chapter hung in the balance. Their offer on a truck was accepted but beaten the same day; they'd been gazumped. Jack would write in his 1971 autobiography: 'The setback in Adelaide completely changed my life. If the chap had accepted our offer for the semi [truck], I'm convinced my motor racing career could have ended there and then. Such very small events can change your life.'

It was not just his life – many futures hung on this moment: his family's and future employees of the team he would found, including future McLaren boss Ron Dennis, the man who bought the team; Bernie Ecclestone, on his the way to running the sport; and the countless drivers of the era who would purchase Brabham-made cars for their shot on the racetrack. The ripple effect from this moment cannot be overstated. But it didn't happen. With no viable vehicle available, the haulage business dimmed in its appeal and Tom and Jack Brabham returned to Sydney to repair the car for the next race. Deep down Jack just couldn't stay away from the racetrack.

With their business dreams dashed, the motorsport journey continued and eventually flourished into a celebrated chapter of Formula One. The Brabham racing legacy is enormous, personally Jack scored 14 wins from 126 races. Practical and forthright as a communicator, he would encourage the Cooper team to enter Formula One before starting his own team in 1962. Jack Brabham became a three-time F1 world champion, astonishingly winning his final title in 1966 in his own car – an incredible achievement unlikely ever to be repeated.

Jack continued to race in Formula One until 1970, winning races into his forties and retiring to universal acclaim with a full day of celebration held at the Brands Hatch circuit. Today's Australian Grand Prix winner's trophy is a reproduction of Brabham's old steering wheel from the 1959 Cooper, highlighting his importance to the Australian motor racing legacy. A legacy which nearly vanished behind the wheel of a haulage truck.

Bernie Ecclestone - The Journey to Control F1

Bernie Ecclestone holds a strong claim to be the person with the single biggest influence on Formula One in its 75-year history.

His extraordinary career shaped the sport into what we know today, transforming the old boys' club mentality of the 1950s into a worldwide professional sports league. Just how do you take control of a sport with so many vested interests and political heavyweights? You start in Suffolk ...

From a very early age, Ecclestone was obsessed with cars. Uninterested in his first job at the Gas Board, he wiled away the hours looking through motorbike listings in the hope of turning a profit by selling parts and then full bikes. This quickly became his day job. He rented the outside plot of a big car dealership and sold so many motorbikes he was able to buy the original owners out. This early hostile takeover displayed a naturally competitive streak from the start.

Ecclestone took his increasing fortune and used it to race anything he could get his hands on – pedal bikes, motorbikes, cars – all while growing his successful second-hand car business with showrooms across the leafy suburbs of outer south-east London. Despite progressing into selling luxury cars to an ever-increasing client list, he moved into driver management. This started with his friend Stuart Lewis-Evans, for whom he quickly purchased two Connaught Altas from a full team that had folded and needed to clear its debts quickly. The plan was to run Lewis-Evans in one car and let the other out to the highest bidder. On two occasions, in Monaco, Ecclestone even tried unsuccessfully to qualify for the Grand Prix himself.

Lewis-Evans' move to the highly competitive Vanwall team in 1957 was overseen by Ecclestone, but tragedy was to strike. In the 1958 Moroccan Grand Prix, Stuart Lewis-Evans suffered a technical failure at speed, plunging him off the track into a solid part of the scenery, which ruptured the fuel tank, causing him horrific burns. He passed away a week afterwards.

Bernie Ecclestone left Casablanca reeling from the loss of his friend, and years passed until he returned to a race paddock. But he was tempted back to motor racing by the charismatic Austrian Jochen Rindt, whom he called the most talented driver he'd ever seen. Both driver and manager knew the risks of racing for the Lotus team, but Jochen wanted to win a title and retire, having become a big celebrity in his homeland. The two were very close – Ecclestone was even a part owner of the Lotus Formula Two team that Rindt drove for in 1970. Unfortunately, Bernie would have to suffer losing another friend after Rindt speared off the road and hit an incorrectly fitted guard rail at Monza. Ecclestone had just turned 40 at this point and waited for his 28-year-old friend to arrive in hospital, but he never did. The loss of a second driver in horrific circumstances again led to a period of self-imposed exile.

Despite the horrors of losing two close friends in two inescapably brutal accidents, the intoxicating mix of sport, politics and endless deal-making opportunities in motor racing paddocks meant Ecclestone would or could not stay away for long. He made his next decisive move after hearing the Brabham team were in a tough financial spot and sensing the chance to become a team owner. At a knock-down price, Ron Tauranac sold the team to Bernie, along with the contract of talented engineer and car designer, Gordon Murray.

Ecclestone was able to utilize Murray's ingenuity to develop a series of sleek, innovative designs, including the beautiful

BT42 in 1974 and 1975. Unfortunately, Ecclestone's love of a deal hurt track performance when he agreed to run heavy flat Alfa engines at the exact time you needed space on the floor to run tunnels to create the ground-effect phenomenon. (The switch to ground-effect cars had changed the balance of performance from wings above the car to driving air underneath to suck the car to the floor.) After many years of waiting and looking for the performance, Brabham found a driver to extract the best from the car. Brazilian Nelson Piquet went on to win the title on two occasions for the team. Then, in the mid-1980s, both Piquet and Murray quit within a year. Ecclestone saw the writing on the wall; he sold the team he'd initially bought for just £120,000 for £5 million. The team folded within two years of the sale.

But Ecclestone had a bigger prize in mind. A year after purchasing Brabham, and after attending meetings with other owners and managers, Ecclestone spied an opportunity for modernization and reform. This would involve combining his role running Brabham with a representative role for the Formula One Constructors' Association (FOCA). Essentially, the teams had a club he negotiated for, in return for a cut of whatever he could obtain for the group he enthusiastically represented. This group consisted of Colin Chapman of Lotus, Teddy Mayer of McLaren, Ken Tyrrell of Tyrrell and Frank Williams of Williams, with legal assistance from Max Mosley. Indeed, he was a key participant in the intense war between FOCA and the FIA. However, the moment team boss Ecclestone willingly gave up the Brabham's 1978 fan car innovation (*see* Chapter 27) and its mammoth lap time advantage to keep the other members of the FOCA happy, it was obvious his ambition went all the way to the top of motorsport.

One of Ecclestone's greatest insights into Formula One was fan access to the sport. In sharp contrast to the ad hoc way the season was broadcast in the 1970s, he could see the power of an organized TV rights deal and the revenue and exposure it could achieve. In

1978, Ecclestone fully took the reins at FOCA, with Max Mosley as his legal counsel. The pair worked well together and set about trying to unpick the one-sided revenue-sharing deal known as the Concord Agreement. This was the key deal that bound all teams to Formula One – crucially it dictated the prize money and how it was divided. For Bernie it meant constantly fighting FIA president Jean-Marie Balestre who became Ecclestone's number-one roadblock to the huge fortune he knew was obtainable.

The FIA had the backing of the big boys: Ferrari, Alfa Romeo and Renault. They suggested banning ground effect for 1981 – but this would hurt the front-running FOCA teams the worst and change the outcome of the title. Ecclestone continued to ensure the teams got prize and appearance money from the promoters. But the Concorde Agreement was under strain and talk of breakaway championships ensued. The 1980 Spanish Grand Prix was a flashpoint in the question of who got to run things; FOCA teams and drivers were fined and threatened with bans. It was just the fight Ecclestone had been waiting for, and in the end the race only proceeded due to a direct order from the king to the FIA that the event needed to happen.

Ecclestone's negotiating tactics became more extreme. He threatened to boycott races, especially in France, causing maximum embarrassment to Balestre on home soil.

Amid the rancour, Ecclestone set about re-negotiating television rights and secured the teams a greater revenue in the Concorde Agreement. Max Mosley then ran for president of the FIA's sporting branch before taking the main presidential role. The two old friends had accumulated nearly all the power, and in the 1992 Concorde Agreement Ecclestone achieved his long-held aim: he was given full control to run the sport's commercial interests.

With his elevation to F1 supremo effectively complete, by the end of the decade Ecclestone would have bought and sold the commercial rights, making himself a multi-billionaire in the process.

4

Murray Walker Defines Modern Sports Commentary

Graham Murray Walker had a day job and it wasn't broadcasting Formula One.

Motorsport was his passion and his commentary would go on to define sports broadcasting, but Monday to Friday, Walker was a highly successful ad man. He had worked his way up from account executive at firms like Dunlop, Aspro and Esso to eventually joining the board of Masius in the late 1980s (he'd joined when it was a startup, but by the time he left, the company had billings of over £1 billion). His iconic taglines of the 1960s and 1970s became part of everyday British life – although he had to point out he never wrote, 'A Mars a day helps you work, rest and play', despite it being widely attributed to him.

Always proud to be associated with his home city of Birmingham, he came from a racing family. His father, Graham Walker, was a rider for the Norton Motorcycle Company and was one of the best in the world on two wheels, winning his class in the 1931 Isle of Man TT.

When the day job allowed, Walker spent his weekends commentating at motorcycle racetracks, starting first as a pit lane interviewer with his father. His first commentary was the Shelsley Walsh hill climb in 1948. It came about due to a mix-up – no one had arranged for a commentator for the public announcements. Graham suggested Murray, who gave it chapter and verse, trying to impress the suits. It worked. A year later, he joined the BBC for his first Formula One commentary at Silverstone – a role he would keep until 2001! During the 1950s, a regular slot alongside his father came up for the Isle of Man TT; after his father's death in 1962, he took the lead role.

Over the next two decades, Murray's reputation grew as he covered all kinds of racing, including motocross and rallycross for Saturday afternoon sports programmes on national television. Until 1978, Formula One was rarely covered in full, except for the Italian, Monaco and British Grands Prix. After James Hunt won the championship, the BBC began regular highlights programmes and recruited Walker as its lead commentator, producing some of the most memorable lines in sports broadcasting.

'Damon Hill exits the chicane and wins the Japanese Grand Prix. And I've got to stop because I've got a lump in my throat.'

'AND LOOK AT THAT – COLOSSALLY, THAT'S MANSELL!'

'SENNA IS TRYING TO GO THROUGH ON THE INSIDE, AND IT'S HAPPENED IMMEDIATELY.'

'A bu-uh-rilliant race for Michael Schumacher, who exits the chicane for the 53rd and last time win the Japanese Grand Prix and the World Championship for the third time.'

'This is the opportunity that Senna was looking for – OUT! Oh my goodness, this is fantastic.'

Walker was as famous for his enthusiasm as for his iconic 'Murray-isms' – the hilarious heat-of-the-moment mistakes that were unavoidable across a half-century of broadcasting at the top. Clive James famously wrote that he commentated like his 'trousers were on fire'. With his fast-paced delivery, on-air gaffes and malapropisms were common, such as: 'This leading car is absolutely unique – except, of course, for the one immediately behind it, which is identical' and 'There's nothing wrong with the car except it's on fire.' They endeared him to his audience and provided content for his lucrative after-dinner speech routine. 'Far too often I'd operate [my] mouth before engaging [my] brain,' he would later admit, 'but the action in front of me was always happening at such a lick.' Some more of his funniest lines included:

'Mansell's now totally in front of everyone in this race, except the two in front of him.'

'"If" is a very long word in Formula One. In fact, "if" is F1 spelled backwards.'

'Unless I'm very much mistaken, I am very much mistaken!'

'I'll now stop my startwatch.'

They're terrific fun, but make no mistake, few had higher broadcasting peaks than Murray Walker. He had a peerless ability to convey information with clarity and emotion at rapid speed, and this is best displayed by an often-overlooked moment, when Mika Häkkinen spun out from the lead in 1999:

> And off goes Häkkinen, Häkkinen the race leader, he's out of the race, he's out of the race! Mika Häkkinen retires on lap 30 and Heinz-Harald Frentzen leads, and this could blow the world championship widddddddddddde open, and Mika Häkkinen, after the misery of Belgium, is consumed with rage, and the tifosi are consumed with delight. The Italian Grand Prix has gone mega!

Firstly, the delivery is Royal Shakespeare Company-worthy. It's exciting but controlled, competing against the riotous noise of a Monza crowd when something goes well for Ferrari. Secondly, you're given seven pieces of information in 30 seconds. All of his experience tells with his top lines of what's happened: the race leader is out; here's the stage of the race; this is the new leader; here is the significance for the big prize. Finally, he was seventy-six when he improvised this! You can hear him running out of air as he completes his masterpiece: it was commentary perfection.

Walker's general attitude, to emphasize the positive and not to score points or punch down from his position of power, created a warm broadcast, in sharp contrast to the 'Should have scored'-style scorn and grumpiness which permeated many sports broadcasts of his era.

His voice would come to define Formula One for English language audiences. Over the course of his career of influence, in league with Britain's golden generation of sports broadcasters, he commentated on more than 350 Formula One Grands Prix and more than 200 motorcycling events.

Over the years, Murray had many famous co-commentators. From 1980 to 1993, he was accompanied by former British world champion, James Hunt, until Hunt died unexpectedly from a heart attack. It was a partnership built on contrasts, with Hunt's input – often dry asides – delivered in a haze of cigarette smoke. The relationship did not get off to a great start when Hunt turned up late, barefoot and half-drunk with a bottle of rosé in hand. They even nearly got into a fight at one point, but animosity turned to friendship over 13 years sharing the microphone. His other iconic pairing was with Martin Brundle, who still commentates today with Sky. When the BBC lost the rights and coverage moved over to ITV, the British press even ran an (unnecessary) 'Save Our Murray' campaign.

Despite 'officially' stopping in 2001, Walker kept attending races and undertaking TV and radio commitments well into his nineties. In 1996, he was appointed an OBE, which he followed up with by being voted 'the greatest sports commentator of all time' in 2009.

In recent times, the entire sports broadcast industry gravitated towards Walker's ethos: warm broadcasts laden with narrative, told enthusiastically and with a smile.

In 2007, Walker made a final appearance for BBC Radio, where he filled in on the European Grand Prix at age 83. It was fitting that his final TV commentary was at Indianapolis and his final radio broadcast at the Nürburgring. Grand stages for the pioneering man who created the rules of modern commentary.

5

Enzo Ferrari Sends Stirling Moss Home

In 1951, Enzo Ferrari offered a 21-year-old Stirling Moss a sensational contract.

Underneath the prancing horse masthead on thick cream paper was the outline for a two-race offer that would see Moss drive for the team at the French and British Grands Prix. Ferrari were beginning to run competitively in every discipline at which they raced, whether it be Formula One, Formula Two or sportscar competition. The Formula One World Championship was not yet the established pinnacle of motorsport and drivers were not yet compelled to run in every round of the season; Moss had committed to racing elsewhere during the French Grand Prix weekend. Feeling that he had to honour his original agreement, Moss sent a message to Enzo Ferrari that he could only accept the drive at Silverstone. Ferrari wasn't interested in a compromise and handed both races to José Froilán Gonzalez. The Argentine racer then created a landmark moment, winning Ferrari's first Grand Prix in Formula One at Silverstone and claiming his place in the history books. Moss could only watch on, wondering what might have been, from the Formula Three paddock.

The chance with Ferrari remained open, and the Scuderia later invited Moss to Italy for contract discussions; the new offer was a try-out in F2, a drive in the season concluding at the Italian Formula One Grand Prix and a full contract for F1 in 1952. Moss duly travelled to the Formula Two race in Bari, Italy, but upon arriving in the paddock he was astounded to find another driver sitting in his car. A furious row erupted. He'd been dumped and, worse still, he'd not been informed about it.

There are suggestions that the British BRM team had loudly proclaimed Moss would be driving for them and Ferrari had got cold feet. The fact was, Moss had been replaced without being told. Understandably, after what was then a long journey to Italy by road, he was incandescent with rage and vowed he would never race for Ferrari again. It was a source of regret for Enzo Ferrari, who in the decade that followed lavished praise on the Englishman.

Ferrari placed Moss' abilities alongside his personal hero – the man who he considered to be the greatest: Tazio Nuvolari, a pre-war Grand Prix giant. Ferrari felt Moss had let his emotions and fierce patriotism affect his decision-making when he came to choosing teams. He cited this as a reason Moss never won a title.

The saga created a huge motivation for Moss who was now obsessed with beating the scarlet machines. With the retirement of Juan Manuel Fangio in 1957, and Moss' refusal to work for the team, Ferrari's driver shenanigans ensured they would not have access to the accepted strongest driver in the field until Niki Lauda joined the team in the 1970s. Arguably, this only made the Ferrari team and brand stronger – no driver would be bigger than the team, no matter who was behind the wheel and no matter their previous success. It all added to the mythology that surrounds the marque.

In 1961, one of F1's great cars, the 'Sharknose' Ferrari, completely dominated championship races. The team were defeated only twice all season, both times by Moss, who recorded memorable wins at Monaco and Nürburgring – the two greatest extreme variations of circuit in the sport: Monaco with the walls close and the Nürburgring a 14-mile behemoth that terrified drivers with its rolling hills, blind corners and wild high-speed sections.

Astounded by the calibre of driving he had witnessed trackside, Enzo Ferrari professed the grandest apology possible and offered Moss a car he could run privately, even forgoing the legendary 'rosso corsa' colour on the car. Devastatingly, before the partnership could begin, Moss suffered an enormous accident at the Goodwood Circuit in Sussex, effectively ending his career as a frontline Formula One driver.

To this day, it is still not clear why Ferrari replaced Moss that day in Bari, or why they did not tell him they had done so. Much like Lewis Hamilton's move to Mercedes in 2013, this sequence of events changed the course of Formula One history for a full decade, deciding the destination of at least six world titles, sadly none of which Moss would ever hold.

6

The Creation of the Constructors' Championship

Every year in Formula One, the multi-stop tour around the world to crown the best on earth is dominated by the narrative of the Drivers' Championship.

But for 67 years two World Championships have been contested: the original Drivers' Championship and the FIA World Championship for Constructors.

While the latter has always been important inside the sport, given a team's standing in the championship table determines its prize money, it has traditionally been considered less relevant to fans than the Drivers' Championship. The Constructors' Championship has gone through several iterations but has traditionally been dominated by only a few teams: out of 170 chassis constructors, only 15 have won championships in its 63 seasons. Ferrari hold the record for the most wins with 16, followed jointly by Williams and now McLaren with nine each after the 2024 season.

In its current form, the Constructors' Championship sees points from both cars fielded in the race count towards the championship. The tally from the cars are added irrespective of who the drivers are, and up to four drivers can be used in a season, with all their points counting.

Formula One allocates prize money based on a team's position in the Constructors' Championship. This can then influence the budgets a team has for the next year, making even the battle for ninth and tenth in the standings as competitive as between first and second. Differences in position can be worth millions, though it's worth noting that unlike other sports, prize money isn't directly awarded for the Drivers' Championship. For the drivers, it's all about the bonuses paid directly to them, often dependent on Constructors' prize money. Aerodynamic testing time using a wind tunnel is also allocated inversely to the Constructors' standings, while garages in the pit lane are allocated according to finishing position.

While the Formula One Constructors' Championship was set up eight years after the start of the first Formula One season, an earlier version existed prior to the start of World War II. In 1925, the Manufacturers' World Championship was set up by the forerunner to the FIA but only lasted for three years. French magazine *L'Auto* suggested the idea of a global series of Grand Prix races as early as 1923, with the inaugural series in 1925 including just four races with a minimum distance of 800 km. To make it truly global, the first race was to be the Indianapolis 500, where only one European car turned up – a Fiat. This was followed by Spa-Francorchamps, the Grand Prix de l'ACF in France, and an Italian Grand Prix.

That first iteration of the Constructors' Championship had all the (unfortunate) ingredients that would later come to characterize Formula One. At the French Grand Prix at Montlhéry, Antonio Ascari Senior, father of two-time world champion Alberto Ascari, did not survive a crash while in the lead. That first Championship was won by Italian car maker, Alfa Romeo, who also happened to be heavily involved in setting the rules – politics being another key feature of Grand Prix racing even then. A laurel wreath was added to Alfa Romeo's badge, where it stayed until 1972, in recognition of this great glory.

In 1958, a Constructors' Championship known as the International Cup for F1 Manufacturers was introduced. It was part of several changes introduced that year by the FIA. Key components of the championship included racing limits – either 300 km or two hours of racing. Points were also only awarded to drivers who completed the full race and did not share the car! Only the highest-scoring car could be awarded points contributing to the Constructors' Championship, and this lasted until 1978. The aim of the Constructors' Championship, whatever its iteration, was to recognize the team behind the car. The team with the most points was to win in a reversal of the scoring system used in 1925.

In that first year, six teams were listed in the Constructors' standings. While the names may be a bit different to those seen today, Ferrari was present. The series ended up being a head-to-head between the scarlet cars of Mike Hawthorn and Peter Collins and the British racing green-clad Vanwalls of Stirling Moss and Tony Brooks. Vanwall went on to take the inaugural championship with Stirling Moss and Tony Brooks splitting their wins three races apiece. Despite the first Constructors' and Drivers' Championships being split between teams, this is quite a rare event that has only occurred 11 times in history.

Ferrari had to wait until 1961 before they achieved their first Constructors' title. The team were well prepared for a change in engine rules with a new purposeful V6-powered 'Sharknose' 156, in contrast to their numerous British rivals. At the first race in Monaco, Richie Ginther led before being overtaken by Stirling Moss in a Lotus. Ferrari, however, dominated the next four races with wins at the Netherlands, Belgium, French and British Grands Prix. A final win by the American Phil Hill in a tragic race in Italy rounded out their season. The other Ferrari of Wolfgang von Trips had been leading, with Hill in second. Unfortunately, von Trips collided with a Lotus and was launched into the crowd. Ferrari missed the last race of the season at Watkins Glen, USA but held on to both the Drivers' and Constructors' Championships.

While Ferrari has had its ups and downs within Formula One, the longest-standing constructor is also the most dominant in Formula One history. As of 2025, Ferrari has the most Constructors' titles at 16, race wins at 248 and Drivers' Championships at 15. They won again with John Surtees in 1964 and achieved four more Constructors' Championships with eminent racing drivers such as Niki Lauda and Jody Scheckter. Two further wins in 1982 and 1983 were followed by a fallow period, until future FIA boss, Jean Todt, and future Formula One managing director Ross Brawn led the team to six back-to-back Constructors' titles, five of which were with Michael Schumacher. The last two Constructors' titles were won in 2007 and 2008 – at the time of writing, they are currently on their longest ever title drought.

Although a midfield team today, Williams is the second joint most winning constructor in Formula One, with the team being dominant throughout the 1980s and 1990s. Team founder Frank Williams with designer Patrick Head entered Formula One in 1978 and had won their first title by 1981. Williams tended to switch drivers, believing the car was more important – no driver ever won multiple titles with the team. McLaren equalled Williams' nine Constructors' Championships with its 2024 win – the first since 1998. In a head-to-head with Ferrari, the team's championship was decided in Abu Dhabi at the last race of the season, something that has happened in only 19 other seasons of Formula One. McLaren is in an unusual position to have won more Drivers' (12) than Constructors' Championships. The team, founded by Bruce McLaren, entered Formula One in 1966, and won its first Constructors' title in 1974 with Brazilian Emerson Fittipaldi winning the Drivers' Championship for the team that year. One of the most iconic and competitive pairings in Formula One history was that of the two McLaren drivers, Ayrton Senna and Alain Prost, both of whom won titles for the team. Mika Häkkinen helped the team to victory in 1998 in the Constructors' Championship, although he won back-to-back Drivers' Championships in 1998 and 1999. Lewis Hamilton in his time with the team won one Drivers' Championship but no Constructors' title.

While the Constructors' Championship has always been important for the team, given its value, there has traditionally been less focus on it outside of the paddock for both broadcasters and viewers. However, with the 2024 championships being split between McLaren for the Constructors' and Red Bull for the Drivers' with Max Verstappen, it appears that this is changing. With McLaren's win widely celebrated, the Constructors' Championship has never been more prominent. The Netflix series *Drive to Survive* has contributed to making stars of the team principals. Strategists and engineers are becoming important partners on the sport's broadcasts, which is highlighting their roles in the sport; an engineer's voice and relationship with their driver can often be a key element of the race broadcast. While the drivers will always be fan favourites by virtue of the risks they take, in the modern era fans are rightly celebrating their favourite teams too.

7

Stirling and Alf Change the Game

The plan had been hatched the night before.

Stirling Moss' bid for victory in the opening round of the 1958 World Championship would begin at the bar.

He could be heard complaining that he was snookered for the following day's Argentine Grand Prix in Buenos Aires; his last-minute entry just hadn't been designed for pit stops … he would lose so much time … he had no hope! It was all completely on purpose. This was poker disguised as motor racing: Stirling and his solitary Cooper mechanic, Alf Francis, had a plan.

The strategy was simple: don't stop, just race – stay out there, nurse the rubber and hope the tyres don't fall apart. The next day, Formula One would change forever as Stirling Moss upended decades of motor racing convention and completed one of the most audacious drives in history.

The morning signalled the first element to fall Moss' way. The normally boiling Argentine weather didn't materialize; it was cool and breezy for the start of a new season. Just 10 cars took to the grid, as teams and drivers were not required to attend every race back then, and the field was down another one when Peter Collins' driveshaft broke on his Ferrari.

The fact Moss was even on the grid wasn't a given. His team Vanwall were not competing because they hadn't managed to adapt their engine for the new fuel regulations imposed for the 1958 season. The race officials wanted the biggest names at their season opener, which had seen its field size depleted because of the cost of freighting cars to Argentina and the time of year. There was a near five-month gap before Round Two in Monaco, and with the World Championship rules insisting you had to drop your two lowest scores, some didn't bother to make the journey.

By 1958, Stirling Moss was one of the biggest sports stars on the planet, and the organizers needed him in their race. They even offered to pay for the expensive air freight if he could find a ride. Despite a contract with the Vanwall team, Moss was free to look for another drive if they didn't show up. He turned to legendary privateer team operator Rob Walker – the go-to man for a customer car, which was permitted at the time. Moss enquired about Walker's available options. Incredibly, the best available amid the rule change flux was a Formula Two spec Cooper with an improved engine. Walker agreed to send the car with just one mechanic, Alf Francis, to service it. This left Moss driving a lightweight, nimble 2-litre Cooper-Climax up against the might of the 2.5-litre Ferraris and legendary Maserati 250F piloted by the home favourite, Juan Manuel Fangio.

Few in the paddock took Moss' chance of a podium seriously. His wheels were designed to race in Formula Two; where in 1958 the short races had no pit stops, it meant stops of three minutes if you were to undo all four bolts on all four tyres, plus he only had one mechanic on hand. They took the only decision which gave them a victory chance: a no-stop strategy, and plenty of amateur dramatics to disguise their intentions.

The strategy was only possible because of Moss' mid-engined car, which was significantly lighter than its competitors, making it stronger on this type of circuit and reducing the punishment the tyres took. For the first six decades of motorsport, the engine had been at the front and no other solution had ever won an F1 race. Moss bided his time as the rest peeled off to change tyres; few were paying real attention to the Cooper's pace, which was vastly reduced by design. Moss had qualified down in seventh, two seconds slower than the pole time set by Fangio.

Both Maserati and Ferrari were firm favourites to dominate the race, with the advantage of quick pit stops (both had quick-release wheels, making stops under a minute). Moss used his skill to dart past the Ferrari Dinos of Musso and claimed fourth place. Another piece fell into place on lap 30, as Ferrari's Mike Hawthorn pitted with an engine losing oil pressure, and Jean Behra of Maserati spun to leave Moss in second.

A few laps later, race leader Fangio suffered a puncture, losing so much time trailing back to the pits he was now out of contention. Moss led by a minute, followed by Musso, Behra and Hawthorn, who had all made a stop for new rubber. Despite knowing the threat from behind, Moss stuck to the plan, deliberately running seconds a lap away from his true pace, only concerned with the condition of the tyres. Ferrari and second-placed Musso waited for Moss to visit the pit lane, looking after their cars at reduced pace. In the pit lane, the carry-on continued; Alf Francis would lean over the pit wall holding a tyre, to which Moss responded with a nod and a wave and continued in his tiny Cooper.

With fewer than 20 laps to go, panic and uncertainty brewed at Ferrari. With 15 to go, the penny dropped. Moss wasn't stopping! Remarkably Moss, looking for ways to preserve the tyres, was now deliberately running wide onto the grass and seeking out patches of oil, all in an effort to cool his tattered tyres.

Ferrari signalled to Musso to begin the charge. There were crucial seconds lost as he didn't understand the instruction, but after much waving and gesticulating he got the picture and attacked. He began taking huge chunks a lap out of Moss' economy drive but it was too little too late. Moss and Francis had bluffed their way to victory; their ruse had thrown their rivals off the scent. A plan 24 hours in the making had come good, creating an underdog story for the ages. Moss had beaten full factory teams in a modified Formula Two car; it was the first win for a mid-engined car and the first victory for strategy beating pure performance. A true landmark day, all in a Grand Prix he should never have raced in.

8

Stirling Moss, the Gentleman Racer

Stirling Moss never used to give his address to journalists: 'Ask any black cab driver,' he'd say.

'It's part of The Knowledge.' His legacy was woven into the fabric of the sport, as was his place as Britain's first post-war sporting hero. In 1958, Moss defined a fabled career with an act of sportsmanship almost unthinkable in the modern era. By knowingly coming to the defence of his only title rival, Mike Hawthorn, he would enshrine two things in motor racing legend: the integrity of his character and the fact he had never won the Formula One World Championship, despite being one of the greatest drivers the sport has seen.

With three races to go in the World Championship of 1958, the Portuguese Grand Prix was due to be held at a brand-new venue in Oporto – a collection of 1950s streets cordoned off with basic hay bales, banner advertising, telephone poles, cobbles, tramlines and – most importantly for the championship – pavement.

Moss started on pole for the Vanwall team, the car draped in British racing green. Mike Hawthorn was alongside his compatriot adorned with a shock of blond hair, flat cap and bow tie; he would start second in his Ferrari. This was the era of the post-war gentleman racer: stiff upper lips served with a side of suave Bond-esque fast living.

After racing closely in the early laps, Moss tore into a commanding lead. His advantage was so great that victory was assured as long as the car kept going. Reliability was one of the reasons Hawthorn had dropped away; he'd lost time in the pits fixing his ailing brakes. With so much time lost, Hawthorn focused on finishing second and minimizing the damage in the championship standings, but such were the car problems, he suffered the ignominy of being lapped by his title rival.

While Moss coasted to his ninth F1 career victory, he charitably let the Ferrari driver unlap himself to provide the crowd with the highly unusual sight of Hawthorn in second, crossing the line metres before Moss won the Grand Prix. As Moss took the adulation from a huge crowd of over 100,000, Hawthorn was starting his last lap before inexplicably spinning at the first turn. Even more astonishingly, Moss had seen the whole thing and, having just won the race, promptly parked up and stopped to watch if his rival could dig himself out of the hole.

Marshals swarmed the car as Hawthorn waved them away for fear of a penalty. He leapt from the car, trying to push-start it back into the race, and to his immense relief he succeeded. However, reports had been submitted that Hawthorn had restarted his car when it was facing backward, meaning instant disqualification. In an act barely credible given the sport we know today, Moss stepped forward with the information that saved his competitor from disqualification. As the only driver to witness the whole thing, Moss stated that yes, the machine was restarted when facing towards oncoming cars but, crucially, on the pavement, not the road. Track limits still mattered, even in 1958.

With the winner of the race arguing in favour of his rival and the marshals agreeing he'd witnessed the whole thing, the circuit officials relented and Hawthorn's second place stood. Two Grands Prix later, Hawthorn would deny Moss the title by a single point to become Great Britain's first world champion. Moss would never have the honour of calling himself world champion, finishing second four times in a remarkable career of 1,000 victories at races worldwide.

Years later, it was put to him that if he had stayed quiet rather than come forward to aid his rival, no one would have known the truth. Moss' answer was emphatic: 'I'd have known.'

The Great Fangio Gets Kidnapped

The lobby of the Lincoln Hotel was alive with the buzz that only an international motor race can bring.

Havana, Cuba, was welcoming a Grand Prix crowd for only the second time in the nation's history.

It wasn't a full round of the World Championship, but back then racing anything anywhere was the order of the day. The drivers drifted around the world to where the prize money could be found. Every room was taken in the seven-storey art deco hotel.

Enjoying the break from the heat after a hard day's practice on track was the best driver on the planet, Argentinian Juan Manuel Fangio: a five-time champion and author of many tales of legend behind the wheel. After losing out on Formula One's first ever championship in 1950, Fangio had won five titles in seven years for Alfa Romeo, Ferrari, Maserati and Mercedes. In one season he drove for multiple teams in the same campaign – such aggressive team switching was only possible because every outfit wanted him in their possession.

On 23 February 1958, that list grew to include the Cuban rebels of the '26th of July Movement'. Fangio was making small talk with friends, when suddenly two men orchestrated their plan. One cast a shadow across the doorway, the second moved to the driver's back, and with a flash of a pistol clearly spoke his instructions. Fangio calmly complied. Within seconds, the world champion was ushered into the street and bundled into a getaway car. His friends, stunned and horror-struck, called the police.

Instantly, the radio carried the story. Juan Manuel Fangio had been kidnapped at gunpoint by Cuban rebels.

The news travelled so quickly, Fangio heard it in the car. It was all by design; the Cuban rebels led by Fidel Castro had kidnapped the champion and wanted the world to know – they publicly claimed responsibility. The socialist revolutionaries had sought to embarrass the Cuban government who were hosting the race in the hope of attracting tourism from nearby America. Back at the hotel, the other drivers were immediately given police protection, with officers so motivated to prevent a second kidnapping the drivers reported being woken up every two hours to check they'd not been abducted. It would be a sleepy grid for the following day's street race.

Fangio's abduction made the front pages of America's leading papers – but now what? Though his kidnappers had completed their mission, they still needed Fangio to miss the race for the maximum PR impact – and they were astounded to find their captive so calm and understanding. Thus, an unlikely tour of Havana began from safe house to safe house as the kidnappers showed off their man. Fangio met his captors' friends and family, and they even dined together before watching the race he should have been part of on TV.

Eventually, 26 hours later, Fangio was handed over to the Argentine embassy. He was released the next day and answered questions from journalists, saying he wouldn't identify his kidnappers but had been 'well fed' and would be 'back to race again in Cuba'.

Juan Manuel travelled back to New York, appearing on *The Ed Sullivan Show*. In the host's gushing introduction, Fangio was called one of the greatest champions of the twentieth century before it was casually mentioned that he had recently been kidnapped by the Cubans. Fangio would later say he thought this was appropriate, as it mentioned the two things he was most famous for!

10

Jackie Stewart Stares at Death

Jackie Stewart strained desperately, but he was trapped.

The remains of his BRM were crumpled into a terrifying mess. He had left the road at the Masta Kink, the headline corner of the original Spa-Francorchamps circuit in Belgium. He was instantly fearful because he smelled fuel. He felt the cold horror of the petrol swell around him in the cockpit. He was seconds from an excruciating death, with professional medical help as much as 25 minutes away. He had entered the cruel purgatory of crashing in the 1960s.

The Spa circuit in June 1966 resembled nothing that we'd recognize in 2025. It was 8.7 miles of a super-fast public road with no barriers, meaning if things didn't go to plan the extraordinary machines of the day would meet very ordinary objects: telephone poles, lampposts, garden walls, and the ominously dark green pines of the Ardennes forest. Beyond the immediate edge of the track sat houses, barns, pubs and churches. It was plainly unsafe in the dry, let alone the typical sodden conditions the drivers had faced that race day.

Around a minute before the start, the circuit commentator announced heavy rain had been reported at Malmedy, a few miles away. Crucially, the message had been conveyed in French and the majority of the grid drove towards a wall of water without warning. Things were so severe, only seven cars made lap 2 from the 15 who left the grid.

Jackie had put in a stunning effort in qualifying, his time

good enough to haul his underpowered BRM to the front row, but on race day this meant he hit the conditions first. He aquaplaned with that sickening weightless feel at the point the grip expires, he was hurled from the tarmac. Hitting a telegraph pole then a wooden cottage, he finally came to a stop, upside down, drenched in fuel, unable to remove the steering wheel.

Moments later, the second BRM left the road in the undrivable conditions. Jackie's teammate Graham Hill did not travel as far or as fast. His engineering background allowed him to switch off Jackie's fuel pump. Then two became three as American Bob Bondurant joined the unintended carpark. One man was stuck, two men were risking their lives to protect him.

After a hellish and helpless period, Graham and Bob finally extricated Jackie 25 minutes later. Doused in petrol, lightly simmering his skin, and with a broken collarbone to boot, Graham Hill had no choice but to strip his friend naked and throw him into the nearest van. With profoundly ridiculous timing, a group of nuns appeared, stunned by the sight, before the ambulance finally arrived.

Finally in the ambulance, Jackie nursed his broken bones and he grimaced and groaned from the petrol burns. He was firmly instructed to hide the reality from his wife. The ambulance would get lost in the forest roads and the pain was extended. The physical wound would heal, but the emotional toll of the experience was inescapable – it's one thing to rationalize the risk, another to delude yourself. To be a spark away from death could only be transformative. Some might have stopped, others might have been forced to stop by family, but Jackie resolved not only to continue but to remake motorsport. Everything unsafe was now a target, regardless of personal cost.

It would make Stewart unpopular with circuit owners, governing bodies, team owners and drivers, but his path was set. He'd passed the point of tolerance, and would only accept broad and sweeping change. He'd happily take the brickbats and the barbs if it meant progress and change, even if it was considered 'unmanly' and 'unromantic'. As Jackie quite rightly pointed out, many of his critics weren't the ones crashing at 150 miles per hour or risking odds of two out of three drivers dying if they raced for five years. The reality is, the change had to be instigated by a driver, and a brilliant driver at that – it was hard to smear the fastest man out there. The ancient standards were only swept away by an unrelenting campaign of a man who would not tolerate a repeat of what he experienced at Spa that day; he knew he'd cheated death and wished to bury no more friends.

Jackie Stewart's safety crusade saw the creation and implementation of run-off areas, barriers, permanent then advanced medical facilities, and marshalling with training and procedures. He insisted on the introduction of full-face helmets and seatbelts. Everything a modern fan takes for granted had to be fought for across decades and all emanated from that crash site at Spa. The 1960s F1 superstar and three-time world champion spent his political capital wisely to protect countless lives over the subsequent decades.

11

The Original Hollywood Fight to Take Racing to the Big Screen

Back in 1966, only a handful of races were broadcast live on TV.

In the UK, they usually included the British, Italian and Monaco Grands Prix, with the possible addition of a live title decider if a championship season had captured the public's imagination sufficiently. The footage was broadcast in a grainy black and white to living rooms the world over. At the track, it was a basic broadcast set-up, with just a few cameras spread around the circuit, yet the pictures still enthralled fans. Motor racing had never been shown in its true glory.

In 1966, Hollywood director John Frankenheimer looked to continue a strong run of hits, including *Birdman of Alcatraz*, *The Train* and *The Manchurian Candidate*, the latter starring Frank Sinatra. It left Frankenheimer rated as a successful if not absolute A-list Hollywood director, and he'd now won a chance to shoot a big-budget picture. He felt showcasing Formula One in all its glory across three hours of shot 70-mm film was a dazzling pitch. The problem was, Frankenheimer wasn't the only one taking Formula One as inspiration. Steve McQueen and John Sturges, who had together as leading man and director routinely wowed audiences with classics such as *The Magnificent Seven* and *The Great Escape*, also planned to make a motor racing movie.

Both films were inspired by non-fiction book *The Cruel Sport* by US journalist Robert Daley – a brutal no-holds-barred view of a sport that exhilarated and killed in equal measure. It spoke in terms studio executives would understand: death, glory and glamour. McQueen and Sturges confidently pitched to Warner Brothers, Sturges set about obtaining the book rights and only when sat next to Frankenheimer at an industry lunch did he realize he was in a battle to make a movie about racing. John Frankenheimer had gone directly to the author while Sturges had been dealing with the publishing house, which was always bound to provide a slower response.

The very next day, Warner Brothers and Metro-Goldwyn-Mayer (MGM) announced two racing movies based on the same book: Warner Brothers' *Day of the Champion* would compete against *Grand Prix* at the box office.

This was more than just a passion project for McQueen, who truly loved motor racing. It even influenced the film roles he took: 1961's *The War Lover* was filmed close to Snetterton in Norfolk, where McQueen raced Formula Junior cars. McQueen then travelled the country racing at Oulton Park and Brands Hatch at club level; the film part was just an excuse to try out the British racing scene.

Indeed, Frankenheimer had wanted McQueen for his leading man but somehow missed a meeting between his producer and the star. Worse still, his producer notoriously didn't get on with McQueen and with no one to chart the waters diplomatically, the encounter had quickly turned sour. Now they were on opposite sides in this bizarre quest to be first. 'If we'd had McQueen in *Grand Prix* it would have been bigger than *Jaws*,' Frankenheimer would later claim.

As it was, MGM insisted on McQueen's fellow *Great Escape* cast member James Garner being leading man. After accepting the part, Garner phoned McQueen to tell him the news, but it went badly: 'He didn't talk to me for about two-and-a-half years.'

Remarkably, both movies began pre-production at the same race. McQueen attended the Monaco Grand Prix with Stirling Moss, a driver adviser to the project. The *Day of the Champion* team then tested camera cars at the Nürburgring, filming with Moss behind the wheel of a sportscar. The camera operator alongside was plainly having the time of his life and captured spectacular footage in the process.

Then came a key turning point for both productions. Steve McQueen journeyed to Taiwan for a two-month shoot of Chinese war epic *The Sand Pebbles*. When it was complete, he'd return to Europe and begin filming his motorsport epic with a crew of drivers, which included Jim Clark and Jackie Stewart, who had picked the famous leading man over *Grand Prix*. But filming for *The Sand Pebbles* overran by a full five months. McQueen had no choice but to honour his contract and found himself trapped as competitor *Grand Prix* took the lead and began shooting on location. With *Day of the Champion* unable to film until August, Warner Brothers knew there'd be no catching up in time and pulled the plug. McQueen's Formula One film would never make it to the big screen.

Grand Prix now had a clear run to the box office and a chance at success with a sizeable $10 million budget – good news considering the huge cast and crew they had to pay for, including 3,000 extras to stage their very own French Grand Prix after the circuit hosting the real thing turned them down. Frankenheimer set about the practicalities of recording the speed and danger of the era, creating special camera mounts to capture all the footage accurately, and attaching huge Panavision 70-mm film cameras to F3 and F2 cars with modified bodywork to resemble the premier class. 2025's *F1: The Movie* would replicate this tactic, commissioning F2 outfit Carlin to bulk up an F2 machine to F1 specifications.

The production won a typically sceptical grid over by recruiting the American drivers first: Bob Bondurant, Dan Gurney and 1961 world champion Phil Hill, who would drive a specially fitted Ford GT40 with a huge Panavision camera. Frankenheimer employed real drivers, including big names of the day such as Graham Hill, Richie Ginther and Jack Brabham. Jochen Rindt, Bruce

McLaren, Jim Clark and Jackie Stewart all signed up after *Day of the Champion* collapsed; as Jackie put it, they got paid twice! The great Juan Manuel Fangio was even paid for a cameo.

The on-track action was captured before and after the real sessions, often creating highly pressurized shooting windows of less than half an hour, leaving little room for error. This placed stressful demands on incredibly complex set pieces, including using a hydrogen cannon to pitch a modified F3 car into the Monaco harbour. Another perilous moment involved James Garner having to drive and open taps of butane tanks to create a fire sequence. When the fire was much bigger than expected, his frantic jump out of the car was real. When Garner's insurers found out they hit the roof.

The Sand Pebbles and *Grand Prix* were to be released the same week in the US. *Grand Prix* opened to varied reviews but it was a significant commercial success, making double its budget at the box office. Frankenheimer later reflected, 'It was certainly one of the most satisfactory films I've made ... To be able to indulge your fantasies with 10.5 million dollars is, marvellous.'

McQueen would fume for years that he'd been denied the chance to make both movies in the same year, especially when *Grand Prix* went on to win three Academy awards for Best Sound, Best Sound Effects and Best Editing (on the same night he'd miss out on Best Actor). A few years later, McQueen was the biggest movie star in the world and could make any film he wanted – but he chose to return to motor racing again, starring in 1971's *Le Mans*, a beautiful visual document of the era's machines that seemed to be almost plot free.

It would take Hollywood 42 years to return to the subject when Ron Howard's 2013 film *Rush* retold the epic 1976 season battle between Niki Lauda and James Hunt. This began a second wave of big-budget motorsport productions, including the remnants of *Day of the Champion*. After the footage shot at the Nürburgring was found decades later, the story was brilliantly told in Alex Rodger's 2021 *Steve McQueen: The Lost Movie*.

12

Cosworth DFV Engine – A British Engineering Achievement Worth Celebrating

Since the beginning, Formula One has loved rewriting the rules.

The FIA rule change on engine size for the start of the 1966 season was no different, leading to the creation of an engineering work of genius that will be referenced for decades to come. The creation, performance and dominance of the Cosworth DFV (Double Four Valve) V8 engine across F1 and single-seater racing is one of the great pieces of Formula One history.

Prior to the rule change, Formula One engines were 1.5 litres, and faster sports cars were starting to make the pinnacle of Grand Prix racing look a tad slow. In 1963, a meeting between the FIA and the teams was held to gauge their opinions before the 1966 rules were agreed. Many British teams reportedly hoped the standard would be set at 2.0 litres, rather than the 3.0 litres that was finally approved; this would have allowed teams to use enlarged versions of the engines already in use. Instead, revolution was now required and a mad dash ensued to ensure new engines could be found and developed in time.

The Lotus team, headed by charismatic but complicated founder Colin Chapman, had been one of the teams pushing for the larger engine size, but they still had a problem or two, including where to source the engine. The BRM engine manufacturer chose to stack two 1.5-litre engines – one on top of the other – while Ferrari and Maserati reused older engine designs from the 1950s for their V12s. The British manufacturer of choice, Coventry Climax, had chosen to withdraw from supplying engines to Formula One.

To create the engine, Chapman turned to two former Lotus engineers, Mike Costin and Keith Duckworth, who in 1958 had set up Cosworth. That Mike Costin had been the Lotus technical director played a substantial part in this decision. Duckworth, who ultimately designed the DFV engine, was noted as a remarkable engineer and designer with an impressive understanding of physics, who was capable of thinking around a problem. In contrast, the older Mike Costin was considered to be a more hands-on practical type.

Duckworth first ran Cosworth on his own in a mews in Kensington, with Mike helping him out whenever he had time. Soon, the company established itself as a trusted supplier of engines for Junior single-seater racing. The work that was carried out on the engines for these championships directly impacted on the future design of the DFV, and Cosworth became known for light, efficient and reliable racing engines.

With Chapman on the hunt for a new engine, he asked Keith Duckworth if he could build it. Keith reportedly replied that he thought he could, but he would need £100,000. Chapman's next problem was now apparent: where to find the money? Many doors were knocked upon, including the Ford Motor Company, the British government and Aston Martin. With time precious, Chapman approached an old acquaintance, Walter Hayes, head of public affairs at Ford of Britain (the British affiliate of the Ford Motor Company). Despite Ford not wanting to enter F1, Hayes got Chapman a dinner with a genial American engineer called Harley Copp, who had worked on NASCAR with Ford in the 1950s. Copp was on board. He and Hayes developed a two-stage plan to get Ford's backing and secure the £100,000 funding.

Cosworth were to develop a four-cylinder engine for Formula Two competition for £25,000, and then produce a V8 Formula One unit for the remaining £75,000. This plan was presented to the Ford of Britain board, headed by Stanley Gillen, who approved the initiative and made it public in 1965. Ford's change of course was a remarkable vote of confidence for Walter Hayes, who went on to have an impressive career at the company, ending up as a vice president.

With time now of the essence, Duckworth went about creating the bottom-up designs for the engines that would make his name, regularly working 16-hour days. The engine showed promise during initial dyno running, where it produced over 400 bhp; the engine's ability to better mix air and fuel improved combustion and generated more power. It took just under two years from putting his pen to paper to handing the engine over to Team Lotus in April 1967. The engine's low weight and compact size was designed to perfectly suit the Lotus 49's design.

The Cosworth DFV made its debut at the 1967 Dutch Grand Prix in Zandvoort. Lotus driver Graham Hill took pole, but teammate Jim Clark went on to take the win, giving the engine a victory in its very first race and initiating the legend of the Cosworth DFV. Clark went on to win three times that year but only came third in the championship as engine reliability issues hampered his campaign. Duckworth continued to work on improvements, with the impact of this shown in 1968. Tragically, Clark was killed early that year at an F2 race in Hockenheim and so it was left to Graham Hill to take the Drivers' Championship, marking the engine's first title.

Whether it was solely Ford's choice or pressure from Formula One, Chapman agreed that the Cosworth DFV engine could be made available for other constructors for the 1968 season. Ford Cosworth-powered entries from Lotus, McLaren and Matra won all but one of the World Championship races in 1968. Only Jacky Ickx with his Ferrari was able to beat them. It was a boon for Ford, which got some nice PR every time a Cosworth DFV car won a race, as the engines were badged as Fords. The engine ended up being used by every specialist team up until the mid-1980s, with a few notable exceptions such as Ferrari, Alfa Romeo and Renault. Its significance was that smaller, single-owner teams such as Tyrrell and Williams could put together cars based around the best engine, and it also forced the teams and their engineers to find other solutions to create performance advantages, in order to win races, as the cars' power units were an even playing field.

The Cosworth DFV and its derivatives (essentially updates) won 155 World Championship races starting with Clark's win at the Dutch Grand Prix and ending with Michele Alboreto's victory in the 1983 Detroit Grand Prix. A DFV-powered car also won every championship until 1975; only the arrival of turbo power in the 1980s stopped the engine's dominance. A Cosworth DFV also powered two Le Mans victories and 10 Indy 500 wins. The Cosworth company grew from a one-man show run out of a London mews in the 1950s to a company with an annual turnover of £33.3 million in 1988 and a work force of 600 people. An incredible achievement for Keith and Mike. More than 30 years later, Ford veterans went on to describe the Cosworth DFV as the 'bargain of the age' – it remains a British engineering achievement worth celebrating.

13

The Making of Colin Chapman

No retrospective on Formula One would be complete without considering the impact Colin Chapman had on the sport.

Widely considered to be one of the greatest engineers, Chapman had a substantial and controversial impact on Formula One over his 24 years in the sport. As the founder and chairman of Lotus, he won seven Constructors' titles, six Drivers' Championships and the Indianapolis 500. The cars he designed and the ideas he pioneered have become icons due to their success, but innovation came at a cost: the machines could be fragile and driver death and injury weren't uncommon. In the end, his legacy is further convoluted by his involvement with the DeLorean sports car company.

Chapman's first exposure to car engineering came in his second term at university – not through his studies, but through dealing with second-hand cars. The London used-car market in the late 1940s was not for the faint of heart, and before long he began to fix the vehicles up a bit, applying his own modifications to the factory designs. Chapman abandoned university and joined the Royal Air Force; by joining directly he avoided national service and spent less time in the forces by design. He did finally end up knuckling down, and after a year of resits he earned his degree.

In his spare time, he decided to enter a car he couldn't sell into a trial, beginning his love affair with motor racing. He produced the Mark II from prize money and drove it in his first meet at a club race at Silverstone, winning a five-lap race. From this, a series of Marks was developed, with MKIII the first to be known as a Lotus. The reason for choosing the name Lotus is not particularly clear – theories included a pet name for his wife Hazel or a random word he saw on a bathroom fitting. Either way, the name stuck. In 1952, with a £25 loan from Hazel, he founded the Lotus Engineering Company. In the early days, Lotus ran out of the stables behind Chapman's dad's pub.

One of the first cars to be produced was a kit car, the MKVI, which could be purchased to be built by the owner. It was a commercial and racing success. The early days of Lotus featured engineer Mike Costin, of Cosworth DFV fame. Mike's brother, Frank Costin, and friends Peter Ross and Gilbert McIntosh also helped Chapman. Their aerodynamic expertise was particularly useful, which Chapman utilized in the design of his cars. In 1953, the team came up with the Lotus MKVIII, which had an all-enveloping body – it looked like a space rocket. The car did well at races and won its class at Silverstone in 1954, later becoming the basis of all future Lotus sports cars.

In 1957, Chapman and his friends further pushed the design of the cars to come up with the Lotus 7. It embodied Chapman's car ideals – high performance driven by low weight and simplicity – and was based on calculations of stress rather than what looked right. Incredibly, the Caterham company still makes a version of the car today.

Chapman was defining himself by his small team of enthusiasts and engineers, who developed a reputation for making uncompromising sports cars for serious enthusiasts. After Lotus finished seventh in the 1956 running of the 24 hours of Le Mans, there was only one place left to aim for – the bright lights of Formula One. After successfully consulting for Vanwall in 1958, it was time for his first design. The sleek, slimline Lotus 12 would begin a legacy of innovation, with a five-speed gearbox and light wheels. The Lotus 18 would push boundaries – the engine was swapped from the front to a mid-engine design, which continues to this day. It was incredibly light and low; Chapman's calling card for the decade to come. Stirling Moss won the Monaco Grand Prix in crushing fashion to record Lotus' first victory in the championship – from stables to the red royal steps of the Monaco trophy presentation.

Popular Scot Innes Ireland was the first non-Moss victory for the main team at New York State's Watkins Glen International circuit at the end of 1961, a pleasing return to form after a wheel had failed and the resulting crash had broken both of his legs. 'Colin's idea of a Grand Prix car was that it should win the race and, as it crossed the finishing line, it should collapse in a heap of bits,' Ireland said in his book *All Arms & Elbows*.

That year also saw the signing of the quintessential Lotus driver Jim Clark, a sheep farmer from Scotland. The Lotus 25 of 1962 then ticked another innovation box, introducing a full monocoque to F1 (a monocoque is when the body and chassis of the car are all connected as one, whereas with road cars, the body of the car is bolted onto the chassis). By 1963, Lotus was the class of the field, winning the Formula One World Championships for both driver and constructor.

The rulebook of the day stated only the six best scores would count for the World Championship. With seven victories in the year, Jim Clark and Chapman had achieved something remarkable together – the Drivers' title had been won with a perfect score of 54 points, something only previously achieved by Alberto Ascari in the early 1950s and never since. Clark's domination to lead 71.47 per cent of the laps in 1963 was referenced for modern audiences after Max Verstappen beat the mark in 2023.

Colin Chapman had designed his way to the top with a monocoque that was stronger than the old cars. But they'd miss out on more titles, with Clark agonizingly falling short in 1964 after an oil leak with just two laps to go of the title decider, costing him the win and the championship. The following season, the Lotus 33 had been tamed just like the 25 had been in its second campaign. Another dominant championship followed, with six victories – a year made even sweeter by success in the Indianapolis 500. In an unprecedented feat, Chapman's Lotus had won it all in the same year.

By 1967, the Lotus 49 raised the bar once more, winning straight out of the box at Zandvoort, the beautiful green and gold machine equipped with the legendary DFV engine (*see* Chapter 12). In 1968, the death of Jim Clark in a Formula Two race in Hockenheim (*see* Chapter 14) rocked Chapman and led to an intense period of introspection. In the aftermath of the horror, Chapman was petrified that his designs – aggressive and light from the modified used-car days – had killed the finest exponent of his work, and more importantly one of his true close friends. Chapman was so distraught he changed the car badge colour to black for a time. He commissioned a full investigation and the car design was cleared.

14

Jim Clark's Death – It Could Happen to Anybody

Few days have caused motorsport such deep sorrow and introspection as 7 April 1968.

Motorsport had lost drivers before – it had lost *champions* before – but this seemed a different class of horror. I have personally experienced the dreadful silence when a circuit should be alive with the sound of engine roar. I recognize similarities from the accounts of the day, some spoken, some implicit. This wasn't just the day two-time world champion Jim Clark died, it was a day that confronted drivers with an obvious truth they all knew, but which, for their sanity, they placed just out of their day-to-day periphery.

James Clark, known to the paddock as Jimmy, had embarked on a remarkable journey from farmer to F1 driver, to international superstar recognized as the greatest of his generation. Twice a world champion, he also became the first Brit to triumph in the famous Indianapolis 500 race, all while driving for Lotus. Those who knew him marvelled at his transformation from a cripplingly shy man to an international star, who in his final years relaxed into celebrity status. When Clark passed away, he held the record for the most F1 victories, with a record 25 Grands Prix wins.

The Hockenheim circuit at the time was a long, thin layout through the forest, with just a few corners. The one the drivers were taking when Jimmy died on lap 6 of the race was driven through flat out, approaching 150 mph even in the sodden conditions. Eyewitness reports say the Lotus' rear instantly stepped out, with Clark unable to correct the slide, and the car then spun towards the inside of the track. 'Suddenly Jim's car broke out,' said Chris Irwin, a British driver who was driving about 200 metres behind. 'It looked like something mechanical. They passed at maximum speed – for a late-1960s' Formula Two car, that was about 150 mph.'

The back end of the car snapped to the left. There had been no barrier on the inside of the circuit and a policeman watching from behind the internal circuit wall built for spectators recounted that the car, 'somersaulted three or four times before smashing broadside into the trees'. Clark struck the biggest tree, the severity of the impact tearing the car into three separate pieces. The gearbox and engine travelled far beyond the chassis and the front end was obliterated. Clark's death at the age of 32 was confirmed at the nearby hospital.

Despite the accident the cars continued racing in the rain. Graham Hill was running near the back of the field. 'He looked in his mirrors, went down through the gears, slowed from 150 mph to walking pace, stared at the debris and shook his head. I could see the shock on his face. Then he accelerated slowly away,' marshal Winfried Kolb told *F1 Racing* in 1998. Kolb had witnessed the frightening sight of a man registering the loss of his teammate, friend and the driver above all others in his generation. Two years later, in his autobiography Graham Hill said of his lost teammate: 'He had the will to win. This tremendous urge to win, which you've just got to have. Some people have got it more than others and he had it more than most. He was a fighter whom you could never shake off ... He invariably shot off in the lead, set up a lead and just sat there dictating the race. He was the ideal racing driver.'

Jim Clark's horrible, violent death ended a notion that drivers had kidded themselves with that 'the greats are safe'. If Jimmy could die, anyone could die, at any point in any race. Future champion and Clark's close friend Jackie Stewart said: 'Jimmy's death is probably the most tragic thing ... in the history of motor racing. Jimmy was not only a famous driver, he was also an international personality, loved by all his fiercest rivals.'

Clark's death showed that ability and skill played no part. The rules of the game had been redefined, cold reality replaced myth. If Clark could go mid-race, they *all* could. The dismay at the loss of this pure racing talent was summed up by *Motor Sport* magazine not even attempting to write an obituary for their edition; they simply ran a picture of Jim Clark on a black background. Formula One was shaken.

The horrid irony was that Clark could have been racing elsewhere that day. His sponsor, Ford, had offered him the opportunity to drive their brand-new sports car at Brands Hatch in Kent, UK. But he was a man of his word and stuck with the agreed, though fairly minor, Formula Two race with Team Lotus, with whom he'd won his Formula One World Championships in 1963 and 1965.

Reading accounts of the day, it's hard to convey the loss, but the effect on team boss Colin Chapman seems to get closest. Distraught, Chapman missed the next race in Spain. This was understandable given what had happened, but the manner in which he'd gone AWOL was unprecedented. Nobody in his team was aware of where he was and they couldn't contact him; Chapman had simply disappeared in his grief. For a Formula One team to not know where the team owner and principal was showed the rawness of what had happened. As the next Grand Prix weekend began, Jim Clark's replacement, Jackie Oliver, turned up to find no car built for him as Team Lotus was operating in the haze of a nightmare. It was left to teammate Graham Hill, who had personally retrieved the pieces of the wreckage by hand, to run the team for a weekend alongside the shell-shocked mechanics.

Ten years later, Colin Chapman would tell *Motoring News* that Jimmy 'was the finest man I ever knew. As a driver, he was a complete genius.' Chapman seriously considered quitting the sport, and as mentioned in Chapter 13, he commissioned a full investigation to find out if he was responsible. They knew the manner of the accident meant only suspension or a puncture could have been at fault, and after an exhaustive process, it was found that a newly designed tubeless tyre had failed. In 1968, contemporary accounts suggest there were more than 100 motorsport fatalities, but nothing compared to the sense of despair that greeted the loss of one of Formula One's greatest.

Colin Chapman
– After Jim

After Jim Clark's harrowing fatal crash in a Formula Two race at Hockenheim, Colin Chapman returned to the helm.

He rejoined his Lotus team at the Monaco Grand Prix in 1968, and there he was forced to display his rare leadership qualities to talk down his furious team. Chapman had gone AWOL for the preceding race in Spain, effectively leaving driver Graham Hill in charge, and the mechanics didn't take kindly to his sudden reappearance, the lack of explanation about his absence and the fact he'd issued them with an enormous task list. But this was Chapman; the rules didn't apply to him. Still, by the time he'd finished speaking to the mechanics, they were ready to fight – inspirational leadership finds a way, even in the most extreme of circumstances.

Team Lotus, fresh in a new livery, as they'd introduced sponsorship to F1 after years of seeing American teams make big money from it (*see* Chapter 16), set about the task list. Amongst rebuilding the car, the mechanics were also asked to attach small wings to it. Chapman had been inspired by the aerodynamic elements he'd seen on a sports car team. Graham Hill duly won the Monaco Grand Prix with the new design of a single-element front wing on either side of the nose. By Silverstone, a few races later, giant rear wings were rife across the grid – the rate of change in Formula One was unrelenting.

Chapman was regularly winning races, lived a jet-set lifestyle and was one of the most prominent technical minds on the planet. He'd listed Lotus cars on the stock exchange and wanted for nothing, yet he was repeatedly dogged by criticism – not of his work but of his character.

Some in racing circles argued he was only interested in the car and took risks with the designs that were borderline unethical. The rapid Austrian Jochen Rindt had been signed by the team in 1969, and his stint brought the criticism to a head. He'd been told by his manager, Bernie Ecclestone, that the Brabham team would be the safest route to the title, while Lotus would be faster but potentially risky. World champion and racing rival Jackie Stewart implored his friend not to switch teams.

Rindt, like any driver, wanted the title above all else. He chose Chapman but railed against the risks he perceived he faced, constantly arguing for a more cautious approach. The uneasy relationship blew up at the Spanish Grand Prix of 1969, with Lotus' large wings being extended and modified in the pits. The end result: the rear wings of both cars collapsed at the same fast corner of the already risky Montjuïc circuit. Hill was unharmed but Jochen was badly shaken, concussed and furious with his boss. In an extraordinary move, he wrote two open letters, one to prominent journalists calling for wings to be banned and one to Chapman highlighting how he'd had three accidents in his four months with the team.

Rindt dreamt of creating his own team but his favoured designer formed the group owning the March team (*see* Chapter 17) and Brabham did not have enough funds to pay his wage demands. And so he'd found himself at Lotus in a marriage of convenience. Things were improved by the mighty Lotus 72, which featured wings moulded to the chassis, side-mounted radiators and innovative brakes, with the chassis shaped like a wedge. It was instantly iconic and incredibly effective in a straight line. After a mess of a Spanish Grand Prix in 1970 with poorly calibrated suspension, the 72 was reintroduced at the Dutch

Grand Prix and Rindt won four races in a row to edge closer to the title he craved before a planned early retirement.

The second part was not to be. Rindt was fatally injured in a horrible crash at Monza after his car struck a barrier that wasn't fit for purpose. Chapman was again under the microscope; an eventual inquiry found a brake issue and the poorly installed barrier as the causes of the accident. Rindt had amassed enough points to become Formula One's only posthumous world champion. The 72 would win for four years, netting Lotus yet another Constructors' title in 1973, but its replacement would fall badly short and a period away from the front began.

Big ideas were required to end the bust and return to boom times. The Lotus 78 was a blockbuster. After a career of quantum leaps, Chapman and his increasingly large design team introduced ground effect, tightly forcing the air underneath the car in order to seal it at the side and push it to the track, with devastating effect. Mario Andretti had shown faith in Colin during a fallow period and now enjoyed the rewards of his patience with a car that had almost impossible levels of grip. After five wins in 1977, Lotus was confident for 1978 with two excellent drivers in Andretti and Ronnie Peterson. Andretti's extraction of the Lotus' capabilities gained him number-one status from Chapman. Driving the Lotus 79, Andretti created the highest cornering speeds seen in Formula One to date.

Andretti strolled to the championship, but the day the title was won was overshadowed by the crash sustained by his teammate Ronnie Peterson after a first-lap crash that left him with badly broken legs. The team celebrated the titles, albeit in muted tones for their poor teammate, who would recover in time, surely. Except he didn't. Overnight, an embolism caused kidney failure and another Lotus driver passed away. It was another title attached to tragedy, and the Lotus 79 wouldn't win another race as the pack finally caught up.

The Lotus 80 was meant to take things even further, with the entire car acting as a wing. The entire underside was designed to generate aerodynamic grip, but the car was so powerful it would trap the air, hit the floor and stall before the airflow would spring back up and begin the whole process again. Mario Andretti would call the phenomenon 'porpoising'.

After three decades at the cutting edge, one of motor racing's greatest stories ended on 16 December 1982. At just fifty-four years of age, Colin Chapman died of a heart attack. His team were working on a new idea he'd hoped would revise their fortunes – active suspension. In the final months of Chapman's life, he had been doing business with the notorious American businessman John DeLorean, who had secured government funding to build the car featured in *Back to the Future*, from a factory in Dunmurry, Northern Ireland. The project fell apart quickly after DeLorean was charged with drug-dealing offences, and £12 million of government funding had been lost. The funds were eventually traced to Chapman, DeLorean and Lotus financial head Fred Bushell's controlled bank account. Bushell was an integral key to Lotus, who had kept the car company from financial ruin on many occasions.

If he'd survived, Colin Chapman's complex legacy would have almost certainly included a high-profile Court Case. A strange last act for a genius engineer who created a title-winning dynasty powered by design and innovation. Even in death, he is debated with rumour and conjecture, with some of his former drivers believing he fled his former life. What is undeniable is that his racing record was incredible: 72 Grands Prix wins, 88 poles, six Drivers' titles and seven Constructors' titles. More than that, he planted the flag on territory still used in modern motor racing today. The term 'visionary' is overused in sport, but no one deserved the title more in Formula One than Colin Chapman.

16

The Ad Men Arrive

Mid-March 1968 and a full media frenzy had descended on Brands Hatch.

It was a busy race weekend with TV crews, written media and thousands of spectators. Far from the on-track action taking centre stage, the Kent circuit's paddock was abuzz with the news Lotus had a sponsor! Team Lotus was now Gold Leaf Team Lotus. The mechanics set to work on a gleaming red car with a gold stripe painted down the middle. On the side was the sticker of a sailor – at the time, the instantly recognizable emblem of the Imperial Tobacco Company Gold Leaf brand. The brand had insisted on being first in the naming order, creating the very first Formula One title sponsor and changing the look of motorsport forever.

Since 1903, each team in European-based motor racing had been designated a colour by the governing body. The British had Green, the French blue, and – as you may have guessed – the Italians had Red. The tradition is the reason Ferrari still runs in red to this day. But Lotus' days of running British racing green were over. Soon the national colours would, for the most part, be a thing of the past as sponsors' brand colours took over and repainted the grid. This was not some dastardly scheme of enrichment for the Norfolk-based team; it was entirely within the rules, with the FIA voting to allow sponsorship logos on the cars. It was suggested and approved in the face of fuel companies tightening their belts and F1 costs rising with every technological development made; the teams had appealed to the authorities to broaden their opportunities for funding. It was a perfectly timed move.

Cigarette companies were facing a crisis; they had been banned from advertising on TV, with governments all over the world beginning to intervene in the face of mounting evidence of the detrimental health effects of their products. However, they were still permitted to sponsor events, and the rules around sponsorship on TV hadn't been rewritten. The marketing men had their answer: no other sport combined speed and glamour like Formula One, it lent instant cool to any brand and nothing was easier to sponsor than a giant banner travelling at 150 mph.

The TV channels covering the race went ballistic. They feared fines and a huge amount of negative coverage for Lotus' actions. If they were to broadcast the race then the Gold Leaf sponsorship logo would need to be changed. A compromise was reached, and the second milestone of the weekend was achieved with the introduction of subliminal cigarette advertising – the same colour scheme, the same font, but a slightly altered logo.

This quirk would remain a prominent feature in motorsport in the late 1990s. Marlboro became a barcode, West became the driver's name, Rothmans logo became 'R?' and Benson and Hedges became 'Bitten Heroes'. Ferrari was still doing this as late as 2018, when various governments asked why Philip Morris International continued to pay Ferrari millions of pounds for sponsorship, despite the brand logos being banned since the early 2000s. Back in the 1960s, though, the compromise worked, with Gold Leaf remaining on the Lotus, as it appeared on the entry list as the official team name, and over the coming decades millions of pounds flooded into the sport.

Sponsorship controversies would continue and, incredibly, would prevent the British public watching one of the most remarkable seasons in championship history just eight years later. The Surtees team had launched a livery adorned with Durex condom logos. Murray Walker was due to cover the race for the BBC and was told by a producer that as far as the BBC was concerned, a visible Durex logo was totally unacceptable for family viewing. They were not going to transmit the race unless Surtees agree to take it off their cars. John Surtees refused and the BBC packed up. Thankfully, things would be resolved so the final round in Japan could be broadcast on both BBC and ITV as James Hunt became Britain's sixth world champion. The Durex logos were prominent on both the BBC and ITV broadcasts, but fears for family values apparently vanished in the face of James Hunt's success and British patriotism.

For all the controversy around sponsorship, the upside was considerable. The early adoption of brand association put F1 ahead of other sports – no football shirt was sponsored in England until 1983, by which time multiple brands had taken their funds to motor racing. Beyond the money, the true legacy was the litany of liveries dictated by cigarette packet colours, always to be associated with legendary teams and drivers of the era.

By 1999, Big Tobacco was fighting a losing battle trying to continue sponsoring sporting events. British American Tobacco therefore decided to bypass the sponsorship bit and bought an entire team for marketing purposes. They instantly caused a stink by wanting to run the cars in split liveries: Jacques Villeneuve in a red and white Lucky Strike, while Ricardo Zonta was to be in the blue 555 that had been so associated with Subaru's rallying heroics. Fears of the grid running in 20 separate liveries put a stop to it. The new team were forced to run both with a big zip down the middle, and the car looked as muddled as the year which followed on track. The car's low/high point was in Spa when 1997 champion Villeneuve challenged Zonta not to lift the throttle through Eau Rouge. The bet ended with two huge accidents, and both cars were written off. Unsurprisingly, the team scored no points that year, and the livery was plain white the following season.

March Burst on to the Scene and Win

You don't just rock up and win in Formula One, but in 1970, four friends did.

Using an acronym of their names – Max Mosley, Alan Rees, Graham Coaker and Robin Herd – the quartet who'd met at various points across school, university and racing set up March Engineering in 1969. Gentleman racer Mosley was to head up the commercial side of things, with Rees managing the racing, Coaker looking after manufacturing and Robin Herd the key man as designer/engineer. The team debuted on the racing scene at Cadwell Park in August 1969 with a Formula Three (F3 693) car driven by Ronnie Peterson.

The team seemed ambitious, although there were questions over their financial backing – where had the money come from? They announced they were building F1 cars for 1970 in their new factory in Oxfordshire, but this was met with some scepticism. At the season opener in South Africa in 1970, there were five March 701s present after a 12-week design and build. They'd originally been designed for Jackie Stewart at Tyrrell for himself and Johnny Servoz-Gavin. Mario Andretti, Chris Amon and Jo Siffert also had works cars, with the March 701 chassis built around Cosworth V8 engines.

Despite the scepticism, the March 701 had an unprecedented and impressive start to its F1 career. At the first race of the new season at the Kyalami Circuit in South Africa, it took a while for the March 701, racing under the Tyrrell team, to be set up properly for the first day of practice, but by Thursday Jackie was away and setting the pace. Stewart was expected to be fast even in a new car; the paddock started to take notice when Amon, racing with the works team, also managed to set a fast practice time in the new and unraced car. At the very first race, Stewart took pole and Amon was second behind him on the grid!

The paddock expectation was for Stewart to run away and hide in the Grand Prix, but Jack Brabham in his eponymous car had other plans. Despite a knock from a Lotus, driven by Jochen Rindt, Brabham began to whittle away at Jackie's lead. Stewart focused on ensuring the car finished rather than pushing it to its max to get a win, particularly as his Dunlop tyres began to struggle in the heat. This allowed Brabham, using Goodyear tyres to overtake Stewart on lap 20, to take his final Grand Prix victory – a win scored at the age of 43, making him the fifth oldest driver to ever win in F1. Stewart eventually finished third in the race behind Brabham and Denny Hulme in a McLaren. A podium for March after a 12-week design and build was incredible.

Other March cars were not as successful. Despite his promising qualifying times, Amon got caught up in the Rindt crash and ended up 18th. Amon managed to make up six places, but his water-system had broken and the engine overheated, leading to a DNF. Siffert was never in contention but was able to battle with Jacky Ickx in a Ferrari and Jean-Pierre Beltoise in a Matra before ultimately coming tenth. Andretti's water system blew right off in a cloud of steam, resulting in a DNF. Servoz-Gavin in the second Tyrrell was also a DNF. Despite the mixed bag for all five cars in the race, the strong qualifying and a podium finish was a pretty good showing for an untested car.

The next event for the March 701s was the 1970 Race of Champions at Brands Hatch. Stewart took pole after a determined last shot. The race was not easy as he struggled with the combination of the Dunlop tyres and the car's loose rear end. Stewart won the race with his usual Scottish tenacity, while Brabham suffered an ignition failure, delivering the March constructor their first win in only their second race!

At the second round of the F1 World Championship, four of the five same drivers were back with their March 701s at the Jarama circuit in Spain. While the March team were buoyant after the first two races, engineer Herd responded to the drivers' concerns and redesigned the rear end of Stewart, Amon and Siffert's cars to be lighter, with the brakes adjusted to further reduce weight.

Brabham took pole but Stewart in his Tyrrell had an excellent start and led Hulme in the McLaren and Brabham into the first corner, which he maintained by pushing the car far harder than at Kyalami. Brabham did look to be closing in on the Tyrrell, but Stewart just managed to pull away. Stewart fought hard to maintain his lead, and then Brabham's Cosworth engine gave up.

The March 701, operated by the Tyrrell team, had won its first World Championship Grand Prix in only the car's third race! Andretti came third, providing the constructor with another podium. March Engineering ended up third in the 1970s Constructor standings in their opening season.

March would expand rapidly into Formula Two, Formula Three, Cam Am, Sportscars and Formula Ford. After the incredible start, Formula One was somewhat less successful, with the team only sporadically running a winning Formula One works team, though they did still supply custom cars to the smaller single-owner teams, such as Williams. Despite their early success with Stewart at Tyrrell, March didn't win their own Grand Prix until 1975, with Vittorio Brambilla in Austria, who was so surprised to see the chequered flag out early, he spun after winning and completed his victory lap with a broken front wing.

Popular Swede Ronnie Peterson became a regular at the front for March and won at Monza in 1976. A year later, March had run out of steam and the Formula One team was sold. The company continued producing racing cars in other categories, with notable success in IndyCar, until the early 1990s.

While March may not be a household name, the considerable early success by a group of friends is quite the achievement. They were one of the first teams to run a woman, Lella Lombardi; early hirers of fabled engineer Adrian Newey (*see* Chapter 31); and the first to give a young Niki Lauda a drive in Formula One in 1971. Commercial brain Max Mosley went on to run the FIA, and alongside Bernie Ecclestone set the sport on its path to becoming an entertainment giant.

Ron Dennis Crashes Through his Windscreen

Ron Dennis' move to management was not sealed in a boardroom; there was no handshake or small talk.

Instead, he woke up dazed in a hospital bed, seriously injured, where he would remain for several weeks.

As Dennis lay there, his whirlwind early-twenties momentum had finally been arrested. He had a badly cut face, both eyes were damaged with glass in them, and the contact he'd made with the steering wheel had punctured his lung. Dennis had fallen asleep at the wheel of his Jaguar E-Type. Having been hurled through the windscreen at speed after striking a lamppost, he could easily have been killed in the crash.

For several weeks, he was consigned to his own thoughts, and inevitably began to picture what could come next. Ambition took hold amid the pain. There would be no more getting his hands dirty; instead, management and ownership was the path ahead for him.

Dennis had a narrow escape, but the fact he was driving a Jaguar E-Type in his early twenties was a sign this was no ordinary operator. As a child, he'd been taken by his older brother to a race at Brands Hatch on Boxing Day, but instead of catching the typical driving dream he'd been hit by a desire to work on the cars; that's where all the creativity lay.

A key aspect of any great is their ability to make the difficult happen; for Ron Dennis, this meant talking his way into the Brabham F1 team after he'd offered to sweep the floor and make the tea. Two mechanics at the team took the teenager under their wing, exposing him to the workings of a top-line F1 team. Dennis credits the mechanics' kindness and sharing of knowledge as key to his obsessive, immaculate approach. After studying motor vehicle engineering at college, Dennis was able to work for the Cooper car company, again showing considerable skills beyond his years. Using this as a springboard, he was able to obtain a coveted place working for a Formula One team at just nineteen years of age.

Dennis would first enter an F1 paddock during the 1967 season, his passion for the job taking up every waking hour At the time, Cooper was running an exciting pair of drivers: Pedro Rodríguez and Jochen Rindt. Rindt loved the industry and graft of his young mechanic, who kept the standards of a surgeon in the normally messy workshop and garages. The next year, when the charismatic Austrian moved to the Drivers' and Constructors' title-winning Brabham team, he insisted on taking the young Dennis with him. Rindt didn't stay long, transferring to Colin Chapman's Lotus team for 1969, and this time Ron stayed put, helping to service the great three-time world champion Jack Brabham's entry at just twenty-one years of age.

In 1970, Jack Brabham finally brought his glittering driving career to an end, and it was a testament to the standards Dennis had set that he was crucial to one last moment of reluctance from the Australian giant, who recounted his final day as a driver in his autobiography: 'Ron Dennis, my chief mechanic, packed my driving bag away in a crate of things, to be shipped home, so I promptly whipped it out and said, "In case I need it some time!"' Stressed and conflicted about abandoning driving, Brabham found the spectre of retiring a hugely stressful ordeal. Wanting to escape the place where it had all ended, he left Ron Dennis in charge to collect the prize money. Dennis was getting experience of team management processes way before any other of his peers, and by an Acapulco hotel pool, he found himself at a personal crossroads – if team management wasn't beyond him, there was no point just taking a wage as chief mechanic.

The only logical next step was to run his own operation. The pitch was simple: to introduce Formula One standards to Formula Two. But starting up this young and with no money turned heads. How would he start a team from scratch without paid drivers or cars? The answer was to lean on his contacts. Dennis brokered a deal to buy Formula Two-spec Brabham's at a preferential rate from Brabham head honcho Ron Tauranac. Crucially, he wouldn't be charged until the end of the season – time enough, he hoped, to prove himself and then later sell on winning cars.

The team was called Rondel Racing, the name formed with Neil Trundle, another mechanic at Brabham. With only enough money to pay operating costs, every penny counted; Dennis kept the pit, garage and transporter gleaming, hoping sponsors would be impressed.

He also found a technicality in the rule book that saw big established names paid more for their appearance in the field. In those days, F2 had different chassis and engines, while F1 drivers would regularly compete. Incredibly, on occasion Dennis persuaded two-time world champion Graham Hill to race for the team, and they also fielded Australian Tim Schenken. At twenty-four years of age, Ron Dennis was a team owner – and a successful one. Rondel finished second in the first round before winning second time out at the Thruxton F2 international race, thanks to Graham Hill.

Rondel were winners, and sponsors, approving of the immaculate facilities, wanted to invest. French oil company Motul approached the team, and Rondel Racing went from nothing to a three-car entry in just a few months. This would rise to four in 1972 and a planned six in 1974. Dennis had proven himself in the second tier and believed it was time to return to F1, this time as team owner and principal. The team moved quickly, purchasing a factory building in Feltham and hiring a designer, with staff being added every day. Motul were so impressed with the Formula Two project, they'd bankrolled the step up to Formula One. Unfortunately, the 1973 oil crisis saw prices soar and production falter. All luxuries were scrapped – and so was the entire project. Dennis was out of pocket from the initial outlay of building a team. Devastated, he sold the factory to Graham Hill, who was starting his own Formula One team, just to break even.

Ron Dennis had experienced more before twenty-seven years of age than some do in a lifetime in the sport, but this really hurt. He was off the big stage and short on offers. Then a huge brand came calling. Marlboro had enormous budgets when it came to sponsorship in motorsport. The marketing men wanted to run two Ecuadorian drivers they knew to be tailenders in Formula Two, in the hope of increasing their market share in that region of South America. Running two backmarkers wasn't much better than not having a team, so Dennis worked out the total it would take to re-establish their pre-oil crisis position and hoped the Philip Morris Tobacco budgets really were that big. They were, and the team was back in business.

The 'Project' teams went through various iterations, running March cars in F2 and winning the British Formula Three title on two occasions. By 1976, Project Four Racing was a serious player in the lower categories and had a great reputation. When BMW started the Procar competition on the Grand Prix weekend, they needed 40 beautiful M1 cars built rapidly. Project Four would build 20; Lamborghini would build the other half. It was all hands on deck to complete the build, with the mid-engined cars sprayed all over the site: indoors, outdoors, every inch of space was used to construct the orders to an exacting schedule. With a huge sense of satisfaction, Project Four finished the final car. Then the phone rang; BMW had just discovered Lamborghini had only finished one car! Dennis both cursed and blessed his Italian counterparts; they'd have to do it all again, but the price BMW paid set the team back on the path to Formula One.

In 1980, it was Dennis who approached Marlboro, suggesting he could build them an entirely new racing operation after their F1-backed McLaren team had faltered, failing to win a race in three years. Marlboro didn't want to abandon McLaren, having won multiple titles with them, so Dennis bought in. Marlboro essentially forced a merger of Bruce McLaren's original team and Project Four. By 1982, Dennis had gained full control, beginning a period of incredible McLaren achievements. In Ron's 32 seasons as team principal, McLaren won 138 races. Out of 21 world titles (Drivers' and Constructors') won by the team – including the 2024 Constructors' Championship – 17 came during Ron Dennis' reign. A mighty legacy for someone who grafted his way into Formula One. In 2024, he was knighted – only the ninth motor racing knight in British history.

19

The Used-Car Deal that Gave Hunt a Shot

Hunt's big break came from an unexpected meeting.

On 9 November 1967, racing driver and member of the British aristocracy Charles Lucas married socialite Antoinette Von Westenholz in a society wedding held at the Church of Immaculate Conception in Mayfair.

While Charles Lucas' wedding suit was stylish enough to end up in London's Victoria and Albert Museum, the most important moment from that day was not the joyful union of the couple but a meeting between two of Lucas' guests – and a failed used-car deal that unfolded at the reception. The main long-term beneficiary of this deal, James Hunt, wasn't even there.

Public schoolboy, former racer and second-hand car dealer Anthony 'Bubbles' Horsley had been buying and selling Mercedes, Rolls-Royces and Bentleys. He'd developed a sales approach of turning up at weddings in one of his cars – reportedly a Bentley at Lucas' wedding – to try to sell to his target audience. At this wedding, he met Thomas Alexander Fermor-Hesketh, 3rd Baron Hesketh, and offered him the Bentley. Somehow, instead, Lord Hesketh offered Horsley his Mercedes to purchase – a Mercedes that would in fact turn out to be Hesketh's mother's. With the confusion settled over lunch the next day (and one assumes a hangover), a firm friendship between the two men was set in motion.

In 1968, the young Mini car driver James Hunt had just graduated to single-seater racing. He was born in August 1947, the rebellious and hot-headed son of a London stockbroker. Hunt had seen his first motor race at a club meeting at Silverstone on his eighteenth birthday and decided that this was the sport for him. With his parents refusing any support, he scraped together the funds to buy a wrecked Mini and soon developed a reputation as a fast but accident-prone driver over the course of his junior racing career, as epitomized by his nickname 'Hunt the Shunt'. He started in Formula Ford, where in one crash the off was so big he ended up in a lake, where his car duly sank. Despite the damage to his wallet and reputation, he graduated to Formula Three, earning a place with March in 1972. Hunt later described F3 as being incredibly useful in learning how to crash, or not crash, in close racing.

However, all was not plain sailing at March. A confrontation with Max Mosley came to head at Monaco. Formula Three was the support race for the Grand Prix that year, and Hunt wanted to make a good impression to improve his chances of getting to F1. He felt the car had mechanical issues and was not generating enough performance, while Mosley was fed up with all the expensive crashes. James went to old friend Chris Marshall and ended up driving with his team for qualifying. Mosley threatened the sack, and then followed through when Hunt drove in the main race with Marshall's team. No matter who was right, James Hunt no longer had a permanent seat in Formula Three.

At the next Formula Three race, in Belgium, Hunt raced in an old car, again borrowed from Marshall, but this was not a long-term solution. With no sponsorship and no earnings, Hunt needed another option. While he had been climbing the junior ladder, Horsley and Hesketh had been busy setting up a new Formula Three team funded by Hesketh's new inheritance. As fate would have it, Horsley needed a driver and Hunt needed a drive. Horsley had been impressed by Hunt's speed earlier in the season, and they met at the race in Belgium – in an old World War I tent being used as a loo – where they began to discuss the driver's future.

Horsley offered Hunt the drive, on condition of his meeting and being vetted by Hesketh. First impressions were not great; Lord Hesketh was concerned about Hunt's reputation as 'The Shunt', as crashes would be expensive to fix. He also felt Hunt was 'well pleased with himself'. Despite these concerns, however, Hunt was duly signed up as second driver. While these things are rarely obvious at the time, Hunt had taken his first steps to the big time.

The first race at Brands Hatch was not an auspicious start for the new team. Number-one driver Horsley crashed one of their Dastles in practice and Hunt smashed the other up in the race. This could have been the end of the team, but Lord Hesketh was not your usual patron, and instead the team went looking for a new car. Hunt and Horsley managed to convince Max Mosley into lending them a year-old March F2 chassis, and the money was stumped up to purchase a Ford engine.

Perhaps unexpectedly, Max Mosley appeared to become something of a fairy godfather to the team, which, dabbling in peak public-school hijinks, would get up to all sorts. Mosley came across the team praying to the 'Great Chicken in the Sky' when their newly acquired Ford engine eventually gave way. Mosley lent them a spare and the fairy godfather was christened 'The Great Chicken of Bicester' in recognition of the March team's factory location. No good deed goes unpunished in F1, and Mosley was met with chicken noises every time he was spotted in the paddock by Hesketh Racing, something which strangely enough he didn't find very funny.

At the end of 1972, Horsley quit racing and became team manager as Hunt entered the last F2 races of the season. These races were slightly more successful, with Hunt finishing in the points twice, and he achieved a third behind Ronnie Peterson and Niki Lauda in their Marches at Oulton Park. For the 1973 season, Hesketh Racing decided to return to Formula Two after purchasing a Surtees car with a Ford engine. However, the car wasn't competitive enough at the first race at Mallory Park.

Jean-Pierre Jarier in his works BMW-engine-powered March outcompeted Hunt and the other Ford engine cars. Hunt still managed to finish fifth, but it wasn't quite the result the team had wanted.

After this, Hesketh Racing went for an unusual but familiar team tactic in trying to race in the series above if the current series wasn't quite turning out how they expected. The team entered a non-championship Formula One race, the Race of Champions, to see how they would get on. They borrowed a Surtees TSB9 F1 car and the gamble paid off as Hunt achieved third, just behind 1967 world champion Denny Hulme in a McLaren. The more power a car had, the better Hunt appeared to drive. With the test race a success, Formula One and the Monaco Grand Prix beckoned. Hesketh and Horsley went back to Mosley and leased a March F1 car for £8,000. And with the help of some white Burgundy, they also secured the recruitment of two talented young engineers, Dr Harvey Postlethwaite and Nigel Stroud. Finally, Hesketh also stumped up for two Ford Cosworth DFV engines.

The team made their Formula One World Championship debut in Monte Carlo to great fanfare; Hesketh had gone all-out with the team's 192-foot support yacht, complete with butlers and minimally clad women serving champagne. Despite the nerves, Hunt did well. The car qualified 18th out of 25 starters, and Hunt managed to move up to sixth place before having to retire five laps from the end after an engine failure. The rest of the season went better; Hunt scored points at the next race at Paul Ricard and then went on to finish fourth at Silverstone, while managing to avoid Jody Scheckter's famous multi-car crash. Hunt the Shunt returned for Monza, but he did better at Watkins Glen, finishing second. In 1973, despite only entering eight races, James Hunt came eighth in the World Championship.

Hesketh Racing, and James Hunt, were popular with the British press and public; less so with the Formula One paddock. Lord Hesketh's aristocratic champagne-and-caviar ways, coupled with

James Hunt's volatile temperament and playboy lifestyle, were met with suspicion. But behind the glitzy façade, a determined team of dedicated mechanics and talented engineers worked steadily on improvements to make the team more competitive.

In 1975, Hesketh Racing decided to race their own car. The Hesketh 308 first raced at the Race of Champions, with Hunt taking pole. The team finally achieved their maiden victory at Zandvoort after a clever strategy to stay on dry settings despite the rain. With the sky clearing, Hunt was the first to pit to slicks and took the lead. Despite Niki Lauda of Ferrari's best attempts, Hunt managed to hold on to the lead to just take the win. Both Hunt and the team came fourth in the Drivers' and Constructors' World Championships.

That was to be Hesketh Racing's final year in Formula One; with Britain in a recession Hesketh struggled to fund the team, and with no sponsorship imminent the fun had to end. Postlethwaite went on to have a great career in Formula One, working for Tyrrell and Ferrari. Lord Hesketh became a Conservative peer in the House of Lords in the British Parliament, and James Hunt – he joined McLaren and won the World Championship in a famous rivalry against Ferrari's Niki Lauda. If Horsley had not offered a young and wealthy Lord Hesketh that Bentley, it's unlikely James Hunt would have become the iconic playboy F1 driver who epitomized British racing in the 1970s. And to that, we raise a glass!

Slowing Down F1 - Introducing the Safety Car

The safety car first made an appearance over 50 years ago at the 1973 Canadian Grand Prix.

The car was introduced in response to the horrible death of Roger Williamson at the 1973 Dutch Grand Prix; racer David Purley had bravely stopped his own car and attempted in vain to help his friend. The unflinching report into the accident cited the need to remove the decision to slow down away from the drivers. Those still in the race believed Williamson's overturned alight March to be Purley's car and did not stop. Such horror could not be repeated. A 'pace car' rule was introduced, with the aim to freeze the race and stop all overtakes while a clearly recognizable pace car with flashing lights and bright colours left the pits. The race leader was to catch up to the car and the rest of the field was to follow behind.

After the introduction in 1973, the safety car did not become a regular fixture in Formula One until the 1990s. Currently, Formula One has two forms – the physical car and the virtual safety car – and they have the same objective: to make the track safer for marshals to remove crashed cars and debris. The quickest lap the safety cars are expected to do with fresh tyres is around 40 seconds a lap slower than normal race pace. In addition, there is a separate medical car that brings an FIA-certified doctor to any accident. Whether the physical car or the virtual car is used, the aim is to slow down the pack of drivers, reducing risks to marshals, spectators and competitors. A side effect of this is that it can upend team strategy and lead to some exciting developments once the racing is allowed to be restarted.

The virtual safety car is based on the 'Slow Zone' systems used in the Le Mans 24 Hours race. It too was a response to a horrible moment, introduced after Jules Bianchi's death at the 2014 Japanese Grand Prix. The aim isn't to bunch the cars up together, but instead the drivers stick to a set time that is flashed on the screens on their steering wheels. This is meant to be less disruptive to racing. It works by yellow flagging a race, while a VSC sign is flashed on illuminated signs. A delta time is shown to the drivers on their screens – this time is the difference between their current racing speed and the safety car time (usually the reduction is about 30–40 per cent of a normal race pace) and overtaking is not allowed.

At the 1973 Austrian Grand Prix, a test run of the pace car was carried out – a bright-yellow Porsche with yellow flags out the back. It was not subtle, and unfortunately the safety car's first official outing in Canada was far from auspicious. Prior to the Canadian race getting started, there was a torrential downpour. As the racetrack dried up, this led to many tyre changes and some commotion in the pit lane, then Jody Scheckter in a McLaren and Francois Cevert's Tyrrell crashed, blocking the circuit. With a breakdown truck out trying to clear the debris and bedlam in the pits, the Porsche driven by Eppie Wietzes was released – only to cause more chaos. The safety car picked the wrong lead driver in the days before electronic timing, meaning most of the field ended up a lap down. Several hours later, Peter Revson in a McLaren was confirmed the winner.

The safety car was not used again until 1976 at the Monaco Grand Prix, despite opposition to its use. It then returned for the 1981, 1982 and 1983 Monaco Grand Prix race weekends as a Lamborghini Countach. In 1992, another safety car was trialled at the British and French Grands Prix, with the car becoming a permanent Formula One fixture in 1993. By this time, the car looked a bit different, with each racetrack providing their own version. A Fiat Tempra was used in Brazil, a Ford Escort in Britain, a Honda Prelude in Japan and, my personal favourite, a Renault Clio in Argentina. A little different to the high-performance sports cars used today.

It wasn't until 1996 that Mercedes started supplying the official safety car, to be consistent across all races. Over the years, the car brand remained the same, while the model was upgraded every few years. In 2010, Mercedes introduced the gull-wing SLS AMG car, which has a top speed of over 200 mph, and in 2021 the car was changed from silver to red to improve drivers' visibility during poor conditions.

The next step in safety car progress following the standardization of the car was the appointment of German Bernd Maylander as the driver for the opening 2000 Australian Grand Prix. Maylander is an experienced sports car racer, having driven in the DTM and won the Nürburgring 24 Hours race, as well as being a podium finisher at the Le Mans 24 Hours race. Over the past two decades he has only not driven the safety car twice, and he is always accompanied by a co-driver. Both of them have to sit in the car for the whole race so they are ready at a moment's notice. In 2021, Aston Martin provided a car for the first time – including its most controversial deployment in the 2021 Abu Dhabi Grand Prix (*see* Chapter 73).

The safety and medical cars began as important innovations that help to make Formula One what it is today – with the added element of its deployment creating a closed-up pack for fans to enjoy from an entertainment point of view.

Project 34 – The Legendary Six-Wheeler

In 1975, Ken Tyrrell really enjoyed showing off his new car design to trusted friends.

The biggest secret in F1 would always conjure the same reaction from individuals staring at the vehicle for the first time. Pure astonishment. The Tyrrell 'Project 34' became the stuff of motor racing legend, created in an era of converging competition where teams felt compelled to take greater and greater technological leaps in the search for lap time. This was not the era of marginal gains; everything was up for debate, including the number of wheels on the car.

After allowing for stunned silence, team owner and principal Ken Tyrrell would bellow with laughter as another onlooker gawped, amazed at his car with four tiny wheels at the front and two giant rear tyres. The bold design theory was to hide the front wheels within the bodywork, setting the four wheels behind the bulbous front wing to improve aerodynamic performance and to give Tyrrell an advantage of straight-line speed. Designer Derek Gardner ascertained it would be worth the equivalent of 40 extra horsepower. F1 had never seen anything like it; this was at a time when most teams were running the Ford Cosworth DFV engine. It was Tyrrell's hope it would take the team back to the titles they'd won in 1969 (as Matra), 1971 and 1973.

The snag came from the tiny front wheels – the small tyre size needed a bespoke design. Thankfully, most who heard the concept became engrossed in the romanticism of it all, and

Goodyear mainly agreed, only insisting on a change from 9- to 10-inch rims. The new front of the car was actually based on an old idea. Derek Gardner had first envisaged a six-wheeler for the Lotus entry at Indianapolis in the 1960s, but neither Lotus nor their wealthy sponsor were interested in building it and so the blueprints had been stowed away in a drawer. But with many teams running similar or identical gearboxes, tyres and engines, any radical concept was now being entertained by those not at the very front. Tyrrell had slipped from third in 1974 to fifth by 1975.

The team's drivers had decidedly mixed opinions about the machine. South African and future world champion Jody Scheckter was highly suspicious, clearly aware he'd be risking his life in an outlandish design; meanwhile Frenchman Patrick Depailler found himself swept up in the furore. Both drivers agreed it was highly different to drive, with Scheckter likening it to a roller skate sensation, as he couldn't see the front wheels for a turning reference from the cockpit. The solution was a so-called porthole, a see-through panel in the side of the car allowing the driver to see the lower, smaller wheels.

The on-track debut for the six-wheeler, at the Paul Ricard circuit in southern France, would decide the car's fate. Would it become an expensive test failure or a revolutionary race car? Each driver was given their preferred machine: Jody Scheckter got the traditional four-wheeled Tyrrell 007 and Depailler was given the new P34. After running low-fuel, high-fuel and in-race scenarios, it was clear the Project 34 was an all-round better car. Formula One was getting a six-wheeler on the grid and it was time to show the world.

The press conference and car launch were held at Heathrow Hotel. The Tyrrell mechanics created fake wooden wheel arches under the royal blue cover to create the illusion of a set of traditional front wheels. Silence greeted the final reveal of the car. The assembled press was stunned and then sprang into motion: some journalists laughed, with a gaggle believing they had wasted their time on a publicity stunt.

Four races into the 1976 season, the instant fan favourite made its race debut. Depailler again in the six-wheel P34, Scheckter in his preferred four-wheel 007 at the Spanish Grand Prix. Depailler qualified third on the grid, but the more conventional machine was left mired outside the top 10. It was clear the new car was the way forward. Things continued brilliantly for the P34 with Scheckter, now also using the new car, scoring a fourth in Belgium, and then both cars were on the podium for the Monaco Grand Prix. The paddock was beginning to discuss whether four wheels would soon have to be left behind.

In Sweden, halfway through the race, Tyrrell's cars sat second and third again, but there was a mid-race argument about whether the leading car, driven by American hero Mario Andretti, had jumped the start. Before the debate could be resolved, his Lotus broke down and, incredibly, two six-wheelers now led the Formula One field. Tyrrell had completely upended convention. Scheckter led Depailler home to win the Swedish Grand Prix. Dennis Jenkinson observed in *Motor Sport Magazine*: 'The revolutionary six-wheeled Tyrrells, brain-children of Derek Gardner, cruised round in complete control in only their fourth Grand Prix, so that any "doubting Thomases, Michaels or Leonards" must have felt a bit uncomfortable.'

It was a false dawn, the six-wheeler would never win again – it worked best on smooth circuit surfaces and these were few and far between in the 1970s. The extra wheels created reduced drag but extra problems – the small brakes constantly failed, and balancing two front axles proved extremely complex. The greatest issue, though, was the tyres: the Goodyear rubber that had been created for the tiny fronts was never developed. As the traditional-sized tyres received improved rubber throughout the season, Tyrrell were stuck with the same compounds in 1977 as 1976. You couldn't be competitive with old rubber. A concept that had won in just four races was abandoned at the end of 1977. Tyrrell reverted back to four wheels for the start of the 1978 season and the team would win just three more races in the next 20 years.

The Tyrrells of 1976 and 1977 continue to run in historic championships around the world and the six-wheeler remains one of the most remarkable cars to triumph in Formula One. Anything over four wheels is now banned in the rule book, but the six-wheel P34 will never be forgotten.

Lella Lombardi Makes Her Point

Motorsport is one of the few sports where all genders can compete together and, with a few exceptions, this right has existed since the sport began.

Despite this, the reality is that only five women have ever entered a Formula One Grand Prix, and only one, Maria Grazia 'Lella' Lombardi, has ever scored points in the F1 World Championship. The second woman ever to compete in an F1 Grand Prix and openly a member of the LGBT+ community, she was a true trailblazer. The daughter of a butcher, her first drive was her family's delivery van. Despite her Italian father's reluctance, Lella competed in karting and then went on to race in Italian junior Formula racing, including becoming Italy's Ford Escort Challenge champion.

Lombardi followed in the footsteps of the first woman to race in Formula One – her fellow Italian, Maria Teresa de Filippis. Despite a ban from the 1958 French Grand Prix for being a woman, de Filippis went on to enter five Formula One races over the course of 1958–59. Her best result was a tenth-place finish with Maserati in the 1958 Belgian Grand Prix. She retired in 1959 after losing too many friends to motor racing accidents, including Jean Behra, the leader of the Porsche team she raced for. Her involvement in Formula One continued behind the scenes as she joined the International Club of Former F1 Grand Prix Drivers in 1979, eventually becoming a vice president in 1997.

Lombardi's first opportunity to race in F1 came with Brabham in 1974, when she entered the British Grand Prix held at Brands

Hatch, where she failed to qualify. Let's be clear here, Formula One in the 1970s, at the height of its macho era, would not have been an easy place to be a woman. Over her racing career, she would be ganged up against and face rough treatment on track from her fellow (male) drivers.

In 1975, she joined March Engineering and qualified for the South African Grand Prix but did not finish. Her second race was the Spanish Grand Prix, which, tragically, was overshadowed by Rolf Stommelen's crash in a Hill – he survived but five bystanders lost their lives. Lella was in sixth place when the race was called off halfway, leading her to win a half-point.

'The Tigress from Tivoli', as the press labelled her, erroneously with a focus on alliteration at the expense of accuracy, was a staggeringly tough and determined woman. She continued to race in Formula One until 1976, with 17 entries and 12 starts. After Formula One, Lella raced in NASCAR at Daytona and then moved over to sports cars. She passed away from cancer in 1992, aged fifty.

A further three women went on to enter Formula One races. The former British Olympic skier Divina Galica raced in 1976–78, with three entries, but she unfortunately failed to qualify for any. South African Desiré Wilson also entered the 1980 British Grand Prix but did not qualify. She did go on to win the 1980 Regional British Formula One Series race at Brands Hatch, but it didn't count as part of the full Formula One World Championship. There is a grandstand named after her at Brands Hatch in recognition of the win. The last woman to enter a Formula One race was Italian driver Giovanna Amati, though she failed to qualify during her three entries while racing for Brabham. Other female drivers have worked within Formula One as test and development drivers, including Susie Wolff, and in 2023 Formula One launched the F1 Academy, for which Wolff is now the managing director.

F1 Academy, and its predecessor, the W series, aims to increase female participation in the upper echelons of single-seater racing, such as F2 and F1. Time is needed for this to take effect but, crucially, an ever-increasing number of female viewers are tuning in to the sport. The next female Formula One driver will be the beneficiary of those who blazed the trail in the early days, and those who seek to provide a platform in 2025.

23

Niki Lauda Chooses to Drive

Across multiple sports there have been great comebacks, but nothing gets close to Monza in September 1976.

It was beyond reason, logic and taste. The act remains the benchmark of mental control in a sporting arena, but so extreme are the details of Niki Lauda's 42-day comeback to his cockpit that it transcends sport. Niki Lauda not only refused to die, he also raged that anyone would interrupt his immediate return to racing.

Two months earlier, Niki Lauda was refusing to race. He attempted to call off the German Grand Prix held at the enormous, rapid, undulating North Loop of the Nürburgring, the Nordschleife Circuit. An extraordinarily plain and forthright speaker, Austrian Lauda had rallied the other drivers on the grid in an attempt to force them to vote against racing on safety grounds. With 174 corners, the 14-mile circuit was clearly unsuitable for racing in the 1970s; crucial safety elements, barriers, curbs, marshals and medical response teams were not in an acceptable condition.

But safety pushes were always greeted with resistance. *The Times of London* newspaper accused any Formula One driver who proposed not racing of being weak or frightened. The drivers voted, Lauda lost. The race would take place as planned. Lauda, who had eloquently prosecuted the case for postponement, clicked shut his visor and accessed another part of his brain. By the end of the practice session, he was fastest of all, keenly aware of what he was risking but able to find a route to performance.

After practice, the driver's extraordinary words summed up the extremity of what they were being asked to do: 'The most important thing is to get through the weekend alive.' Niki's title rival, James Hunt, agreed the place really wasn't suitable anymore for topline motor racing. He told a press conference: 'I don't mind telling you, I'm frightened.' Bewilderingly, the weekend continued. The German Grand Prix started in the wet, only adding to the trepidation. Hunt led Lauda on the grid, but the circuit was drying quickly and being on the wrong tyre for a full 14 miles could finish your afternoon at the front.

Now on the second of 14 scheduled laps, Lauda took a very fast left-hander before the Bergwerk corner. His Ferrari snapped on him; at 140 mph, he spun to the right through flimsy catch fencing, sickeningly crunching into a grass bank. Instantly, the left fuel cell ruptured and ignited as Lauda spun back across the narrow track. Brett Lunger couldn't avoid the car and hit it; the fireball grew worse.

Lauda was trapped in the car, his helmet ripped off in the impact. His face was exposed to the flames. Four drivers stopped: Guy Edwards, Harald Ertl, Brett Lunger and Arturo Merzario. Lauda's life was saved by Arturo Mezario's knowledge of the safety belt system Ferrari used, and his bravery to put his hand into the fire to release the belts. He later said, 'It wasn't easy. Niki was in agony straining against the flames; it's only when he lost consciousness that I could free the buckle.'

The drivers hauled Lauda clear. His face and hands were horrifically burned from first to third degree, his thorax was badly injured and he had blood poisoning from the toxic fumes. His lungs were severely damaged and he had to be sent to a specialist hospital after two previous hospitals decided they couldn't save him. His third hospital in Mannheim was a university teaching hospital specializing in lung trauma.

Lauda had lost his eyelids and severely burned his lung. Despite his constant agony, he had to be intubated to drain liquid from his lungs, and 48 hours later doctors didn't expect him to live. Lauda concentrated on holding on to consciousness and life. The priest administered the last rites and his fury built. He wasn't going to die like this. He lay in agony, broken, disfigured but alive – resolved not to be written off.

Within days, he could breathe unaided and blood transfusions reduced the immediate danger to life. Soon he could walk, and when he talked, the conversation was firmly set to when he'd go racing again. The path back would be utter torture. This comeback was powered by a superhuman will and an otherworldly pain threshold. He'd lost half his right ear. He suffered from horrendous swelling, then he was subject to painful skin grafts to repair his disfigured face. The eyelid graft was necessary, but Lauda declined more reconstructive surgery.

To design a recovery plan, Lauda turned to leading Austrian physiotherapist, Willi Dungl. In a regime years ahead of its time, he controlled Lauda's diet and exercise, and incredibly, he would throw balls of paper set on fire at Lauda to check he could cope mentally with the prospect of returning to F1 and the dangers it brought.

Niki was really motivated by this point. Amateur footage of the crash had surfaced and he believed it clearly exonerated him of driver error. He was therefore distressed when Ferrari refused to rule out driver error.

Ferrari believed Lauda would never race again and immediately prioritized the Constructors' Championship. In solidarity with Lauda, former champion Emerson Fittipaldi and race winner Ronnie Peterson refused the drive before Carlos Reutemann signed, his desperation to escape the Brabham team trumping any honour among drivers.

Lauda was absolutely incensed with the Scuderia, both at being replaced and at a perceived lack of loyalty from Ferrari. Furious, he redrew his plan. His return was brought forward, the original plan to return at the Canadian Grand Prix shelved; he did not want Reutemann driving a Ferrari without him there. Lauda resolved to drive at Monza, despite plainly being in no state to jog, let alone drive a Formula One car at the world's fastest circuit. Just 38 days after his Ferrari had hit the banking and burst into flames, Lauda returned to Ferrari's Maranello factory.

Then Ferrari team manager Daniele Audetto was stunned by the seriously ill man who walked through the gates. 'When he arrived, that is a vision that I can never forget in my life. He was so pale, plenty of scars, he lost hair, he could not close his eyes – he was like a ghost,' he told an F1 podcast.

Lauda had to stop after a few laps, and the mechanics feared the worst as he pulled into the pit. Instead, a request for new belts was forthcoming. He'd lost so much weight in the ordeal, he was sliding around the cockpit. With that problem fixed, 60 laps later Lauda had proven his mettle to Enzo Ferrari, who agreed to prepare a third car for Monza. Audetto stated, 'He was controlling inside him not only the emotion but the strength because you can imagine – 40 days before … I saw him in the helicopter, and I was thinking, "I'll never see you alive."' Only 40 days after his life-threatening crash, Niki Lauda drove through the gates of the Autodromo Nazionale Di Monza. He had missed just two races. On top of everything, he had to endure the emotions of his visual disfigurement being absorbed by the public for the first time.

Lauda seemed unaffected and instead raged at the extra medical he was put through the day before the race; his tear ducts were damaged, he couldn't blink, but he'd passed the governing bodies' checks and was ready for his Grand Prix weekend return. Or so he thought. Torrential rain hit Friday practice. Lauda picked his way through the parkland sick with fear, finishing 19th, the slowest of three Ferraris. He'd covered just two laps as the wet conditions left the cars 20 seconds off the pace.

Physically, he was in agonizing pain as the skin grafts rubbed against his balaclava, but this was nothing compared to the psychological anguish the day had caused. Lauda later wrote that he was completely consumed by the fear, reduced to a quivering shell. He suffered diarrhoea, throat contractions, and his heart was pounding as he threw up. After the mania had subsided, he methodically sifted the tasks ahead, diagnosing that he had mistakenly attempted to find his limit immediately. Next time, he'd drive slowly, build up until he hit the fear threshold. The approach worked and he qualified fifth fastest, leading the Ferraris. Title rival Hunt was excluded from the qualifying results; Lauda could actually extend his championship advantage if he finished! Weary paddock insiders remarked it was highly interesting the only two teams that had been excluded from qualifying were the two teams to recently win races, McLaren and Penske, therefore Ferrari's greatest rivals.

Before the start of a piece of sporting theatre on the iconic main straight, between the art deco grandstand and the timing towers, two Ferraris roared from the pits. Lauda was applauded, a thoroughly restrained un-Monza-like response to an act of defiance. Niki Lauda was just 40 days from the last rites, 42 days from the crash and 45 days from the vote to postpone the German Grand Prix. His tiny, nimble, lightweight red-and-white Ferrari awaited the flag, but the starting system had changed and in the maelstrom of events Ferrari and Lauda had missed the memo: the 10-second signal and flag drop would be replaced by red and green lights. He wasn't even in gear when the green light illuminated to start the Grand Prix. A drop into the mayhem of the midfield was not what his nerves needed, and he spent the opening laps terrified and out of the points.

With each passing lap, however, the fear eased and he worked his way through the pack, climbing to the points by the 14th lap. Lauda symbolically passed his replacement Carlos Reutemann and then worked his way to fourth, fewer than 20 seconds from the lead. Towards the end he repeatedly set the fastest lap. Title rival Hunt had spun off, and after the race he led the tributes: 'To virtually step out of the grave and six weeks later come fourth in a Grand Prix was an amazing achievement.'

Lauda told Reuters the real target was Canada, and Monza was 'just a test'. Some test. After the race, when he removed his crash helmet his balaclava was soaked in blood. Niki Lauda had blended gladiatorial determination with a mental control unavailable to all but the great. He had produced a sporting comeback without equal.

He had chosen to race.

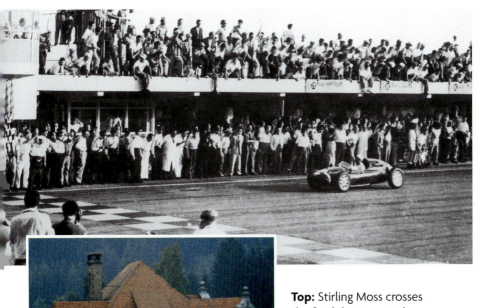

Top: Stirling Moss crosses the finish line to win the Argentine Grand Prix in 1958.

Middle: Graham Hill rushed to help teammate Jackie Stewart from his upturned BRM at the Belgian Grand Prix in 1966.

Bottom: Jack Brabham won the 1966 Grand Prix of the Netherlands, becoming a three-time F1 world champion.

Top: The Lotus team at the 1967 Grand Prix of Belgium, including Jim Clark, Colin Chapman and Keith Duckworth.

Bottom: Jim Clark moments before the crash that took his life at Hockenheim, 7 April 1968.

Top: Piers Courage in Frank Williams' Brabham BT24 at Casino Corner in the Monaco Grand Prix of 1969.

Bottom: Hollywood star Steve McQueen during the shooting of his film *Le Mans* in 1970.

Top: James Hunt came fourth in the 1973 British Grand Prix, and despite only entering eight races that year he came eighth in the World Championship for Hesketh.

Bottom: Tyrrell test their innovative six-wheeler Tyrrell Project 34 car during a Formula One testing held at Silverstone in 1976.

Top: Still in recovery from his previous race, Niki Lauda raced at the 1976 Italian Grand Prix with gladiatorial determination.

Middle: In the first ever Japanese Grand Prix, Niki Lauda, the defending champion, dropped out after the second lap due to the weather conditions, saying the speedway was too dangerous to race on.

Bottom: Niki Lauda in action at the wheel of the revolutionary Brabham-Alfa Romeo BT46B 'Fan Car' in the 1978 Swedish Grand Prix, which he won.

Top: A happy Team Lotus on the morning of the 1978 Italian Grand Prix. A few hours later, Ronnie Peterson (right) would lose his life in a crash at the start of the race.

Bottom: The finish of the 1979 French Grand Prix. Gilles Villeneuve came in second place for Ferrari and Rene Arnoux finished in third for Renault after one of the sport's greatest ever battles.

Top: Marshals race to the scene of Gilles Villeneuve's fatal accident during the 1982 Belgian Grand Prix.

Middle: Brazilian Nelson Piquet leads teammate Nigel Mansell at the 1986 Australian Grand Prix.

Bottom: After a collision at the 1989 Japanese Grand Prix put both Alain Prost and teammate Ayrton Senna off the track, Prost abandoned his stalled car while Senna restarted his, getting pushed back onto the track and driving on to take victory, only to be later disqualified.

Top: Eddie Jordan with his new driver Michael Schumacher, who qualified seventh in his first race, the 1991 Belgian Grand Prix.

Bottom: At the 1993 Formula One Championship's European Grand Prix, Ayrton Senna scythed through the field in difficult conditions, overtaking both Williams cars by the end of the first lap.

Niki Lauda Chooses to Stop

The World Championship of 1976 had broken past the normal realms of sporting competition by the time the championship had reached its 16th and final race.

McLaren and Ferrari had feuded, protested and boycotted. Such was the political battle that qualifying and race results became semi-permanent. While such antics would become common sporting fare across the next decades, thankfully the sight of one of the all-time great drivers severely burned would disappear. Lauda continued to stun the world by processing what was required to compete while circumventing horrific injuries; it was sport in the major key, a great epic that required a conclusion. A circuit in the shadow of Mount Fuji was the setting, the sky dark and foreboding as a field of drivers faced one final hurdle, and a title battle since immortalized by Hollywood required its ending. Would Lauda complete F1's greatest comeback as the champion or would playboy James Hunt rule the world?

After the comeback in Italy, Ferrari and Lauda had struggled to match the form of McLaren and Hunt. In Canada, Lauda railed against the team management publicly as the Ferraris struggled: 'I'm very disappointed that no development or testing was done while I was away,' he said.

His disappointing eighth place offered no points; at the next race at Watkins Glen, he was a stronger third, but James Hunt had won both races and closed the gap in the championship to just three points with one race to run. Lauda and Hunt were good friends away from the racetrack, but McLaren and Ferrari were constantly bickering. This wasn't helped when it turned out McLaren had broken a gentlemen's agreement not to test at the season-deciding venue of Fuji the week before the grand finale.

Despite missing two races after his accident and lacklustre results after the triumph of Monza, Lauda was still leading the championship. He was just three points ahead of Hunt, and in the hours before the Grand Prix was due to start, that looked to be how the championship would end.

Sunday had brought rain, which had clearly made the track unraceable. Conditions were extremely wet, with low-lying clouds severely impacting vision. Could the race go ahead in such conditions? Lauda's injuries were inescapable, all but a few competing had driven past his wreckage just months earlier. It was so wet it is arguable whether personnel would even be allowed on site in 2025, should the same events be replayed today, let alone allowed to race.

As expected, the start was delayed and replaced by a reconnaissance session of 15 minutes. When it was complete, the drivers voted overwhelmingly for the postponement of the first-ever World Championship Japanese Grand Prix. But it was a significant day for Japan, and such was the titanic nature of the year's championship battle, the race was to be beamed all over the world to a massive live TV audience. This was unusual at the time and, frankly, the drivers didn't get a say. Bernie Ecclestone and the race director informed the drivers that while they understood their vote, the pit lane would be opened. The race had to take place, and sunset dictated they'd run out of light if they didn't start in the next few moments. For the first time, the pressure to put on a show for TV was going to change the title's destiny.

It was raining heavily, with the track still flooded at multiple corners when the race began. Standing water was everywhere and the low-lying cloud created a true gloom. For the pack, the visibility was as tough as it could be. Pole-sitter Mario Andretti lost the lead at the start and described what he found on track as 'the worst conditions I ever experienced at the start of a race ... Never, ever, ever had I experienced anything like it.'

Amid the storm, Lauda's vision was impacted further due to his injuries. He couldn't stop his eyes watering, further reducing the already minimal vision available. After a poor getaway that had left him outside the top 10, Lauda did not think the conditions were safe. At the end of the second lap, he brought his Ferrari back to the pits and undid his belts. He chose to stop.

He watched the pack speed by for a few laps before leaving the circuit and driving to the airport. Ferrari wanted to say he'd had a car issue, but Lauda refused to play along, comfortable with his choices and the truth. 'I stopped because of the conditions – nothing to do with after-effects from the accident. I know that – for me – what I did was the right thing ...' he told *Motor Sport Magazine*.

With Lauda out, Hunt had an opportunity he'd never expected. His driving in the McLaren had surprised even him. Hunt led from the start, establishing a gap in the wet, but as conditions began to ease the McLaren's tyres were seriously worn. Hunt was in a horrible position, aware this was probably his only shot for the championship. He couldn't communicate with the pit wall because team radio didn't exist yet; this was still the era of signal boards and hand gestures.

Hunt led and was heading to the title watched by millions around the world – but then the rain relented, and on the drying track his tyres were finished. Suddenly, it was all in the balance again as first Depailler and then Andretti got by. Hunt was still safe by one point, but on lap 68 – just five laps from the title – the tyre totally failed and a pit stop would be required to continue. Hunt dropped down the order, the championship slipping away; he was no longer in position to win the title, but suddenly the tyre problem was affecting others.

As Alan Jones' Surtees machine slowed with an identical failure and others hit problems with just two laps to go, Hunt was back to third, ready to collect the four points and the championship of the world.

The adrenaline-fuelled chaos fitted a grand season that had captured the hearts and minds of so many. In the end, James Hunt won the World Championship and completed his victory lap utterly furious, thinking he'd fallen short because of the puncture. Exiting the car he was animated, swearing at his team with them swearing back. Only once McLaren boss Teddy Mayer held up three fingers did he believe he was the champion.

At Tokyo airport, Lauda was informed by a journalist he'd been beaten to the title. He didn't care. He liked James and had total conviction in what he had done, all he wanted now was to escape.

Enzo Ferrari did not understand nor was he interested in an explanation of Lauda's actions. Enzo suggested to Lauda he should not have returned in 1976, and their relationship would never recover when, in the following season, Lauda announced he was leaving the team with three races to go. Nothing epitomizes this more than the morning after. Lauda awoke in his Maranello hotel and unfurled the curtains to find his sportscar had been stolen! He immediately phoned Ferrari to report one of their vehicles missing. The voice on the end of the phone said, 'No, it has not been stolen. Ferrari has taken back the car.'

For many drivers, Lauda stopping usurped what he had achieved in Monza. The drivers understood defiance – it was built into their personality, the motivation from fear of failure was almost standard issue. But willingly choosing to withdraw, that was different. In a sport and in a season where these qualities were rare, to see them displayed at the crucial moment of a championship finale was unreal.

Lauda would have known the dissent he would face from those who hadn't experienced the conditions. 'My life is worth more than a title,' he later said, when discussing the events of that day. Over the off season, it was proposed he should stop driving and become Ferrari's team manager. Lauda took this incredibly badly, but the doubt did not hurt his motivation – he returned to the cockpit and won back the World Championship in 1977.

The 1976 season captured the imagination of the sporting public, becoming a defining championship because of Hunt, McLaren and Ferrari – but it was Lauda's heroism that elevated it from mere sport to something akin to ancient legend. In Monza, he chose to race; in Fuji, he chose to stop. In retaining the ability to choose in the face of the opinion and noise from the public, paddock or even Enzo Ferrari, Lauda had defined himself as a giant.

The Yellow Teapot – Renault Build a Turbo Engine

You know a turbo instantly. Even from miles away, it sounds unique. For many, it recalls a golden age.

In 2024, Renault announced what had long been feared: its F1 engines would no longer be produced at the Viry Châtillon facility in Paris from the 2026 season onwards. The facility is a key part of both F1 history and created one of the sport's defining moments. Renault were responsible for the introduction of the first turbo engine in 1977.

Turbocharged engines were developed in the early 1900s and were a crucial component of making planes in World War II both faster and more efficient with fuel use. However, development of Formula One's first, the Renault 1.5 litre turbocharged V6 engine, was far from straightforward.

A turbocharger is an air compressor that force-feeds air into the engine cylinder, known as forced induction; this forces more air to be mixed with the fuel and should result in more power. The turbocharger is powered by the kinetic energy/flow of the exhaust gases, which can lead to one of the drawbacks of turbochargers: turbo lag. It takes time for the engine to increase the exhaust gases enough to reach the turbine to create enough speed and generate the resulting power boost; this can make the car slower to reach peak speeds. Turbocharged engines can also reach very high temperatures, but their improved fuel efficiency and greater speeds generated with smaller engine sizes are useful attributes in an F1 car.

The engine was developed by the technical trio of Francois Castaing, Jean-Pierre Boudy and Bernard Dudot. Francois Castaing and Jean-Pierre Boudy were both engineering graduates of France's most famous engineering school, l'École nationale supérieure d'Arts et Métiers. Both went on to work for the sports car racing team, Gordini, which was under contract to Renault the manufacturer's motor racing activity. While there, Castaing and Boudy designed a 2-litre V6 engine that became the basis for the later F1 turbocharged engine. That car did well in sports-prototype racing, with a European Championship win in 1974.

The 1974 merger of Renault with Gordini and Alpine brought together the duo with Bernard Dudot for the first time. An engineer educated in Nancy, he had been working on turbochargers while at Alpine; one of their cars had almost won the 1973 Rally of Cevennes, with a 1.6-litre turbocharged engine, until a pesky stone got in the way. The team went on to develop an engine for 1,000-km racing in the 3-litre category, although 2-litre turbocharged engines were allowed. Cars with that engine won a race at Mugello in 1975 and then at Le Mans three years later. After those successes, Renault was open to returning to top-line racing for the first time in 70 years, but as Dudot later flagged the challenges ahead were faced with a fair bit of naïve optimism.

Halfway through the 1977 season, the gorgeously bright yellow Renault with the turbocharged engine debuted midway through the season at the British Grand Prix at Silverstone with what you could charitably call an uninspiring start. The driver, Jean-Pierre Jabouille, only managed to qualify in 21st, but during the race, the car lasted a mere 12 laps before the turbo cracked. It was fixed briefly, but the car only managed 16 laps in total before the turbocharger blew up. The team missed both the German and Austrian races to make repairs. Renault tried again at the Dutch Grand Prix in Zandvoort, but another DNF occurred after 39 laps.

The car failed to complete a race that year and was given the nickname 'the Yellow Teapot' due to its shape and the smoke it spouted when the engine failed. That year, the team learnt the hard way that turbochargers and pumped fuel cause a great deal of stress on the engine while being slow to respond.

Reliability issues continued into 1978, where the Renault joined the season three races in at the South African Grand Prix. Two DNFs were followed by a rare spark of potential with a tenth-place finish at Monaco. This was followed by seven DNFs out of nine races before the team achieved a fourth-place finish at Watkins Glen (the USA East Grand Prix) in the penultimate race of the season, scoring their first points, followed by a 12th place in Canada.

By 1979, Renault had learnt that switching out the single turbocharger for two smaller turbochargers improved responsiveness, and the team started to see the impact. Both Jabouille and René Arnoux in their Renaults had DNFs in Argentina for the first race of that year's season. But by the third race at Kyalami, the Renault team's fortunes looked to have changed with Jabouille achieving Renault's first pole in the turbocharged engine era. Both cars again failed to finish, but the pole was a sign of things to come.

At the Dijon circuit for the French Grand Prix, the Renaults surprised the paddock with their promising qualifying times. By the end of Friday morning's practice session, the Renaults were fastest and looked to be dominating the field, with Jabouille just ahead of his teammate Arnoux. This was in spite of Arnoux's engine giving him a bit of trouble in practice – the cars' reputation for being fast but fragile persisted. The team's pace carried into qualifying as they picked up a one–two on the grid, locking out the front. While Arnoux struggled after a poor start, Jabouille was overtaken by Gilles Villeneuve in his Ferrari.

At 20 laps, both Villeneuve and Jabouille remained out in front on their own, with Jabouille slowly eating up the time difference between himself and Villeneuve. On lap 46, Jabouille used the distraction of Villeneuve lapping de Angelis to draw alongside and pass him on the straight – the 100,000 strong home crowd roared, engrossed at the prospect of a home win! Jabouille drove his heart out and managed to create a gap by lap 50, but victory was by no means certain as the Frenchman worried about brake wear issues. Villeneuve was unable to respond, with his own worries with the tyres and brakes, and faced a greater threat from behind from Arnoux.

All concerns about reliability were instantly discarded as the second and third cars duelled in one of the greatest wheel-to-wheel battles in F1 history. Pass, repass and pass again in a battle for the ages. Arnoux and Villeneuve sent the crowd into delirium and entered the last lap side by side. Villeneuve getting ahead at one point, then Arnoux, both wrestled the cars under control and remaining side by side as they raced for the line. The Ferrari just beat Arnoux by a quarter of a second. Arnoux was unflustered with finishing third, calling the duel 'my greatest souvenir of racing'. All the while, Jabouille cruised to victory as the drama unfolded behind him. Two years after first re-entering Formula One, Renault and its turbocharged engine had their first win; extraordinarily it came on a day where all anyone could talk about was who came second.

Sid Watkins – Bringing Safety to Formula One

In Formula One, there are characters who transcended their role, people who created an outsized impact on the sport we know today.

Eric Sidney Watkins was one of them. Sid Watkins was the first full-time doctor to oversee medical care across Formula One. As the first safety and medical delegate to Formula One, he implemented significant changes to medical care at the circuits that substantially saved many drivers' lives over the years. Sid, or 'Prof' as he became known in the paddock, joined Formula One in 1978. It was a time where death was a regular occurrence in the sport. Formula One drivers were seen as risk-takers and playboys and the safety was sometimes disregarded as a result. Niki Lauda best described the circuits' medical facilities at the time as, 'haphazard in the extreme; you just crossed your fingers and hoped you would not have an accident at certain tracks'. Watkins took up the battles for safety that Jackie Stewart had started and did more than anyone else to make Formula One as safe as it is now.

The then owner of Brabham and CEO of FOCA, Bernie Ecclestone, had contacted Watkins, explained the issues with medical facilities and asked if he could help to reduce the fatality rate. Watkins was a car enthusiast, having grown up around motorbikes and cars. His father had moved to Liverpool during the Great Depression in the 1930s and set up Wally Watkins Bike Shop, which later expanded into fixing cars. As a child, Sid helped his dad out, pumping petrol and supporting car mechanics. The scholarship boy at Prescot Grammar School went on to the University of Liverpool Medical School. After spending time in West Africa with the army, he specialized in neurosurgery at Radcliffe Infirmary, Oxford. In his spare time, he worked as a race doctor at the Silverstone and Brands Hatch circuits. Later, the State University of New York asked Watkins to become professor of neurosurgery, where he also worked at the Watkins Glen circuit in Upstate New York. Ecclestone got in contact after he'd moved back to the UK and taken up a post as professor of neurosurgery at the London Hospital. He was also medical director for the British Grand Prix in his free time.

Halfway through the season, Watkins attended the Swedish Grand Prix in his new role that he combined with his day job. The issues with the safety arrangements were quite quickly apparent. The helicopter that was to provide medevac was only available on race day and not for any of the earlier sessions in the weekend. At the British Grand Prix at Brands Hatch, there was a medical centre, but it was small and lacked the necessary equipment. Two paramedics overseeing it sat and drank beer during the race. At the Hockenheimring, Germany, the medical centre was a converted single-decker bus and the medical staff camped nearby.

Three races from the end of the season in 1978, the worst-case scenario happened in Monza. Swedish driver Ronnie Peterson was involved in a huge first-lap crash. Watkins was prevented from getting to Peterson by an Italian police cordon. With the delays in medical care and getting him freed from the car, Peterson later died from an embolism – a hugely popular driver had died a preventable death, and it was unforgivable.

Action was swift after this. Driver and circuit safety was turned over to Watkins, which included actively managing incidents requiring medical care. He quickly implemented changes, telling Ecclestone that unless properly equipped medical centres were provided, circuits should not hold F1 races. The whole process in how accidents are handled was first developed by Watkins. He ensured that helicopters were available for all sessions on track and implemented the medical car. Watkins and an anaesthetist were to be driven by a competent driver who knew the circuits in a car with a radio behind the grid for the first lap. This allowed the medical team to be on hand quickly at one of the riskiest times of a race, where the cars are all bunched together. The current medical car, an Aston Martin or Mercedes-AMG, can still be seen today lined up behind the grid. Ecclestone and Watkins had all these measures implemented by the next race, the USA East Grand Prix at Watkins Glen, less than a month later.

The biggest hurdle Watkins faced in improving safety was buy-in from the paddock. He faced pushback, as death was seen as part of the attraction, in some sort of gladiatorial combat that the drivers had knowingly signed up to. An attitude that is unthinkable today. It helped that Watkins had charisma and a great sense of humour. The drivers could go to him for more than medical care – he was a father figure to the whole paddock and was not to be underestimated. Watkins was the only man Ecclestone was known to defer to, and he accepted his opinions on any safety matter without question, even if this meant delaying the start of a race.

A pivotal moment in his time at Formula One was the 1994 death of Ayrton Senna in Imola (*see* Chapter 40). That dark weekend where Rubens Barrichello had a horrific crash in practice on the Friday; on the Saturday, the Austrian rookie Roland Ratzenberger hit a concrete wall and died. The Grand Prix went ahead, and on Sunday, on lap 7 of the race, Senna went through the Tamburello corner and crashed into a wall at 190 mph. Ayrton Senna's death deeply affected Watkins, as the two men had been close, with Watkins asking why he didn't stop racing the day before that fatal crash. Watkins even recounted experiencing Ayrton's soul leave his body as he was resuscitating him. After Senna's death, head of the FIA Max

Mosley set up an expert advisory committee with Watkins as its chairman.

A world-leading surgeon in his own right outside the paddock, Watkins was the perfect man for the job. Despite not being an expert in the engineering that would make the sport safe, he used scientific principles – hypotheses and evidence and data collection – as the methodology to improve the safety of the sport. Yet this wasn't enough; again, his personality came into play to drive through the changes, and he was savvy enough to understand how to navigate the politics of Formula One. The new barriers that better absorbed the energy from crashes, the new asphalt, the changes to the car and the new helmets with head and neck supports that the committee devised went on to save countless lives in the sport. The crash tests for front, rear and side impacts even impacted road car safety design. His experiences as a neurosurgeon influenced his attitude to the sport; at the end of the day, he would be going back to his day job, operating on someone's brain with a very serious condition. Sid could not be told to shut up when it came to the safety of the drivers.

Watkins was integral to saving the lives of many notable names in Formula One, including Ferrari's Didier Pironi (*see* Chapter 29) and Rubens Barrichello at Imola (*see* Chapter 51). In 1995, he performed a tracheotomy on the racetrack to save Mika Häkkinen's life during practice at the Australian Grand Prix; Mika later called him a hero of the paddock.

Former Formula One driver and leading race pundit Martin Brundle credits Watkins with saving his left leg from being amputated when he crashed in his first Formula One season. His care went beyond the confines of the circuits; Frank Williams attributed his ability to live a normal and healthy lifestyle as tetraplegic due to Watkins care in the 11 weeks he spent in hospital after a car accident. Sid was also asked by Max Mosley and World Rally to consult on improving their safety, and helped to look after rally driver Richard Burns, who was diagnosed with a brain tumour before his death.

The role of the Formula One doctor requires a great deal of courage, given the risk of fire around an accident. Formula One would not be the sport it is today without Sid Watkins and the two safety and medical delegates who have followed in his footsteps – Gary Hartstein and Ian Roberts. Sid Watkins passed away in London in 2012, aged eighty-four, his years of work having helped improve the sport, immeasurably.

The Brabham Fan Car

In 1978, Formula One was being dominated by Team Lotus.

Colin Chapman's innovative design – adorned in one of the greatest liveries of all time – was so aerodynamically advanced it left the rest of the field far adrift and rendered the championship a formality. Until the Swedish Grand Prix.

For weeks, the Formula One rumour mill had been talking about the exact nature of the Brabham team's new car; a spy shot photograph had detailed a new part at the rear.

Lead designer Gordon Murray would bring his entirely revised B specification car to race for the first time at Anderstorp, the sixth round of the season. There would be nowhere to hide for the Brabham team, and expectations were high within team ranks. The dark red machine saw the driver sat further forward than today, there was an uncomplicated suspension and just a two-element front wing, with the bodywork sculpted to create the underside of the car as the main downforce generator. At the very back of the car sat the new addition, at the back of the gearbox: a huge fan.

The regulations had evolved for nearly three decades since the championship's inception, but significant innovation was still possible. Privately, Murray believed he had found a huge advantage with the giant wheel-sized fan. The team was so confident in the concept, team owner Ecclestone ordered the Brabhams to qualify on full tanks of fuel, adding weight and hiding the true pace of the car. John Watson was second, six-tenths off Mario Andretti in the supreme Lotus, while Lauda was third, seven-tenths off the leader.

The other teams reacted like a group of pro cyclists who had just seen their competition pull up to the start line with a motorbike. The teams didn't need to see the times, they collectively knew instantly this spelt trouble for them. The giant engine-powered extractor fan created low air pressure under the whole car, sucking the car to the ground and generating massive grip through the corners, which increased cornering speed. It was a true game-changer and everyone knew it.

The pit lane soon filled with photographers taking shots of the new fan design. Other designers had stumbled across the idea before, but no one had been able to make it work reliably, let alone have the confidence to race it. A photograph of the groundbreaking design could be very useful, so the Brabham team were forced to cover the design with a bin lid that fitted the fan size; within a few minutes, the team had attached a sponsors logo.

Lotus, McLaren, Williams, Tyrrell and Surtees were not seeing the funny side and all believed the design to be illegal. All five teams appealed to the stewards of the race weekend. The rule book of 1978 stated: 'Any part of the car whose primary function is to influence aerodynamic performance' is considered to be an aerodynamic device, and according to Article 3, Item 7, 'Aerodynamic devices must comply with the rules relating to coachwork (i.e. heights, widths etc) and must be firmly fixed while the car is in motion.'

The words 'primary function' had caught Gordon Murray's attention. In his book, *One Formula: 50 Years of Car Design*, he recalls, '60 per cent of the air was for cooling and 40 per cent for downforce, meaning that aerodynamics was not the primary function.' The stewards agreed with the logic, stating, 'The primary function of the fan is to assure cooling to the engine and other mechanical components.'

The appeal from the five teams was heard but then dismissed on the morning of the race. The fan car was legal and ready to go. Niki Lauda would later reveal he created the illusion of a race toying with Andretti in the Lotus. After amusing himself for a few laps, Lauda passed for the lead and simply pulled away, winning the Swedish Grand Prix in the Brabham fan car by 30 seconds. The car the Austrian world champion had nicknamed 'The Vacuum Cleaner' had lapped everyone on track, apart from his fellow podium finishers. The Brabham team were delighted. In a season of engineering quantum leaps, they'd found the greatest innovation yet.

For Murray, the victory was vindication after similar attempts at design breakthroughs had failed earlier in the season. Most terrifyingly of all – the system wasn't even close to being optimized; the true aerodynamic performance of the fan car had barely been utilized in its dominant victory. Outside their garage the paddock was in uproar. Many teams still believed it was illegal, but if it was within the rules, every car now required a fan or it was as good as obsolete. The costs would be through the roof!

Before the great fan arms race could begin, Brabham team owner Bernie Ecclestone asked Gordon Murray to remove the very part that could have won them the title. The car was never banned, no rule was ever found to have been broken, but political forces can outweigh everything in Formula One. Ecclestone wanted to win more races and championships but had his eye on a greater prize. He was the head of the FOCA, and it might have been somewhat troublesome to lead a group who were accusing him of cheating at every race. Collective bargaining would be far harder to achieve – and his end goal of running the sport wasn't compatible with winning with the fan car.

At the next event in France, the fanless Brabham was on pole. Before normal service was resumed and the Lotus pair returned their conquering machines to the front of the order by the end of the Grand Prix. Lotus would go on to win the Drivers' crown with Mario Andretti and win their last Constructors' World Championship. A decade later, after years of amassing political power within the sport, Ecclestone would collect the prize that had made him so cautious in 1978 – controlling the commercial interests for one of the world's richest sports as the head of what would become Formula One Management. Murray's design wouldn't race again, but it does occupy the special place of the only F1 design in history to have a 100 per cent win record.

John Barnard's Carbon-Fibre Car

At the 1981 Argentine Grand Prix, McLaren debuted its new MP4/1 car – the first to race with a fully carbon-fibre composite monocoque chassis.

While the car was met with some classic F1 scepticism, it would go on to change how Formula One cars are built to this day. This was not the first car to use carbon fibre: Graham Hill had used it in his team's rear wing supports in 1975 and Gordon Murray had explored its uses at Brabham. Even Lotus had put together the first carbon-fibre car with the Lotus 88 – it just never raced.

Concerns over safety and the material's suitability had restricted the use of carbon fibre up until that point. Colin Chapman of Lotus went on the record to say he did not think a carbon fibre chassis would be safe, and other teams had visions of the car disintegrating into a cloud of black dust on impact. Some versions of the material were even relatively easy to snap by hand if you broke it in the wrong direction. The McLaren Project 4/1 would prove its detractors wrong over the course of the 1981 season.

The car was a testament to the project's main engineer, John Barnard, whose drive and imagination led to its fruition. He started at Lola and then McLaren in the early 1970s but had left to work with Parnelli and Chaparral on IndyCar. Ron Dennis, who at the time had set up a Formula Two and Formula Three team, called Project Four Racing, approached Barnard to join. Drawing inspiration from the rear wing of the BMW M1, the thought process was, why not make the whole car from that material?

Both Dennis and Barnard were keen to enter Formula One, and in 1979 Barnard started working on the designs. At the time, ground effect was the dominant concept in the sport, and he wanted a car that would maximize this. This meant he needed to develop the biggest underwing he could with the smallest section chassis possible – one that was not much bigger than the driver's rear end. He felt that this needed a completely new approach as the aluminium sheet metal joined with rivets used at the time was too flexible. Steel was also considered but would have added too much weight. Barnard decided to explore carbon-fibre composites given their light, stiff and extremely strong properties.

Formula One didn't have the expertise he needed, so he turned to the aerospace industry. He knew Rolls-Royce were using carbon fibre for their engine cowls in the RB211 turbofan engine, which was promising. Barnard and Dennis tried British Aerospace Engineering, who were excited by the project but didn't have the resources to help. What they did do was facilitate a relationship between Barnard and Arthur Webb, one of its aeronautical engineers and an expert on carbon fibre. Webb supported Barnard on the design of an aluminium honeycomb monocoque with layers of carbon fibre. This improved rigidity and reduced weight. The pair also realized that placing inserts within the structure would allow different components, such as the engine, to be mounted to the car without compromising the carbon fibre's integrity.

Project Four had the design, but where to build it and who with? Companies with this expertise willing to help the team were thin on the ground in the UK. The team turned to the US where the material was being used in rocket design; Barnard spoke to a former American teammate from his IndyCar days, Steve Nichols. Nichols had done his apprenticeship at Hercules Aerospace, a defence contractor based in Salt Lake City, Utah. Hercules Aerospace were working on carbon fibre and, crucially, had a research and development team. When Barnard proposed to build a car with a unified chassis and body made of carbon fibre, they saw the commercial benefits. Hercules Aerospace would help to lay the carbon fibre over the aluminium honeycomb using the mould provided by Project Four and place the monocoque in its autoclave. The chassis in five parts would then be shipped together back to the UK for Project Four to construct. It wasn't the prettiest first attempt, but it worked! And five parts was a lot fewer than the usual 50 components an aluminium chassis would require.

While this was all happening, Ron Dennis was struggling to secure the financial backing to continue the team's quest to enter Formula One. Dennis had gone to Marlboro to fund his Formula Two team, but Marlboro had a commitment to McLaren in Formula One. The McLaren team were struggling to create a car with good ground effect and John Hogan, the marketing director at Philip Morris, had doubts about their investment into McLaren. He had the bright idea to get Project Four and McLaren to merge and build a new team with Marlboro backing, which they did in 1980. The new carbon-fibre chassis was integral to this deal. After 18 months, the original team principal and the designer at McLaren both left, leaving Ron Dennis in charge and Barnard his chief designer/technical director.

Three races into the 1981 season, the MP4/1-1 was ready for its first race. In Argentina, John Watson qualified 11th but retired with a gearbox failure. The car, with a Ford Cosworth DFV engine, completed its first race a month later in San Marino in tenth. Midway through the season, competitors woke up to the fact that a carbon chassis may be something they needed to follow. At the British Grand Prix at Silverstone, Watson qualified seventh. He got off to a decent start but dropped to tenth after just managing to dodge an accident that started when Gilles Villeneuve's Ferrari hit the kerb at the end of lap 3. He managed to make his way through the pack and then Nelson Piquet in his Brabham crashed and Prost's Renault expired on him. Watson was up to second but a long way back behind René Arnoux's Renault. At lap 51, the Renault didn't sound healthy and was beginning to slow; Watson in his McLaren made up the gap until he was alongside Arnoux by lap 61. With the home crowd signalling their joy, Watson passed Arnoux to take the lead and win the Grand Prix!

While the British Grand Prix showed the potential of carbon fibre, the 1981 Italian Grand Prix was potentially even more important to the future of the material in Formula One. On lap 20 of the race in Monza, Watson ran wide in the second Lesmo corner. The car hit the right-hand guard rail backward, causing the engine, gearbox and rear suspension to be torn off the monocoque; a sheet of flames appeared before the automatic valves in the fuel lines closed. Despite the rear end of the car having been torn off, the monocoque remained intact and slid to a stop. John Watson walked away from a 140-mph crash and, most importantly, the car had not exploded into a cloud of dust. If the car had been made of aluminium, he is unlikely to have been so fortunate.

The car was not considered easy to drive and tended to porpoise. Indeed, Watson's teammate De Cesaris earned the nickname 'de Crasheris' after collecting a single point in 1981. And yet, the car started a design revolution in the sport by providing new levels of rigidity, driver safety and far more precise designs. Hercules Aerospace were reported to have kept John Watson's destroyed 1981 Italian Grand Prix car – it apparently proved to be a great marketing tool to the military when they explained he had walked away from the crash.

29

Ferrari's Villeneuve and Pironi – A Racing Tragedy

Gilles Villeneuve and Didier Pironi were two super-talented, highly competitive drivers whose racing careers would always be intrinsically linked in tragedy.

They first met at the end of the 1980 season, when Ferrari were race winners but struggling to find form in the new regulations.

Gilles was unconcerned and embraced a new teammate, despite being of opposite backgrounds. Villeneuve was a natural-born racer from Quebec, Canada, who started out in snowmobile racing. Newly married, he sold his house and bought a ride in Formula Atlantic. At the 1976 Grand Prix Molson Trois-Rivières, Gilles beat the legendary James Hunt. This remarkable display of talent led to a call from no less than Enzo Ferrari after the race. As James Hunt stated, 'You didn't have to be too much of a brain surgeon to spot his talent.'

While the pressure was huge, Gilles adored being a Ferrari driver. His first win was at his home Grand Prix in Montreal, Canada, in 1978, with his parents watching on in the crowd. Almost immediately, Villeneuve was on his way to becoming a global star, popular with the crowds for his flamboyant driving persona while remaining a humble family man out of the car.

Across the garage, Didier Pironi was sophisticated, charming, intelligent and hugely ambitious. Born outside of Paris to a wealthy family; he could be forthright and to the point and would have made an excellent politician. He became head of the Grand Prix Drivers' Association (GPDA) between 1980 and 1982. With an impressive junior career, Pironi joined F1 in 1978 with Tyrrell. He also went on to win the 1978 Le Mans 24 Hours race with Renault. Didier joined Ferrari for the start of the 1981 season believing he was the fastest driver in the world, even though he was aware he was entering a Ferrari operation which was very much Gilles' team.

A horrible facet of 1970s and 1980s Formula One racing was how deadly it could be: 13 drivers had died in the 1970s alone. This was the era of ground effect, which meant incredibly high cornering speeds. The Ferrari drivers faced this with different mindsets: Villeneuve point-blank refused to accept the risk, stating it wouldn't happen to him. Pironi, on the other hand, understood the danger but at every moment tried to remain in control.

In 1981, Ferrari constructed a terrible car, but Villeneuve was working wonders behind the wheel. By Monaco, roughly halfway through the season, Gilles was on the front row and went on to win the race, while Didier was two rows from the back. At the next round in Spain, Villeneuve produced one of the all-time great drives, holding four obviously quicker cars at bay lap after lap. When he won the race the top five were separated by just 1.24 seconds across the line.

With the 1982 car looking much stronger, Pironi knew something had to change. In his mind, while Villeneuve had won a fair few races, he'd never won a World Championship. Pironi still believed he would be the man to deliver that World Championship for Ferrari over Gilles. Ahead of the 1982 World Championship, Pironi was reported to have met the main sponsor of Ferrari at the time, Marlboro, to discuss how to move Ferrari towards favouring himself over Gilles. Ever the politician, Ferrari sporting director Marco Piccinini would be Pironi's best man at his wedding during the season. The Villeneuves, in contrast, were not invited.

By the time the championship appeared in Imola, a political battle was being fought over the control of F1, with many teams boycotting the race. Only 14 drivers were on the starting grid versus the 26 at the starting grid in South Africa, the first race of the season. With a truncated grid, the four Ferrari and Renault drivers met ahead of the race to plan tactics and ensure the crowd got a good show. Unfortunately for Prost and Arnoux, both of their Renaults blew up. This meant Ferrari were running Gilles in first and Pironi in second.

Villeneuve also believed that 1982 was to be his season and didn't even think of Pironi's ambitions, even if Enzo Ferrari liked to pit people against each other for motivation. However, Ferrari had a rule that if you were first and second you didn't try to overtake each other; essentially, no racing between teammates to safely secure both podium positions. Gilles was aware of this – in 1979, at Monza, he stuck to the rules and stayed behind Jody Scheckter, losing out on the World Championship as a result.

Back to 1982, this was still the Ferrari rule, and the drivers were given the 'slow' sign as a reminder of team orders to hold position. Gilles backed off to cruise to the end, but then he made a mistake and went off the track. Didier overtook and was now in front. He picked up the pace, only for Gilles to take over the lead again and slow down the race. However, Pironi had other ideas, despite team orders, and passed on the inside at the last overtaking spot on the last lap. That was it, and Pironi won his first Grand Prix with Ferrari. Gilles was so angry and felt so utterly betrayed by someone he thought was a friend that he didn't want to go on the podium: 'If he beat me fairly, I'm good, but if you cheat that's not racing.'

How Ferrari went on to handle the situation post-race didn't help. Pironi knew he could rely on his best man and wasn't reprimanded for ignoring team orders after the footage was reviewed. As far as the team was concerned, they were one–two. Pironi stated that if needed for the benefit of Ferrari, he would do it again. Enzo Ferrari at first stood behind Pironi, but on reflection retracted his support the next day. Villeneuve felt betrayed by the whole organization and declared war on Pironi.

Two weeks later, at the next race at Circuit Zolder, Belgium, Pironi was fractionally quicker than Gilles in qualifying and Villeneuve remained furious. He asked for Pironi's time – something he'd never done before. Villeneuve had used two sets of qualifying tyres already but wanted a third qualifying run. All he cared about was beating Didier's time. It was personal. On his third push lap, Villeneuve was closing in on Jochen Mass and he tried to take the outside line at the exact moment Mass moved his car.

They collided. The Ferrari took off. Villeneuve was thrown from the car into the fencing onto the side of the racetrack, an unthinkably violent accident in a sporting arena; the chassis of his car stuck in the middle of the track with the front smashed up. Didier passed by and stopped; he carried Gilles' helmet back to the pits. The doctors explained that the spinal cord had severed and his life couldn't be saved. Formula One had lost one of the most exciting drivers who ever lived.

The whole of Canada stopped for his funeral, where his coffin was draped in a chequered flag. After Gilles' death, Enzo Ferrari made a personal statement: 'His death has deprived us of a great champion; one I loved very much; my life is full of sad memories, parents, brother, son. I look back, I see the faces of my loved ones and among them I see him.'

Three races later, at the renamed Circuit Gilles Villeneuve in Montreal, Canada, Pironi resumed his World Championship challenge by taking pole. But he stalled the engine at the start of the race. The rest of the field managed to avoid him until one of the backmarkers clipped him, creating chaos. Boesel's March ended up on the right of the track and Salazar's ATS car and Lee's Theodore entry ended up on the left. In only his second Formula One start, Riccardo Paletti, in an Osella, hit the parked Ferrari, killing himself on impact. Paletti was only twenty-three years old. Despite the succession of horrific situations, Pironi kept racing.

By mid-summer, Pironi had won Imola and the Dutch Grand Prix and was becoming the leading contender for the World Championship and the first potential French world champion. At the Hockenheimring, Germany, surrounded by forest, Pironi was on top with the fastest car. But the practice session conditions were highly dangerous at a very high-speed circuit in the wet.

Due to the trees at Hockenheim, when it rained the spray from the cars hung in the air. Didier was one of the few cars to go out; he wanted to show everyone he was the best no matter what conditions. On track, Pironi was closing very quickly on Derek Daly, with maximum commitment. He drove into a wall of spray and was blinded. Pironi's car got caught on Prost's rear wheel, took off, flipped over and was brutally smashed on impact. The accident was eerily reminiscent of Villeneuve's. Pironi later described the car as going so high he saw the tops of the trees. He broke both arms and was aware that the doctors around him wanted to amputate his leg. He was one infection away from losing it and ending up having around 30 surgeries after the accident, such was its impact. The experience haunted Pironi; according to those who knew him he became a shadow of his former self and struggled with regret for what happened to Gilles.

Pironi was only beaten to that year's title by five points, despite missing the last five races. He tried to get back to Formula One, despite struggling to regain strength and movement in his right leg and ankle. In the meantime, he took to offshore boating with the aim, as always, to win a championship. In August 1987, five years after the accident and just as he was about to sign with the F1 Larousse team, he took part in a boat race off the Isle of Wight, UK. As one of two boats leading the race, the leading pair faced a slow-moving tanker ahead on the second lap. The rules of the sea state that if you're the overtaking boat, you must take proper precautions. Pironi hit the tanker's wash straight on. The power boat flipped, killing the crew of three. The pair who met in 1980 were gone. At the time of his death, Pironi's partner Catherine was pregnant with twins. On 6 January 1988, she gave birth to Didier and Gilles. Gilles Pironi continued the family F1 story as an engineer in 2014 with Mercedes, while Gilles Villeneuve's son, Jacques, became a driver, winning the Indy 500 and 1997 World Championship.

After Gilles' death, Pironi had faced a lot of blame and negative press – but never from the Villeneuve family. While they resented the betrayal at Imola, they knew the truth. It's a truth which confronts even the most dazzlingly talented in motorsport: it is each driver's choice to get in the car. No matter how fearless they look, they all know the risk.

The Strike

In one of the great capers in F1 history, this is what happens when the drivers read the small print.

Charles Leclerc stares out of the window, lost in the music as he tinkles on the piano, Liam Lawson sits attentively nearby waiting his turn, all while Lewis Hamilton provides vocals, as the rest of the drivers sit on the floor enthralled.

It might seem preposterous, but in 1982 that's exactly what happened when the Formula One grid went on strike. The story features, quite predictably, some highly complex politics at the heart of Formula One. The details are dense but the repercussions had a long-lasting effect on the sport and its competitors, and it made for great story.

Every driver in Formula One is required to hold a valid licence called a 'super licence', and, like all drivers' licences, this is subject to terms and conditions. Ahead of the 1982 season opening Grand Prix in South Africa, the small print had been changed. Two-time world champion Niki Lauda felt the changed terms were completely unacceptable. The new licence tied the drivers to their teams for three years, leaving them unable to switch cars for an unprecedented length of time.

Not only this, but the team would retain the right to dismiss drivers, leaving them potentially stuck on the sidelines if they fell out with team management. The individuals would also be forced to disclose the financial terms of their contract, promoting fears that the teams would collude to keep salaries down. Finally, there was a threat of penalties if the drivers publicly criticized Formula One. Something that would cause revolt in any era in any paddock.

On opening day of the 1982 season, Kyalami was strangely devoid of drivers. Niki Lauda had set up camp at the entrance tunnel leading to the paddock gates, thereby preventing drivers from entering the pits until they had learnt of the new injustice. Lauda felt he had to take this action because 24 of the 31 entrants had already signed up – most without even reading their licence terms and conditions.

Ferrari driver Didier Pironi was the chairman of the GPDA. With Lauda, he set about convincing the drivers to take action en masse, leading the negotiations. With the drivers on one side, the opposition was led by Jean-Marie Balestre, the FIA president.

Pironi outlined the drivers' position. Unless the three new clauses were dropped, they would strike, forcing the cancellation of the opening Grand Prix of the season. Jean-Marie Balestre stalled for time, replying he could not change anything without convening a committee in Paris. Not only that, the drivers who had not signed the new terms would not be competing. Team managers were now under pressure to control their drivers, with opinions ranging from 'they'll be sacked if they don't turn up' to 'let's see how this plays out'. Team principal and owner of Lotus, Colin Chapman, called it 'mass hysteria'.

Moods were not improved when it emerged Niki Lauda had ordered a bus and the drivers were actually leaving. Almost unbelievably, each driver boarded the bus and made for the circuit gates. But the circuit tunnel played its part. Someone from the teams and FIA had parked a campervan lengthways, blocking the exit. Ligier driver Jacques Laffite was sent to move it – and after much heckling and jeering from his fellow drivers – somehow succeeded. The last barricade failed and the strike had begun.

The circuit was silent, the pits were empty. The farce continued when the March team's race-winning driver Jochen Mass somehow missed the bus, and upon finding out what had happened, slunk off back to his hotel alone. The rest of the grid headed to the Sunnyside Hotel in Johannesburg. Lauda insisted the group stay together in the hotel ballroom; this was to stop angry team managers peeling off drivers by knocking on individual hotel room doors. If anyone wanted to speak to a driver, they had to go through Niki. He was not taking any chances.

It was an unprecedented situation; having nearly the whole grid in the room in a social setting was extremely unusual. Alfa Romeo driver Bruno Giacomelli drew cartoons of his fellow drivers. Lotus' Elio de Angelis and Ferrari's Gilles Villeneuve kept everyone entertained by playing the ballroom piano. Spirits were high.

Back at the track, things were getting increasingly heated. Pironi had joined Ballestre and head of the FOCA, Bernie Ecclestone. The trio could be seen arguing through the window of race control. With everyone – drivers, teams, TV, circuit and sponsors – in various forms of breach of contract, threats of the cars being impounded circulated. The ATS team attempted a recruitment drive, scrawling on a piece of cardboard left at the entrance of the garage: 'Formula One drivers wanted, enquire within.'

Multiple team managers drove to the hotel in an attempt to break the strike. Arrow's Jackie Oliver attempted to enter the ballroom, only to find the piano wedged against the door as Lauda's one-room plan held firm. For hours, the drivers showed a united front but sentiments were shifting. Those in the middle and back of the grid began pondering what they were risking. To the consternation of the driver group, Italian Teo Fabi went to the loo and fled out of the window.

With night approaching, mattresses and blankets were

procured. Alain Prost shared a mattress with Gilles Villeneuve, and Arrows driver Patrick Tambay was said to have remarked, 'If those two have kids tonight I might as well retire now.' Bruno Giacomelli then provided a change of pace with a lecture on terrorism in Italy and how to service an AK47. Every few hours, Peroni would return with news from the bargaining table, with Villeneuve providing dramatic theme music before every announcement. The strike moved beyond midnight, with Williams driver Carlos Reutemann snoring so loudly he kept the rest of the grid awake, before multiple thrown pillows finally allowed the drivers an uneasy night's rest.

The day of qualifying began with Didier Peroni continuing to negotiate in the circuit offices. Two drivers, Mass and Fabi, took to the track but just two drivers on the circuit was somehow more embarrassing than none, and the session was quickly red flagged. The situation was now critical; some drivers had broken with the strike and time was running out quickly to prevent the cancellation of the race. Ecclestone and Balestre had no choice but to back down immediately. The drivers were promised no punishment and the promise of further negotiations about the licence.

Qualifying was scheduled to take place immediately so no recriminations could unfold in team motorhomes. The pit lane crackled into life and Formula One in 1982 was underway with a full grid and an uneasy truce holding. It would last mere hours. Mid-race the stewards suspended all the drivers indefinitely after the chequered flag fell. Alain Prost ended up winning the Grand Prix having made a mid-race pit stop before staging a fight back from a lap down to pass seven cars and take victory.

Afterwards, despite reassurances to the contrary, the drivers were also fined. The next race in Argentina was scrapped amid the acrimony but eventually the clauses were dropped and the drivers felt they had won. There has never been a drivers' strike since.

Adrian Newey Makes His First Mark in F1

Adrian Newey is one of the most important figures in F1 history and is regarded as one of the best designers and engineers to ever live.

His cars have achieved more than 200 Grands Prix victories, 14 Drivers' Championships and 12 Constructors' titles over the course of his career. If Adrian Newey was a team, he would be the second most successful constructor of all time only behind Ferrari, who have been in the sport for 75 years versus his 40. Newey has described his design process as 'thought bubbles popping up' when he least expects it. These bubbles, combined with an uncanny ability to almost 'see' the aerodynamics of a car, have led to some of the most significant innovations in Formula One car design. An uncanny ability to use his talents, particularly at rule changes, have seen his cars dominant across many different years including the ground-effect period, V10 engines, blown diffusers and the current hybrid turbo era.

After attending the same school as former *Top Gear* host Jeremy Clarkson, Newey studied aerodynamics and aeronautics at Southampton University. He struggled to get his first role in F1, but in 1980 he had some success after a highly unusual interview with Harvey Postlethwaite, design chief at Formula One team Fittipaldi. Newey had ridden to the interview on a Ducati 900SS, which Postlethwaite asked for a go on, and that's all it took – Newey got the job. Unfortunately, with limited resources, there wasn't much he could do, and Newey was forced to leave when the team's money eventually ran out. Crucially, though, he had proved he belonged at the top table.

Colin Chapman at Lotus instantly offered him a role, but Newey turned it down to join March (*see* Chapter 17) in 1982. March built junior single seaters, IndyCars and sports cars as well as Formula One cars. This wide-ranging experience across different car types, and crucial exposure to different aerodynamics used in different series, was to prove invaluable. After some success in IndyCar, Newey moved back to Formula One with the Haas Lola team, halfway through 1986. The team was well funded but badly organized. A lot of talented individuals were part of the engineering team, including future Ferrari technical boss and Formula One Management managing director Ross Brawn and future McLaren executive director of engineering Neil Oatley. Ex-McLaren bosses Teddy Mayer and Tyler Alexander were unable to get the most out of their young team, as no one was able to overcome an underpowered Ford engine. When the sponsor pulled the plug, Carl Haas shut the factory down. Newey went back to March and IndyCar working with Mario Andretti, but it didn't take him long to rejoin Formula One.

In 1987, Japanese businessman Akira Akagi worked with March to form a Formula One team, later buying the team outright with the name changed from March to Leyton House Racing. Newey was to be the team's technical director – he'd made it! At the time, F1 cars were bulky, large things with fast turbo-charged engines, but the Leyton team was using an underpowered Judd engine. Newey knew he needed to take a different approach to car design. The car was designed to be lightweight, compact and tight aerodynamically, with a fully integrated nose/front wing assembly. Newey also changed the seating position, lowering the driver further into the cockpit to gain aerodynamic advantages by raising the pedals above where the driver sits. With the driver now in an almost reclined position, the driving experience of a Formula One car potentially has more similarity to a Pilates workout than a road car. While Leyton never won a Grand Prix, much to the paddock's surprise Ivan Capelli drove an excellent race at the 1990 French Grand Prix to snatch the lead on lap 33, only for Alain Prost in a Ferrari to overtake him with just three laps to go. Newey's ideas had taken a small startup to the brink of victory on a fraction of the big boys' budget; he had set new trends that shifted Formula One cars to be more aerodynamically driven.

The March/Leyton endeavour did not last, and Newey found himself again in need of a new role. Thankfully, Williams had already noticed his innovations. Newey joined the team in 1991 as chief designer under famous technical director Patrick Head. The first car he worked on was the 1991 FW14, with which Nigel Mansell won five Grands Prix to come second in the Drivers' Championship. His next car, the FW14B, helped to end McLaren's previous dominance of the sport. So dominant was the Williams team that they took first and second in the Drivers' Championship and the Constructors' Championship with 10 wins and 9 second-place finishes. The FW14B and its successor, the FW15C, successfully used active suspension. Newey saw it as a platform-control device that allowed aerodynamic surfaces to be driven harder. The FW15C was considered to be one of the most technically advanced F1 cars of its time, with power steering, launch control, traction control, anti-locking and power-assisted brakes. In 1993, Alain Prost made the most of the car to win his last title.

Seeing Williams' success, Ayrton Senna sought to make a move to the team and joined for the start of 1994. This was to end in tragedy as Senna died three races later (*see* Chapter 40). Newey was later cleared of manslaughter in three separate court cases, the last occurring as late as 2005. In an interview, Newey admitted feeling guilt but not culpability for Senna's death and shared how at the time he questioned whether he wanted to continue in a sport where drivers could die in his creation. Rarely seen Japanese TV footage shows Newey absolutely distraught at the pit wall during the aftermath of the accident.

Newey continued to make further design advancements at Williams, particularly in 1995 with the undercut diffuser – new step plane regulations allowed for a larger diffuser exit by sweeping the diffuser upwards behind the rear wheels, which created a major downforce-generation advantage. He next found a loophole in the 1996 regulation changes that were meant to better protect the driver's head. Instead of going for the bulky designs of his competitors, Newey lowered the Kevlar-coated foam headrest and added a thin piece of bodywork, ensuring better airflow to the back of the car. This template became widely adopted in 1997. Newey was to leave Williams at the end of 1996, seeking greater control, including input in driver selection. Frank Williams and Patrick Head did not want to lose any more power and did not consult Newey when they fired world champion Damon Hill (*see* Chapter 43). It was the final straw.

Newey joined McLaren for the 1997 season as technical director, with his first job to optimize Neil Oatley's MP4/12. Newey's appointment coincided with the start of a short renaissance at McLaren. Both their drivers, Mika Häkkinen and David Coulthard, ended up winning races that year, having won none the previous year. The car wasn't quite as competitive with his own old design at Williams, who won that year's Constructors' title. However, the new 1998 regulations were an opportunity ready to be exploited. Quite simply, with its narrow track concept Newey's MP4/13 was dominant. The drivers commanded the opening of the 1998 season at the Australian Grand Prix with a one–two. Häkkinen went on to win the Drivers' Championship and the team the Constructors', despite a closely fought battle with Ferrari's Schumacher. Häkkinen would also win the 1999 Drivers' Championship, but this would be Newey's last at McLaren.

Ferrari entered a new era of dominance with the power axis of Schumacher, old colleague Ross Brawn and Team Principal

Jean Todt. McLaren would still compete for wins but not enough to upend Ferrari's five consecutive Formula One World Drivers' Championships. By 2003, Newey had a rare miss with his MP4/18. While innovations in the car, such as the blown diffuser, would later be recycled at Red Bull, the car suffered from reliability problems: overheating, floor delamination and engine failure meant the car never raced. With parallels to the end of Newey's time at Williams, team principal Ron Dennis and managing director Martin Whitmarsh wanted to reign in his innovations. Newey sought more design freedom and accepted an invitation to dinner on the King's Road to meet his old friend David Coulthard ... (*see* Chapter 56).

Ginny Williams Refuses to Let Her Husband Die

Frank Williams had a well-worn adage for what he'd experienced in his remarkable time in motorsport.

When the topic of his accident came up in conversation he'd say he lived one life for 44 years, and then he lived another. The day everything changed was 8 March 1986.

The Williams team were in a buoyant place that spring, four-time World Championship winners and making constant progress throughout 1985. They'd closed the season on top, winning the final three races of the campaign with a raft of effective car updates twinned with the increasingly mighty Honda V6 turbo, which had become the industry standard.

The drivers had noticed. Nelson Piquet – once the hated team opposition when driving for Brabham – had personally approached Frank to join the Oxford-based outfit. He'd be paired with moustachioed Brit Nigel Mansell, whose skills behind the wheel fervently divided opinion in the paddock. Lotus team boss Colin Chapman rated his ability, but with the great designer gone Mansell's reputation suffered. When Nelson Piquet signed the contract in Austria, Mansell had failed to win a Grand Prix and looked like clear number two material to his detractors. But ahead of the 1986 season, both Mansell and Piquet looked very fast behind the wheel of the new FW11 in pre-season testing, including on a temperate day at the Paul Ricard circuit in southern France.

It was a day that defined the Williams story in Formula One.

Frank Williams was ragging his Ford Sierra hire car down the winding hill from near the top of the mountainside the circuit is carved into; this man utterly obsessed with speed was treating the journey to the airport as his own personal time trial. He pushed too hard, ran wide, clipped a rock and the car somersaulted into a field, and so began the journey into his next life. He would later admit it was at least the sixth time something like this had happened.

Frank's passenger on the way to the airport was Peter Windsor – the team's sponsorship manager – who had escaped without injury before smashing a window to drag Frank clear of the wreckage. Williams, awake and aware he was seriously injured, spoke calmly while facing death: 'Tell Patrick that all the existing sponsorship deals have been signed for the year and that Honda has an option with us for '87. Nelson is signed for '87 but Nigel's on a two-way option. And I was raised as a Catholic. If necessary, I'd like the last rites.' Formula One came first, sacraments second.

Nelson Piquet was now at the scene too, and seeing the gravity of the situation, Peter phoned Frank's wife, Ginny Wiliams. Tentatively, he reassured her that while they'd had an accident, Frank was conscious and they were heading to the hospital to get him checked over. Ginny first knew the situation was dire when co-team owner, Patrick Head, said he was driving over to the Williams family home and they should wait for news together. The sickening feeling of not knowing hung over the beautiful mansion in the English countryside.

After an argument between Mansell, Piquet and the ambulance driver nearly ended in a fist fight, Frank Williams was eventually taken to a hospital in Marseille. It was the first sign nothing would be straightforward in the coming hours. Ginny and Patrick Head made the short journey to Marseille's huge Timone Hospital. Professor Sid Watkins, Formula One's in-house doctor, was called to France by Bernie Ecclestone, and soon they all heard the news that would change the Williams' lives forever: Frank Williams had broken his neck.

On being told the news, Nelson Piquet wept and Ginny let out a strangled noise. Her husband was paralyzed, quadriplegic and hooked up to multiple machines. He was badly cut, beaten and bruised by the accident. She couldn't find the words, only tears. On seeing his wife, Frank Williams quietly rasped, 'Now I shall have a different kind of life.' This would be a huge adjustment for anyone, and for Frank it was the robbery of a way of life. He had started running regularly in 1970, to balance the mental toll of the job with physical exertion, sometimes accumulating 80 miles a week.

The only thing that inspired Williams more than running was Formula One. It was part of him. Ever since he saw Peter Collins triumph at the British Grand Prix in 1958, it was all he wanted to do. After trying and failing to race himself without crashing, Williams had wisely become a mechanic, then a team owner in Formula Three, then Formula Two, running the highly rated Piers Courage who was a close friend. Brabham ran a very lucrative customer car business, and Frank Williams – always on the brink of a financial crisis – found enough to purchase a Brabham F1 car for 1969. Frank Williams' racing cars had made it to Formula One, but money was tight – for a few weeks the team was run out of a public phone box, as BT had cut his phone line after months of unpaid bills.

Courage was instantly quick, scoring fine second places at Monaco and Watkins Glen, but the joy didn't last. Courage would be killed at the fast sweepers at Zandvoort. The personal pain of having to tell Courage's parents about the fire and the loss of their boy wounded Frank. Heartbroken, he continued, until the money ran out. By 1977, Williams could no longer defy financial gravity and was forced to sell. He concluded the only answer would be to start again.

Crucially, he persuaded a young engineer to join him in

team ownership and to run the engineering side completely. This decision represented a major moment for Patrick Head; he left behind good wages for the chance of vaulting up the ladder in Formula One. Improbably, Williams were winners within two years of his decision, mastering the new era ground-effect regulations. Frank and Patrick won the British Grand Prix in 1979, and just a year later won the Drivers' World Championship with Alan Jones, while Frank Williams held the Constructors' trophy – the first of nine in the team's history. The following seasons they repeated the feat, and in 1982 Keke Rosberg became the second drivers' champion with the team; Williams had won 20 Grands Prix by the end of the 1985 season.

Back in the hospital, two days after the accident, Williams' previous achievements must have felt like a lifetime ago. Ginny began to think of the way forward. Offers of private jets to transport him back home flooded in from the giants of F1, while Patrick Head was placed in full charge of the race team for the upcoming season.

But deep concern was rising; everyone in the Williams clan was unhappy with the treatment Frank was receiving in the hospital. Bizarrely, no medical staff kept them updated, and sometimes there was no nurse at all. It was clear Frank wasn't receiving the care he required. Panic rose within Ginny; this wasn't right.

After demanding an answer from the staff, Ginny was coldly told the reality. Her husband had been written off by the hospital as a dead man. Frank Williams was not receiving anything other than basic care and no effort was being made to save him; resources had been sent to other patients who had a fighting chance. The situation quickly became clear to Ginny: death was inevitable unless the location changed, fast.

Her husband may succumb to his injuries but not like this, not through neglect. After a furious phone call home, Prof. Watkins dispatched one of his team to survey the latest.

Dr Yates was understandably cautious, believing they needed to stabilize Frank's condition before moving him. After witnessing just one night of the care provided, however, he changed his mind; there wasn't a minute to spare. The family took up the offer of private jets – they would take the risk to get him home and give him a chance of living.

The weather on the flight day was critical, with storms and cloud around London, but mercifully the fog cleared and Frank Williams was flown to London's private Biggin Hill airport. He was then transferred to the London Hospital. Top-line care would give him a chance, but he was still gravely ill. For Ginny, after three days of torture in Marseilles, she could finally stay with her husband and monitor his care.

The next month was a waking nightmare of improvements and setbacks. At one stage, a tracheotomy was performed to aid Frank's breathing, and after completion the surgeon asked, 'Just how much more effort do you want us to make to keep your husband alive?' The astounding lack of empathy Ginny encountered was shocking, but post-tracheotomy, having barely eaten and slept in weeks, she let forth a roar of defiance: 'I want every effort made!'

At every stage, the prevailing opinion from doctors was that he should be allowed to die. But Ginny just wouldn't relent. She brushed off the details of the quality of life Frank would face; they'd face it if he made it. All those around her, including Peter Windsor, implored her – Frank would want to live at all costs.

And so her demanding resolve took over. She utterly refused to accept the stated case without explanation, with utter devotion to the man she loved. In the coming days, Frank's condition transitioned from critical to stable. Then, when he suffered a setback after developing pneumonia, Ginny learnt how to drain the fluid that endangered her husband's life on a daily basis. A month later, after several brushes with death and a recovery that was far from linear, Frank and Ginny left the hospital. Frank Williams returned to the paddock four months after the trip down the mountainside, but it was his wife who collected the trophy after Nigel Mansell had brilliantly passed Piquet and won the British Grand Prix. Virginia Williams' face while hoisting aloft the trophy was incredible. Somehow, it captured every doubt, every snivel, every sexist dismissal she had faced while ensuring her husband was well cared for. Patrick Head would bluntly state, 'She had kept Frank alive.' On the podium at Brands Hatch she had been vindicated, her husband had survived – the team were winners again, and her role in preserving the family business was reflected in the glint of the grand old golden trophy. It is an indelible image in the great tapestry of F1 – a picture of pure defiance.

Frank Williams was told by many experts he would be lucky to live 10 more years after his accident. In 2019, he marked 50 years as a team owner, having redefined what a person with severe injuries could achieve. Thanks to his wife's dedication, Frank and Ginny shared winning World Championships on 12 more occasions before his death, aged seventy-nine, in 2021. Ginny had passed away from cancer in 2013. Her dedication in the face of unimaginable horror preserved a family. In 2025, 56 years after the first entry, the Williams name lives on.

33

Mansell's Tyre Bursts to Break a Generation's Heart

Formula One does not have an official hall of fame when it comes to races, but if it did the Australian Grand Prix of 1986 would be towards the top.

For a whole generation of fans it is an indelible memory.

If Nelson Piquet had his way, 1986 would have been much more of a dreary affair. The Brazilian believed he had a verbal promise from team leader Frank Williams for number-one status in the team, but Williams' car accident in pre-season testing had left Williams fighting for his life and placed technology chief Patrick Head in charge (*see* Chapter 32). Head scoured the written contracts and found nothing to suggest Nelson had any promises of number-one status.

It meant game-on for 1986; Piquet had the best car in the field but so did British driver Nigel Mansell. After the early races, Piquet went to Frank, trying to get the desperately ill man to blink to indicate the status story was true. Eventually, Piquet got first dibs on the spare car but they couldn't make Mansell drive slower and there was an almighty battle to be had on track between the two rivals. Heading into the final race of the season, Mansell only required four points which came with a third place in order to take the title. It was an unexpected shot at glory for a driver who had only won his first Grand Prix the season before.

The teams arrived in Australia with a new winner; after Gerhard Berger in a Benetton had taken victory in Mexico City, he was in the news for leaving the team for Ferrari for the 1987 season.

Ferrari had also tried to sign World Championship leader Nigel Mansell, with Enzo Ferrari, admiring his flamboyant, aggressive style behind the wheel. Mansell said the offer was 'staggering money', but it was suggested to him his championship aspirations could suffer in the way these things can unfold once a driver has signalled their desire to leave their current team for a big rival. Desiring the title above all else, Mansell signed an extension with Williams – it was a team and driver combination that seemed to work perfectly. The Honda turbocharged Williams with more power than grip, making these cars visually spectacular and universally loved trackside by spectators.

Mansell's fifth place in Mexico left him six points ahead of Prost and seven ahead of his teammate, Piquet; one final trip to the podium would be enough for a place in sporting history. Mansell was confident of scoring a tenth podium in 16 races and securing the crown. For Alain Prost, the goal of still being mathematically in contention was complete. His aim in the inferior McLaren was to hang in there to try to force a result at a track where he enjoyed racing.

On the grid, Mansell was on pole ahead of Piquet and Ayrton Senna, who had faded from title contention with an incomplete Lotus. Prost was the title outsider in the McLaren and was fourth, 1.2 seconds off Mansell's time. With this being the biggest day of Mansell's life, he was understandably cautious, slipping behind Senna, Piquet and Keke Rosberg, who'd climbed from seventh to third. Piquet then passed Senna for the lead later in the lap. Senna dropped to fifth out of contention with a car that didn't work around the streets of South Australia.

Keke Rosberg then took the lead from Nelson Piquet and stormed away at a staggering rate. This was remarkable for a couple of reasons: because of the rate he disappeared and due to the dreadful final season he was having in F1 – a single pole position in Germany and one podium in Monaco where he was second. Rosberg and Prost had hatched a plan in order to try to shake up the obvious result. Rosberg would set a fierce pace, trying to tempt the Williams pair to keep up with him and burn through their fuel, which had to be carefully monitored in the 1980s. Realistically for Rosberg and Prost in their McLarens, there was little chance the Finnish driver would make the end of the race. He was devastatingly quick around the 2.3-mile circuit, but this came at the expense of his brakes, which were getting decimated in the process.

With street circuit specialist Rosberg playing disrupter, Williams continued to play it cool, running their own race and letting Rosberg hog the airtime in the lead. Alain Prost began the second phase of his race and began to push. Nelson Piquet then spun, the mistake putting him behind Prost and Mansell, though he still had the ability to fight back.

On lap 31 out of 87, Prost punctured his front right tyre when lapping a Benetton This seemingly dropped the outsider out of contention, but McLaren, looking for any differential to Williams' race, had always planned to tyre stop. Prost rejoined 20 seconds away from Piquet and 24 behind championship leader Mansell. Prost had fresh tyres, his teammate in the lead and 50 laps to make up the time difference.

On lap 44, Piquet passed Mansell for second. For the first time, Mansell must have felt a pang of vulnerability. Nearly 20 laps passed without incident before Rosberg slowed and retired from the lead – his tyre had let go but he'd mistaken it for an engine failure. He parked up after a thrilling starring role in his final outing in Formula One.

Mansell began his 64th lap. He was now second but was easily passed by Prost on fresher tyres. Mansell now dropped to third, the Brit simply had to stay where he was to win the title as he had a mammoth minute-sized gap to fourth position. On the back straight, the TV cameras caught the moment that would decide the title.

'LOOK AT THAT. Colossally, that's Mansell!' shouted Murray

Walker on the BBC. Just moments after Rosberg stopped, Mansell's tyre had exploded on the straight, showering the circuit with sparks and destroying the car. His car and title dreams were blown up in the cruellest way.

The iconic image was caught live, creating an unforgettable moment replayed for decades to come. The recriminations began in the paddock. The Goodyear tyre had let go minutes after Rosberg's. While the team confirmed it was always the plan not to change tyres, Mansell called it 'a terrible mistake' and protested he'd wanted to stop. Worst still, the team had suffered tyre failures with Goodyear in testing early that season. Leading cars hadn't tried zero stops since the second round of the season at Jerez. Goodyear thought the tyres that had come off Prost's car on lap 31 did not show signs of excessive wear, and it had been communicated to Williams that the tyres were fine.

Patrick Head was then forced to make a call about his sole remaining car in the race. Risk an identical failure and potential harm of a driver or pit and hand the championship to McLaren. There was only one ethical option and Piquet was called in to change tyres; the championship lead had changed hands three times in a matter of minutes. Piquet never argued the call, later revealing his car had been vibrating on the straights, indicating a failure was imminent.

Back on the track, Alain Prost was suddenly in position to win a championship without the fastest car – but the fuel gauge in his car said minus five. The Frenchman prayed it was inaccurate. The long final laps ticked by, and Prost coasted across the line to win the race and the championship. He immediately pulled over to save what fuel there was left for a required sample and jumped up and down, consumed with the joy of becoming the first back-to-back world champion since Jack Brabham in 1960.

Prost believed his second title to be his best championship win, revelling in having secured it with the tactical ability that earned him the nickname 'The Professor'. Engine supplier Honda were distraught, despite becoming the first Japanese company to be part of a Constructors' Championship victory. Patrick Head was summoned to Japan to explain why Williams had failed to pick between both drivers and split the points nearly equally across a 16-race season.

Mansell would endure more title heartbreak in 1991 before dominating the 1992 championship. When I interviewed Mansell years later, in the middle of Sebastian Vettel's dominant run of title wins, I asked him whether dominant titles ever got the right respect from the public. 'Mine did … after 1986,' was his reply. It is no exaggeration to say the events of Adelaide haunted Mansell for decades.

Prost vs Senna, Part One - Japan 1989

It all began at Imola.

The picturesque circuit, named for Enzo and Dino Ferrari, has hosted some of the most consequential days of Formula One history and in 1989 it would be the site of the beginning of the sport's greatest rivalry. There had been flashpoints along the way – the politics of stopping the 1984 Monaco Grand Prix in the pouring rain as Senna caught Prost at tremendous pace. Their battles when Senna had raced for the iconic Lotus team had been intense but the pairing of the two at McLaren was a ticking time bomb. When McLaren became the front-running car by a distance, it became zero sum. Prost or Senna would win the titles of this era; everything orbited them.

In Imola in northern Italy, the McLarens had qualified first and second. Senna suggested, with the season still in the early stages, the team shouldn't risk losing points by fighting. Strangely, considering Prost prioritized his set-up around race day, he agreed. The terms of the deal were simple: whoever reached the first braking zone at the turn 3 Tosa hairpin first would win the race. Senna got the better start and Prost honoured the agreement. On lap 4, Gerhard Berger had a huge, fiery crash in his Ferrari at the flat-out Tamburello corner; so serious was the crash that the race was red flagged, which was a not hugely common occurrence at the time.

At the restart, Prost got ahead but Senna outbraked him into Tosa. The rules of 1989 said that all parts of the race counted towards the race time, even parts before red flags. Essentially it was the same race, not a brand-new start and race (as it would be today under a red flag). Senna went on to win; Prost's post-race mood was volcanic and immediately after the race the argument started.

'Afterwards, I said it was finished; as far as our personal relationship was concerned, that was it,' Prost told *Motor Sport Magazine* years later. 'He argued that it wasn't the start, it was the restart, so the agreement didn't apply.'

By July 1989, Prost felt the relationship with Ayrton was damaged beyond repair and was convinced engine partner Honda favoured Senna; with McLaren prizing the best-in-class Honda engine above all else, the Frenchman chose to leave for Ferrari. There was no more peace to keep at McLaren; as the drivers took the title to the wire, just two races remained as they boarded flights for Japan.

By Japan 1989, Prost and Senna weren't close to speaking terms, with Prost telling the media: 'I have left the door open many times for Senna, but I will not do that again.' Senna's previous racing conduct was vital for the next race, because if neither car finished, Prost would be the world champion with a race to spare.

As expected, Senna had the pace edge on Saturday and qualified on pole position, but the margin was an incredible 1.7 seconds! Prost conceded he couldn't beat Senna over a single lap, so focused on his race set-up and securing the front row. At the start, Prost stormed into the lead, believing this was going to be his only chance at victory given the manner of Senna's win the year before. Senna couldn't believe what he was seeing from his cockpit. Prost was seriously attacking, haranguing the car around Suzuka's elegant turns so aggressively Senna thought Prost was pushing too hard and risking the car's reliability. Senna, knowing he had to win, held back; they had switched approaches in the most important race of the year. It was only at the halfway stage Senna began to apply the pressure in the battle for the lead. For many laps, they ran together; finally, after a few test runs, it was time. On lap 47 of 53, Senna boldly attacked into the final chicane.

Prost wasn't playing games anymore. He shut the door. The beautiful red-and-white McLaren cars gently scuffed into each other and ground to a halt.

'This is the opportunity that Senna's looking for, and he's going through ... this is fantastic – this is what we were fearing might happen. And that means to say that Prost has won the World Championship,' Murray Walker described from the BBC commentary box.

Prost's version of events stated that by the time he saw Senna was making the move, he had already started turning in. As advertised, he had no intention of opening the door and attempting to race the corner. His post-race press conference quotes pummelled into his teammate.

'I was sure I'd win the race or have an accident like this ... Ayrton can't accept he won't win and can't accept someone will resist an overtake ... If you have two drivers like Ayrton, there would be a crash at every race.'

Senna's version of the same corner went like this: he had outbraked Prost, accusing his teammate of turning in early. The teammates could continue to squabble between themselves, but the aerial angle left no ambiguity. Prost had turned into the corner very early.

Somehow, the crash hadn't actually decided anything. The cars had come to a halt intertwined, stranded motionless in the middle of the tarmac. Prost thought his car was damaged and could hear both engines were cut. The two-time world champion thought he had secured his third crown as he was convinced Senna couldn't be pushed back into the race. He undid his belts, lingering on the track before spinning around in complete incredulity as he heard an engine note and Senna was pushed back into the race.

The rules clearly banned push-starts, but the marshals were permitted to push a car from a dangerous position. Senna had asked for a second push, which helped the car to start. He missed the chicane and rejoined the race via the run-off. With the front wing damaged and hanging off the car at an angle, Senna would need to pit for a new nose. In third place, Alessandro Nannini had been coasting, looking to bring home the Benetton and secure a podium. He'd only made the top three on two occasions that season and was playing it safe.

After the crash, however, he was now in the lead. Inexplicably, Benetton didn't tell him what was going on, and, having never won a Grand Prix, Nannini carried on nursing the car home rather than pushing. How much was he coasting? Senna, driving like a man possessed, was running four seconds quicker per lap – a huge margin in any era. Nannini was furious when he worked out what was happening as Senna made a clean pass at the chicane, to win the race and continue the title battle to Australia for the first last-race decider since 1986!

But after the parc fermé celebrations, no one appeared on the podium. It was obvious the race result was in doubt. When the podium music blared from the circuit speakers, it was official. Senna was disqualified, Nannini was the winner and Prost was the champion of the world!

FIA president Jean-Marie Balestre appeared, pointed at the TV and shouted, 'Illegal!' at the replay of Senna rejoining having cut the chicane. Senna was no longer fighting Prost; he was fighting the FIA. McLaren appealed the decision, even though their own driver had won the title – disappointingly for them, the winner had been the driver heading to Ferrari.

Ron Dennis held a press conference highlighting previous chicane cutting that went unpunished; he argued for fair play, honesty, integrity and consistency from the stewards. Balestre was seen applying pressure to the stewards to decide the penalty and race result before the podium was held. Ayrton Senna railed against the process: 'What happened post-race was disgraceful. It was clear I'd been disqualified before I'd even got to the hearing.'

The stewards told him he should have turned back towards the chicane as soon as the engine fired to rejoin the race. Raging, Senna pointed out this would be against the rules, as he would have been headed towards oncoming cars. They also said his pass was illegal, because he put his wheels over the pit entry.

It was now clear they were chucking the kitchen sink at Senna. Anything they could think of was being weaponized to ensure disqualification. The FIA accused Senna of endangering the safety of other drivers and listed his accidents from previous seasons. The infringements listed were: the car was pushed backward; the car did not take the chicane; Senna did not rejoin the road at the right place, instead making a shortcut; and Senna had overtaken over the pit entry, which was not allowed. Senna was also accused of driving a car in a dangerous condition and, craziest of all, called the pass on Nannini highly incorrect, despite it being a standard issue overtake on the inside. Things had descended far beyond a questionable disqualification for a push-start; this was now a highly personal hearing on the very being of Ayrton Senna, the driver.

At a later hearing in Paris, the FIA upheld the disqualification, issuing Senna with a six-month suspended ban and $100,000 fine – a punishment so severe even Alain Prost called it 'very high'.

In a box-office press conference, Senna questioned how he could race in F1 with the ban hanging over him. Every quote was explosive as he said he'd been treated like a criminal. 'What we see today is a true manipulation of the World Championship.'

Balestre called Senna's comments defamatory and reminded the drivers he personally had the power to sanction any driver or team who refused to abide by the decisions of the FIA. The sorry incident was resolved in February when Senna wrote a letter saying no pressure group or person had influenced the result of the 1989 championship. What followed would make 1989 look tame in comparison.

Prost vs Senna, Part Two – Japan 1990

In 1989, the two best drivers in the world, Alain Prost and Ayrton Senna, had fallen out beyond repair.

McLaren was split into two teams under one roof. A year on, the same two drivers battled for the World Championship, at the same circuit for the third year in succession: Prost vs Senna for the title, for the final time. The only change: Alain Prost was in the red scarlet of Ferrari, having joined the team at the start of the season. He was seeking to be only the second driver in history to win the title with F1's two most successful teams after Niki Lauda had won with Ferrari in 1975 and 1976 and then beat Prost by half a point in 1984, driving a McLaren.

Senna had repeated his trick from the previous two seasons and took pole position, which began the first narrative of the weekend. The world champion of 1988 wanted the grid changed and pole position moved to the opposite side of the track. He wanted a fast getaway on the right-hand side of the circuit with its rubbered racing line that made the car grip better. Starting from the front was nowhere near the advantage it would have been if the positions were switched. Senna set about lobbying for a change and he believed he'd convinced officials at Suzuka circuit. Jean-Marie Balestre, intervened; pole position would stay away from the racing line again.

But while Senna's battle with the FIA was still being played out in public, Senna hadn't forgiven Prost for turning on him and starting the incredible events of Japan 1989. A full 11 months after the collision in Monza, Senna told the journalist Gerald Donaldson about the first time he'd seen Prost since the crash: 'I told him [Prost] to get lost and watch out for his life.'

Senna's mood worsened during the drivers' briefing held before the Grand Prix; the drivers were told of a change to the rules if they cut a chicane. Senna was incredulous, storming out after what had happened a year before. The paddock atmosphere was boiling. The sporting world held its breath. The lights illuminated in Suzuka: Prost on the right in second in the beautiful Ferrari, Senna on the left on pole in the white McLaren with a luminous red stripe.

The single green light starts the race.

Three seconds into the race: Prost has a chance of the championship because he's ahead instantly! Senna has left behind two thick tyre lines of rubber from pole position; he's behind but not by much.

Six seconds into the race: Prost is upshifting, heading to turn 1, but he's not looking out of the front of his car. He's looking at his right mirror at Senna. Senna is about to commit a premeditated act so aggressive it was without precedent in the previous 40 years of the championship or the 34 years that followed it: 'I said to myself, OK, you try to work cleanly, and you get f****d by certain people. All right, if tomorrow Prost beats me off the line, at the first corner, I will go for it and he better not turn in because he's not going to make it.'

Nine seconds into the race: Senna and Prost make contact at huge speed, both utterly committed to the first turn. Senna goes over the kerb hard into the back of the Ferrari, which loses its rear wing. In a cloud of dust, Senna is the new world champion. Commentator Murray Walker is ready for the act: 'It's happened immediately!' he exclaims on the BBC.

Prost is out of the car and pacing. He doesn't confront Senna; he seems staggered. Eerily, both walk back to the pits alongside the white Armco barrier, separated by about 10 paces as the race continues. By the time the enormity hits, Prost is furious. More than that, he is revolted. 'The World Championship is for sport, not war,' he thundered later. Formula One had entered new territory at turn 1 in the Japanese Grand Prix of 1990. 'What he did today was absolutely disgusting ... he tries to represent himself to the world as a man he is not. He has no value,' he told a press conference.

The race continued, but the sheer violence of the accident to decide the title had stunned observers. Senna's expression betrayed his unease at the brutal tactics he'd unleashed. Senna had been pushed to use his car as a weapon at 130 mph; shockingly, the stewards could find no rule Senna had broken.

Senna never relented from the two trips to Japan that defined his career. After Balestre was replaced by Max Mosley as FIA president, Senna was finally free to tell the truth, telling a pre-race press conference a year later: 'Why do people say I caused the accident in 1990? Because if you get [expletive] every single time ... what should you do? Stand behind, stay behind and say, "Thank you. Yes, thank you"? No. You should fight for what you think is right.'

When the madness of the day had subsided and the McLaren team decamped to the notorious log cabin bar near their hotels, they watched as Ayrton Senna ordered a whisky, raised his glass and said 'Prost'.

Formula One would go 31 years before it saw anything close to this intensity again.

Jean Alesi's Sliding Door

At the season opening Grand Prix of 1990, Jean Alesi was starting his ninth Grand Prix and first full season, and incredibly he was leading the race.

The French Sicilian was in thrilling combat against the legendary Ayrton Senna on the streets of Phoenix, Arizona. Lap after lap, Alesi darted left and right, positioning his car superbly to defend and repass Senna's superior McLaren for the lead.

While Senna eventually prevailed and took the win, Alesi had not only taken an unfancied Tyrrell to the front, but by cleanly scrapping with Senna on the way to second place he'd shown he had front-runner class. His exploits had put him on every leading team's radar.

Alesi's ascent had been rapid. Just 10 years previously, Giovanni Alesi had never sat in a go-kart. He changed his name to Jean after mockery at school and during those early days he dreamt of being a rally champion after his father had competed at local level. Perhaps this was the root of his dramatic and aggressive style behind the wheel that earned him legions of supporters.

A second-tier champion who made his Formula One debut mid-season in 1989, Alesi's strong fourth place on debut put him on the radar of many teams for a full-time drive even before Phoenix. Alesi was twenty-six, with half a season of Formula One and a strong campaign to win the F3000 title in 1989 (the Formula Two of its day) under his belt, but his success came with a paddock reputation for being extremely volatile and combustible.

Frank Williams laughed in the face of moody drivers – were

there any other sort if they hadn't won? The British team, at the time Constructors' champions of the world on four occasions, were beginning to look competitive again after a few years slipping backward in the pack. They were so impressed they offered Alesi not only a lucrative race deal but a contract that would give him clear number-one status at the team. It was a huge moment for a driver who just a few years previously had not been a sure bet to reach F1.

The French Grand Prix arrived and Jean waited for the announcement to be made. In just his second full season, he would lead the Williams Formula One team in 1991! But the news didn't arrive; the weekend came and went. Alesi, who was new to the sometimes-bizarre tactics the F1 paddock could employ, was completely perplexed. He implored Williams to go public with the news, allowing him to focus on matters on track.

Two weeks later, at Silverstone, there was a bombshell. Nigel Mansell, who was racing for Ferrari, announced to the world he was 'retiring' from Formula One. Despite the theatrics and protests to the contrary, Mansell was in fact now back on the driver market and available for hire. Alesi's nerves now skyrocketed. Mansell clearly coveted the Williams seat too and Alesi was stuck, committed under legal contract to Williams who refused to tell the wider world they'd signed him. The delay was caused by Frank Williams trying to persuade Ayrton Senna to leave McLaren – the veteran team principal revealed his position by asking Alesi to drop the number-one clause from his agreement. Worse still, the Tyrrell car's competitiveness had badly slipped and after a fine second place in the fourth Grand Prix of the season in Monaco, Alesi would fail to score a point for the rest of the season.

Despite waiting a full month, Williams held firm and failed to announce their new driver. By August, Alesi had run out of patience. In a stunning turn of events, he signed with Ferrari for 1991. Few careers have swung on a team switch like this one. Earlier that year, Williams had secured the services of Adrian

Newey, whose industry-leading designs would take four separate drivers to the title in the next seven seasons (*see* Chapter 31). This included Nigel Mansell who reversed his retirement and rejoined his old team to the surprise of few in the paddock who had been disbelieving of his willingness to quit without a title in the first place.

Frank Williams pointed out that Jean was under contract and the agreement included a clause clearly stating he did not need to announce anything to anyone until September. Compensation would be paid to Frank in the form of a Ferrari F40 road car and a lump sum. For Alesi, the move would prove devastating to his standing in the sport. He had turned down driving for a team that would contend for the drivers' title for the next seven straight years. Instead, he signed for Ferrari at their lowest ebb. Mansell would push Senna all the way to the penultimate race of the 1991 season racing a Williams; Ferrari, meanwhile, dissolved into shambles.

How dysfunctional did it get at Ferrari in 1991? Alain Prost, who by this time had won three Drivers' World Championships, was fired from the team with just one race remaining, after calling the car 'a truck'. Ferrari finally moved back into contention in 1994, after electronic driver aids were banned, and on multiple occasions Alesi finally looked set to win before heartbreak would strike. He would retire from the lead on multiple occasions, including at Monza where, after mechanical failure had struck, he drove home in his F40 road car at blinding speed, utterly furious at the lost chance.

Behind the wheel, he was daring, flamboyant and exciting. The tifosi adored the aggressive all-action style, admiring his 'heart on sleeve' demeanour and punchy driving.

In 1995, Jean finally took his only Grand Prix victory of his career on his thirty-first birthday in Canada. He led 19 races and finished second 16 times but Jean's decision in 1990 unwittingly opened the door for four drivers: Nigel Mansell and Damon Hill claimed historic title wins, Prost's sealed fourth championship, along with Jacques Villeneuve's stunning last race battle with Michael Schumacher in 1997. Arguably, Jean could have been a Williams driver for this whole period.

The move to Ferrari also denied viewers a repeat of the duelling in Phoenix. Many believed the 24 laps that he'd spent in the lead with audacious pass and repass lunges were a trailer for the full cinematic feature of the 1991 title battle. Even Senna seemed hugely excited about the prospect. 'It was a very exciting battle, and he drove really well; very clean and precise, the sort of motor racing I like.' But it was not to be.

A tale of 'what might have been' haunts multiple drivers – so many have inadvertently made the wrong team move at a crucial time. It speaks to an uncomfortable truth of motor racing – that the difference between a trip to the top step or being a title contender really could be as simple as luck and timing.

Bertrand Gachot Is Late for Dinner

Negotiating with Eddie Jordan was always a battle.

When 1996 world champion Damon Hill considered signing with Jordan's team in the late 1990s, he was greeted with the gentle persuading words: 'You will not f*** me, no one f***s me.' Hill recalled in his autobiography: 'He was doing the perfect impression of the Tasmanian devil cartoon character, he was insane. He was running backward and forward, shouting at people, right at the top of his lungs.' 'He' was Edmund Patrick Jordan: the ebullient leader and team principal of his self-owned Formula One team.

In 1991, 10 years after accepting he would not make it as a driver, 'Eddie Jordan Racing' burst into life in Formula One with an unmissable green livery and a genuinely fast design. Their employee headcount was just 18 and the small team created a welcoming atmosphere. In comparison, Mercedes employed over 1,200 people across three sites in 2025. The team won friends quickly and Eddie instantly became a paddock personality.

Mere months later, things had completely unravelled. The money had run out, there was a 'winding up' order working its way through in the British High Court and then, one of their drivers, Bertrand Gachot, had a prang. Heading to a restaurant in London's Soho district, Gachot had been hit by a taxi driver and entered into a furious argument.

It became physical, fast. In a rage, Gachot reached for the pepper spray from his girlfriend's purse and proceeded to use it on the cab driver's face! 'In France, tear gas is considered as the perfect means of defence,' he protested years later. Gachot fled the scene but was later arrested for Actual Bodily Harm. 'Calm down, we all do this in France' did not hold up in court. Against pre-hearing expectations, he received a custodial sentence. Gachot was sent to jail for 18 months, and Jordan was left without a driver for that weekend's Grand Prix in Belgium.

Requiring a swift replacement, Eddie immediately knew just the man for the job – his close friend and popular Swede, Stefan Johansson. Johansson was former teammate from Eddie's driving days who had progressed through the ranks to drive for McLaren and Ferrari in Formula One. How could you not be romantic about motor racing!? Here were two old friends taking on the establishment – a band of brothers taking on the world together.

But hold on ... what was that? Someone's on the phone offering more cash? Eddie told Stefan he'd call him back.

Mercedes at this time did not race in F1 but they did have a young driver programme. Their new marketing idea was to start moving their talent from sportscars to F1. The first driver they wanted promoted was Michael Schumacher. He came not only with instant Deutschmarks but with the promise of more money in the future. Jordan said yes.

In a pre-internet era, Jordan was uncertain of the new driver he had signed. In fact, he was completely unaware he was being hoodwinked when Schumacher – all unkempt hair and pointy chin – embellished his driving experience around the fearsome Spa-Francorchamps circuit by 100 per cent; Schumacher had never driven a lap there. While in the modern age, talented junior drivers are well known from go-karting onwards, in the early 1990s it was not obvious who would graduate to the elite level, as everyone who had an opinion usually had a financial interest attached to it.

On the Friday of the Belgian Grand Prix weekend, with a seemingly straight face, Jordan told the cameras that his team had 'always believed in youth' and 'Schumacher was the obvious choice.' If Schumacher was expecting glamour to accompany him with his F1 call-up, he was to be disappointed. In September 1991, the man from Kerpen journeyed the short distance across the German border to the Ardennes Forest of Belgium to find he was sharing a bathroom with 10 other Jordan team members.

It did not affect him. He arrived at one of the great tests of driving skill on earth and qualified seventh out of 26 at the first attempt. This performance was only possible with pure driving talent. On race day the fairytale concluded prematurely due to Jordan's penny-pinching tactics of running reconditioned clutches the other teams had binned. The sleek green machine managed no more than a few metres before grinding to a halt … but Schumacher had shown enough in qualifying.

Now the real race began … off track.

The Battle for Schumacher's First Full-Time F1 Contract

The real race began at the Belgian Grand Prix weekend of 1991.

After his strong qualifying, Michael Schumacher's contract was now the prized possession that every team owner coveted in Formula One, even if he had to retire from the race on the first lap with a failed clutch.

For Eddie Jordan of Team Jordan, this would be a defining test. A man smeared by detractors as a fanciful loudmouth at the team launch 10 months previously now had a path to a future champion. That would mean significant sponsorship, especially from Germany. Household-name manufacturers would be interested in giving the team competitive engines exclusively. Suddenly, the same hustle and ingenuity could be applied to blue-chip brands. Schumacher was a ticket to survival, but bigger than that he could solidify Jordan in the big leagues as a well-funded F1 team. Jordan knew Schumacher wouldn't be with his team for long but he could score podiums and, with a long-term contract, the big marques would have to pay handsomely for his services in the future.

This idea had also occurred to the opposition. Flavio Briatore was the boss at the Benetton fashion family's race-winning F1 team; a position he effectively still holds with the Enstone based team in 2025! Enigmatic to some, troublesome to others, Briatore had confounded motorsport insiders by successfully moving from fashion marketing to becoming a motorsport administrator. Flavio had a helpful ally in F1 boss Bernie Ecclestone who also wanted Schumacher in a Benetton for the next race; as the sports ringleader, he would often have the final say on key personnel moves. Mercedes wanted Schumacher with the Italian team because they believed Jordan wouldn't exist within days.

Owing millions and facing collapse, the Jordan cabal attempted to reassure the Schumacher camp verbally; they failed. Jordan was now out of diplomatic options; but this was so big, it had to be fought for. Jordan filed an injunction against Benetton in the UK high court. Within minutes he was summoned to a terracotta-roofed villa hotel on Lake Como for a ferocious wine-fuelled argument attended by lawyers.

As the tourist boats and superyachts bobbed along peacefully, ever more lawyers poured into the villa: side tables became desks and brick-sized mobiles were shouted into. Eddie Jordan had limited cards left to play. The writing in the original contract was vague and someone had leaked to Briatore that Ford engines were now prepared to pull the plug on Jordan. The team had no money and no worthwhile engine.

But then came a dramatic change in luck – Benetton's then current number-two driver Roberto Moreno mysteriously discovered he was being sacked to make way for Schumacher. The Brazilian promptly took out his own shiny injunction, which succeeded. Benetton now had no free seats; it would come down to persuasion and cash. At 3 a.m. on Thursday with the first running of the Italian Grand Prix weekend just a day away, Roberto Moreno surrendered his contract and accepted a sizeable fee to exit his contract seven races early. Defeated, Eddie consoled himself by charging Roberto Monero to be his driver for the next race.

Michael Schumacher would win two World Championships with the Benetton team – they never won a title before or after in their 15-year history.

The German's career would rewrite the history books and yield 91 wins, 155 podiums and eventually seven World Championships – five won with Ferrari in one the greatest combinations of car and driver ever witnessed in Formula One. Schumacher's name will be spoken long into the future, but he drove just once for Eddie Jordan in Formula One. The victors departed by helicopter, and in a stark visual metaphor of defeat, Jordan left in a dented Ford hire car. It would take him hours to find the team chalet even though it was located just a few miles away.

As the Jordan team staggered through the gates of the Monza paddock on Thursday, the boss of McLaren, Ron Dennis, greeted them with a quip that has passed into Formula One folklore. As the Irishman approached him, he said, 'Welcome to the Piranha club.'

Senna's Lap of the Gods

The cliche goes that you can't win the race on the first lap, but you can lose it ... there are always exceptions to the rule.

In 1993, Donington Park would host a Grand Prix that laughed in the face of all that. Circuit owner Tom Wheatcroft had wanted a race for his Donington Park Circuit in the East Midlands for years. The facilities weren't cutting edge but the circuit had a great flow, the Great British public adored motor racing and, amid the Mansell mania of recent times, ticket sales were assured. The problem was Ecclestone did not enjoy racing in Britain once a year let alone twice, preferring to find state-of-the-art facilities that would pay a big hosting fee.

Then for Wheatcroft a break in fortune – the Autopolis circuit in Japan went bankrupt and Bernie Ecclestone suddenly had an empty slot in the calendar to fill. The European Grand Prix had found a new home; Donington would join a select few of British racetracks that hosted a Formula One World Championship round alongside Silverstone, Aintree and Brands Hatch.

The changeable April weather in 1993 led to a wet practice on the Friday but a dry Saturday, and the two Williams of Prost and Hill locked out the front row for the Grand Prix. Michael Schumacher was third with Benetton and Ayrton Senna fourth in his underpowered McLaren. Come race day, the rich dark skies and rain had returned as the crowd braved the traffic to attend the first Grand Prix held at Donington Park since the 1930s, so wet was it that spectators were tumbling down the grassy banks that offered the best views of the sweeping Craner Curves.

It was cold, wet and dismal; even the vivid colours of the F1 grid couldn't improve the reality on the formation lap. Then the lights changed and Ayrton Senna wrote a sporting epic. What would follow was a dizzying minute of brilliance. As the cars left the line, Senna's red-and-white McLaren crawled away, dropping to fifth. He lost more ground as he was squeezed into the pit exit; instantly the Brazilian switched to the very inside of the first turn. His traction was superior and he out-dragged Schumacher's yellow Benetton when applying the power on the exit.

The descent into the sweeping Craner Curves began with the majority of the spectators massed on a steep hill alongside. Senna showed all of his feel by pulling to a soaking part of the circuit, and despite the greater volume of water to clear, he slid past Karl Wendlinger by the time he got to the old hairpin right hander. Things were beginning to look preposterous from the onboard camera as Senna tore towards second-placed Hill. Senna, now on another racetrack to the rest of them by virtue of his racing line, slid to the inside and took second. Everyone else was thinking and fighting; Senna was gliding and scything across the track, almost unnaturally one with the car. Ten seconds later, he was in the lead, darting late on the brakes to the inside of old rival Prost at the hairpin.

Fifth to first without contest – the rest of the field had nothing in response. This was Formula One at its best, the world had watched the greatest driver alive unfold his talent in the conditions where you could see the difference.

Senna remarked that it was 'one of these days where everything came together'. He wasn't wrong. Senna had set the fastest lap by coming into the pits due to a quirk in the pit lane entry cutting the final corner. The winner's trophy was a giant bronze Sonic the Hedgehog; thanks to title sponsor Sega everything seemed to be slightly different, the venue, the gulf in driving. But even in this story, Prost had a part to play; he'd missed his breaking point at the chicane, allowing Senna to move to first in one lap. While Senna would have undoubtedly taken the lead on lap 2, it just wouldn't have the same impact. Prost hadn't seen Senna after lap 1 and hadn't had much fun on his run to second place. The Frenchman made seven pit stops. After an issue with slick tyre pressures, Prost thought he had a puncture and pitted unnecessarily, when actually on the track he had constant gearbox issues.

Senna was running low on sympathy and proceeded to rub Prost's nose in it in the press conference, asking the Frenchman if he would like to swap cars for the rest of the season. Prost had pointed out the McLaren was a very advanced car electronically. Senna had been enraged by Prost's veto of him in the second Williams – it was clear to all in 1992 that whoever had access to the Williams in 1993 would win the World Championship.

So, Senna knew that standout victories would be the best he'd achieve in 1993. McLaren didn't have the best engine, and not only that, they didn't even have the best version of their engine. Ford had agreed its works deals with the Benetton team, leaving Senna with an old spec to power his car. Senna had publicly railed against Ford, telling them Benetton could only win when Williams and McLaren broke down, but it was all to no avail. It all made for a furious champion, outmanoeuvred politically and suffering on the circuit. The Brazilian felt he was wasting his time – so much so, he'd only signed a race-by-race deal. If his million-dollar salary didn't hit his bank account by Wednesday, his manager Julian Jacobi would telephone his client and Senna wouldn't get on the plane.

Sponsor and paymaster Marlboro thought it was probably all a bluff but didn't want to take the risk, so agreed to the weekly arrangement as McLaren set about matching Williams' technological innovation, which was able to circumnavigate Senna's brilliance.

But the reality was Senna won with thrilling ease when others had floundered and the lap legend would only grow.

When Senna died 13 months later, the finite nature of his achievements meant the sense of greatness only swelled for every single milestone. It had been Donnington's first Grand Prix since the pre-war titans of Caracciola and Nuvolari had competed. In the pouring rain, Senna had gifted those who witnessed his opening lap a memory that belonged alongside the names heard long ago.

The Death of Ayrton Senna

1 May 1994 remains the most impactful day in Formula One history, marking the end of an era.

The tragic death of Ayrton Senna was the concluding horror on a fraught weekend with multiple accidents. The world could not look away as one of the greatest drivers of all time lost his life at the Tamburello turn, live on television.

Brazilian Senna was a driver whose name continues to transcend Formula One. He was composed of many elements: God-given speed, intensity, competitiveness and an uncompromising need to win. He showed no fear behind the wheel. Off-track, he was known for his support of his fellow countrymen and social responsibility. His formidable natural talent places him among the all-time greats of Formula One. He advanced his teams with uncompromising determination to win and yet was respected by team principals, engineers and mechanics alike.

Senna, or 'Beco' as his family called him, started driving karts at four years old, going on to become a professional kart racer at 13 and winning the South American Kart Championship in 1977. Moving to Europe, Senna started his junior Formulae career with the Van Diemen team in slim single seaters of Formula Ford at Brands Hatch. He went on to win that championship in 1981, and the next rung up Formula Ford Championship in 1982 for Rushen Green Racing. The following year, he was pitted against future Formula One driver and commentary legend Martin Brundle. In a still-talked-about battle, Senna won the 1983 British Formula

Three Championship in a RALT car racing for the West Surrey Racing team.

His dominance in the junior series saw his promotion to Formula One in 1984 with the Toleman-Hart team, where he debuted at his home Grand Prix in Brazil. Early promise was shown at a rain-impacted Monaco Grand Prix that year, where he finished second to his future teammate and rival Alain Prost, after the race was controversially halted with the Brazilian honing in on the lead at an electric pace. Before the end of 1984, he had committed to switch to Lotus, and by 1985 had won his first Grand Prix in Portugal in similar torrential conditions. But Senna dreamt of the title and joined McLaren in 1988, racing alongside the methodical and brilliant Alain Prost.

At McLaren, Senna won his three World Championship titles, scoring seven victories to win the World Championship in his opening year. Likely the greatest driver pairing of all time, the championship swung between Senna and Prost (*see* Chapters 34 and 35), and the famous rivalry was cemented. After winning two more World Championships in 1990 and 1991, Senna was still on the hunt for the fastest car, which was now a Williams. Prost got the seat first, reportedly blocking the move while he was at the team, but after the Frenchman retired in November 1993 Senna got his wish and joined the British team for the start of 1994.

The San Marino Grand Prix weekend in May 1994 started ominously; electronic aids had been banned after the 1993 season, and the result made the cars incredibly difficult to drive safely at high speed – they were light, fast and incredibly skittish. Senna's fellow Brazilian and mentee Rubens Barrichello suffered a horrific crash in his Jordan in Friday's qualifying practice session. He lost control at the Variante Bassa, hit the kerb and was launched high into the air before landing on top of the tyre barrier. The car rolled several times and laid to rest upside down. It was a close call, as Sid Watkins (*see* Chapter 26) saved Barrichello's life by unblocking his airways. Despite being clinically dead for six minutes, Barrichello survived with broken bones and returned to watch the rest of the weekend's race. This was only the start.

On Saturday, the brutality intensified. During qualifying, Austrian rookie Roland Ratzenberger, in a Simtek, crashed into a concrete wall at the Villeneuve Curve while travelling at close to 200 mph. His car had suffered damage to the front wing in an earlier lap; as he tried to turn into the corner, it broke and lodged under the car. Sid Watkins was at the scene of the crash in 12 seconds, but Ratzenberger had suffered blunt force trauma leading to a fractured skull and a ruptured aorta. Watkins attempted to resuscitate Roland but he was pronounced dead on arrival at the Maggiore hospital after being airlifted there. It was only Ratzenberger's third race weekend. It was inescapably cruel, and Formula One's first fatality at a Grand Prix weekend since 1982.

As he had done with Barrichello, Senna appeared at the door of Watkins medical centre to check in on Ratzenberger. In an awful foreshadowing of what was to come, Senna cried on Watkins' shoulder when he found out what had happened. This led to a charged conversation between Watkins and Senna, where Watkins tried to convince the driver he had nothing left to prove. 'What else do you need to do?' the doctor asked. He pointed out Senna had already won the championship three times and told the driver, 'Give it up and let's go fishing.'

Ayrton's retort was: 'Sid, there are certain things over which we have no control.' Watkins, the older of the pair, was a talented neurosurgeon and had a close and paternalistic relationship with Senna. The driver had stayed with the Watkins family in Scotland and knew them well; in return, they had gone fishing together in Brazil the year before, while Watkins was a guest at Senna's family's farm. Senna's final words to him on Saturday were: 'I cannot quit, I have to go on.'

Despite the events of the Friday and Saturday, F1's attitude of 'the race goes on, no matter what' continued, and the cars lined up on the track with Senna on pole and Schumacher next to him.

Senna got a fast start, but the tension in the air was unnerving; JJ Lehto stalled his Benetton and was hit with ferocity by Pedro Lamy in his Lotus. Both drivers were OK – as were the spectators and a policeman who suffered minor injuries from debris – but the safety car was sent out to allow the track to be cleared. Senna was still leading the race in his Williams; by lap 5 the field was cleared, and racing resumed on lap 6.

On the start of lap 7, Senna went through the left-hand Tamburello corner, leaving the road at 190 mph, and crashed into the wall. While the car stayed relatively intact, Senna's helmet was pierced by a piece of suspension that had been pinned against the wall and sent back into the driver's path in a matter of milliseconds.

Watkins rushed to the scene of the crash. Once there, he looked into his friend's eyes and saw inescapable signs that Senna had sustained a massive brain injury and would not survive. His friend was gone. Movingly, Watkins wrote in his book *Life at the Limit*: 'He looked serene ... We lifted him from the cockpit and laid him on the ground. As we did, he sighed and though I am totally agnostic, I felt his soul depart at that moment.'

The Brazilian national hero and 41-time Grand Prix winner had sustained a fatal injury, broadcast live on television to millions across the world. He was gone, and the future of Formula One instantly hung in the balance.

Never had a star of Formula One been lost like this. FIA president Max Mosley even went as far as to predict to F1 chairman Bernie Ecclestone that this could be the end of the sport, so shocking was the event. Their worst-case scenario was a spiral of decline leading to the car manufacturers pulling out. And yet, as they considered this, the motor race was restarted 40 minutes later, with Michael Schumacher going on to win. The drivers expressed their fury at having to race past Senna's blood on the track for 55 laps.

In the aftermath, the ongoing campaign to improve safety would transform motor racing. The FIA under Max Mosley formed an advisory safety committee to investigate what actions needed to be taken after that horrific weekend. Sid Watkins (*see* Chapter 26) was made chairman – a perfect choice to cut through the political landscape of Formula One racing at the time. He was well qualified to use his scientific training and medical rigour to drive further safety changes throughout the sport. Everything from car design, circuit configuration, crash barrier construction, track run-offs, team protection in the pitlane, and spectator safety were up for debate and consideration.

The championship would have to change or collapse. A number of changes were made to the sport on the guidance of the review. New helmet designs were introduced and more tightly enforced, including the Head And Neck Support system, specifically designed to counter the injury that had killed Ratzenberger. In the short term, the cars were instantly changed mid-season to be made slower while impact testing could be carried out with the aim to develop safer regulations – this was achieved by shortening the rear diffuser and reducing the wing endplates. The engines were depowered, and a plank was fitted to raise the car up. The plank is still used to this day.

Circuit design was also drastically improved. Tyre barriers were made mandatory and secured with conveyor belts, run-offs were made mandatory and chicanes were added where needed to slow drivers down. At Imola, both the Tamburello and Villeneuve corners were significantly remodelled into chicanes with gravel traps. Pit lane speeds were also reduced. And the drivers, led by Niki Lauda, re-established the GPDA at the 1994 Grand Prix to strengthen their bargaining power with the FIA and Formula One and demand safety improvements.

The modern-day giants of Formula One, including Lewis Hamilton and Fernando Alonso, venerate Senna. Even the tough, and highly competitive Schumacher dissolved into tears in Monza 2000 at the post-race press conference when told his win tally was now equal to Senna's.

The work Senna started to support underprivileged children

in Brazil was continued by his sister, Viviane, via the Instituto Ayrton Senna. His life reached a new generation in 2010 with the acclaimed documentary, *Senna*.

On my first visit to Imola, I walked along the track to visit the corners described in this chapter, from Tosa and its Austrian flags, past the Ferrari-installed tribute to Gilles Villeneuve, on to the statue of Ayrton Senna and finally to the site of the crash at Tamburello. The response to the events of 1994 created the modern foundation for what we watch on Sunday afternoons; no audience could accept the loss of their heroes unless every possible precaution had been taken. Without the sizeable and continuing reform triggered by 1 May 1994, motorsport would not be able to run as a mainstream sport and many more names would have been lost. It was the end of an icon's life and the beginning of modern Formula One.

Schumacher's Dark Arts

Michael Schumacher has a claim to be the greatest driver in motor racing history.

When he called time on his career the first time in 2006, he had rewritten the record books: 91 F1 Grand Prix wins, 154 F1 Grand Prix podiums, 68 F1 Grand Prix pole positions, 77 F1 Grand Prix fastest laps and seven F1 Drivers' World Championships. All categories he led when he eventually left Ferrari in 2006. But beyond the awesome work rate and astounding drive, Schumacher possessed an edge; a trait which would create some of the most spellbinding moments in Formula One history.

In 1994, Formula One had experienced 10 seasons in a single year: there were new regulations, accusations about cheating, the first fatalities on a Grand Prix weekend for 12 years, the death of an icon live on TV, black flags, race bans and now a title decider. Michael Schumacher of Benetton led Williams' Damon Hill 92 points to 91. The championship arrived in Adelaide at fever pitch. The backdrop of the race was surprising for a number of reasons. Damon Hill had caused a stir in the week running up to the race by publicly airing grievances against his team. In the era of the red top circulation wars, this went straight onto the sporting back page of every newspaper.

But Hill had reason to be punchy – the Williams test driver of 1992, race winner of 1993 and championship contender of 1994 had just produced the greatest drive of his career. For many, Hill never surpassed what he achieved in Suzuka 1994, beating Michael Schumacher in the wet was an act of pure brilliance. Hill had extracted everything from the car under the most intense pressure, and the result had changed things dramatically in the points battle. Instead of an outsider's chance with the margin between them at nine points, he'd closed the gap to one, and set up a winner-take-all shootout on the streets of South Australia.

Hill had grown in confidence after unexpectedly becoming team leader after Senna's tragic death in Imola. He wrote in his autobiography: 'I felt like I was carrying the main load but still being paid a number two retainer.' Clearly, the stress was beginning to tell in the battle for the crown. At Benetton, Schumacher was dealing with his own strange situation. He was on the brink of losing a title the racing world had already crowned him with months beforehand.

While Schumacher had built a sizeable early lead in the championship, the moment that changed everything came when Schumacher overtook Hill on the formation lap at the British Grand Prix, halfway through the season. This was a pretty odd unforced error, it was against the rules and had been for a while. Mid-race Schumacher was given a stop-go penalty, which at the instruction of the team, he ignored. This led to the dreaded black flag, which meant instant disqualification, but again he ignored race control, continuing on regardless to finish second after the team said on the radio they would appeal the penalty. Schumacher was banned for two races and then risked this ban being extended by appealing it. At the appeal, the ban was upheld. In Monza and Estoril, Hill would race with his main rival on the sidelines. Hill responded brilliantly, converting his open goal opportunities and winning both races to cut his lead by 20 points (with 10 awarded for a win in 1994).

At the start of the Australian Grand Prix, Schumacher surged to the lead with Hill moving up to second, after Bernie Ecclestone had told 1992 champion and pole sitter Nigel Mansell to stay out of the way at the start. What followed was a classic title-deciding pressure-cooker race. As the leading pair sprinted away from the rest of the field, they surged clear of the pack, daring each other to the edge with the biggest moment of their lives ahead.

Schumacher left in the lead with his thoughts. After 10 laps … 20 … finally, he built a cushion of a couple of seconds, but Damon was driving out of his skin – they were both on the very edge. Until Schumacher cracked. Lap 36, suddenly a snap! Schumacher caught it, corrected, but he was slewing wide to the wall. He'd hit it badly! The rear wheel was bent, the suspension broken. He was going to lose the World Championship to a driver who hadn't even go-karted!

Michael faced a choice at this moment: win or lose. There was no time to process, no time for reasoning or considering the repercussions, what came next was pure instinct. Hill had been two seconds back. He'd not seen the light-blue and green car hit the wall. The architecture of the circuit prevented him from seeing the Benetton's rear right wheel at an angle, until he'd rounded the corner. All Hill saw was his chance – his rival was slow and while the Eastern Terrace corner wasn't a traditional passing place, he saw a gap. This was it.

Schumacher made his choice with a broken car and he shut the door. Waiting, then turning in, he made sizeable contact with Hill's Williams, considering the relative speed. Schumacher's car was tipped into the air, and he made contact with the barrier for the second time in two corners.

Schumacher was out.

'Damon Hill will be world champion if he can keep going, but can he keep going?!' asked Murray Walker from the BBC commentary box. But the kink in the front suspension was visible. The car couldn't continue. Schumacher had won by a point. He looked decidedly sheepish watching the big screen by the catch fencing but he had achieved his dream. By the side of the circuit, he celebrated in front of the grandstand. For the third time in six years, the championship had been decided by a collision.

Williams declined to lodge a protest, the team had multiple

active legal proceedings against them due to Senna's death. They all needed to go home. Hill took the defeat gallantly, although from this point onwards he would always race Schumacher like he could still see the gap on the Eastern Terrace. Many judged what Schumacher had done as betraying his staggering talent.

Earlier that year, Schumacher had finished second in the Spanish Grand Prix despite being stuck in fifth gear, displaying an astounding ability to calibrate around a problem. Then two years later at the same venue he took the rough, clunky, cumbersome Ferrari F310 to a victory of astonishing dominance. Hauling a car that had qualified 0.9 seconds slower in the dry and outpacing everyone in the race. At one point he was three seconds faster than anyone else in the field. The sort of sentence you read about drivers at the Nürburgring in the 1960s, not a three-mile circuit built in the 1990s – nothing short of driving genius. Did this driver need to resort to collision?

Schumacher strolled to a second title in 1995 with Benetton before his big-money move to Ferrari, the aforementioned car was slow and expectations were low heading into 1997. Williams were expected to easily win the title, so Ferrari shifted their attention to the new regulations in 1998. But halfway through the year they had to switch back as Schumacher had dragged the car into contention. The combination of the best driver not having the best car made these seasons of Formula One so compelling, and 1997 would again see Schumacher lead a title rival by a point heading into a winner-take-all decider.

The score of the championship table read Michael Schumacher 78, Jacques Villeneuve 77 at the 16th round of 17 races. Jacques Villeneuve, the son of Gilles Villeneuve (*see* Chapter 29), had been poached from IndyCar by the leading Williams team. Jacques had promptly arrived at the championship and taken pole position on debut before finishing second to Damon Hill in the World Championship. With Hill sacked and his replacement Heinz-Harald Frentzen not clicking with the direct or downright brusque way the team was run, Villeneuve was team leader in just his second season. The team privately fumed they should have easily strolled to the title but Villeneuve would point to the loss of Adrian Newey (*see* Chapter 56). The guru's exit had left a design office uncertain of the development direction.

A huge European audience tuned in to watch the decider. Schumacher took the lead, Villeneuve eventually taking second place from Frentzen who had tried to slow at turn 1, confusing Villeneuve who was being cautious. This gave Schumacher a huge early gap, and Frentzen then jumped out of the way on lap 7. Just like at Adelaide in 1994, the top two eased their way from the pack despite the near comical efforts of Ferrari-powered backmarkers trying to hold the Williams up. On lap 22, Schumacher made his first pit stop, with Villeneuve marking him off one lap later.

Frentzen stayed out and slowed the pack by two seconds a lap, allowing Villeneuve to catch his title rival. This was made possible by a Jerez circuit, which provided incredible motorbike races but by 1997 was incredibly tight and small for a modern F1 car. There was no clear safe overtaking opportunity around the circuit, but by lap 26 Villeneuve had a favourite corner in his mind – the hairpin at turn 6 shaping for a move late on the brakes. The dummy run would prove crucial in what was to follow.

After Schumacher had built a cushion before the final stops, Villeneuve pitted and chose his moment to unleash the full pace of the Williams. Lapping consistently faster, he knew lap 48 was the moment; lunging from way further back than normal, he sought to catch Schumacher off guard. Schumacher had been checking the mirror; he squeezed his rival, then in a crucial second movement of the steering wheel he attempted to cause contact on the apex again.

Martin Brundle in the ITV commentary box instantly diagnosed what had happened: 'You hit the wrong part of him, my friend. I don't think that will cause Villeneuve a problem.'

Villeneuve's Williams crawled away from the dry sack corner

on his way to a maiden World Championship in just his second season. Schumacher's Ferrari sat a metre off the racetrack, limply beached in the gravel; the contact hadn't worked, but it came mighty close. The collision had broken the Williams car's battery mounts and the battery was hanging by a wire while circulating at 180 mph.

Out of the race, and beaten in the championship, Schumacher stood on the wall at turn 6 watching with the world as Villeneuve cruised around, only needing two points to take the title. After a while, Schumacher conceded defeat, returning to the pits completely furious with Villeneuve's tactics. The two-time champion was then shown the onboard of what he'd done and there could be no hiding. It was a professional foul from behind the wheel. On the telecast, Ferrari team principal Jean Todt looks at his driver with the broken heart of a parent who has watched their child commit a crime. By the time his driver returned to the pit wall he is almost in tears greeting him.

At an FIA hearing in Paris, Michael Schumacher was disqualified from the 1997 F1 World Drivers' Championship standings, though he kept his wins and his podiums for the record books. It was clear the verdict encapsulated what he'd done in 1994; the second offence was inescapable. A man who had advanced what it meant to be a frontline driver still embodied human fallacies and inadequacies under pressure. In truth, it was emblematic of what makes motor racing so wonderful. Flesh and blood in the middle of the machine. He could drive absolutely anything to the limit, but at that limit the examination of how far he was prepared to go had stunned the sporting world.

I once spoke to a highly successful driver about rough tactics in key moments. He said in the crucial seconds you 'choose what sort of driver you want to be'. But Schumacher never appeared to choose; it was like it had all been predestined. The drivers who shared stewards' rooms with him at the peak of his powers say he possessed a blinkered certainty in himself and his actions that rendered debate impossible. Nine-time winner Mark Webber got closest to putting Michael on the record about the dark side of his driving. 'Sometimes you go down a certain path and you cannot go back,' Schumacher said to the Australian driver after he'd faked a mistake to prevent anyone from stealing his pole position at Monaco in 2006.

Wherever the actions came from, Schumacher played a huge part in saving F1 post-Senna. As a flawed sporting colossus, it's undeniable that he provided the championship with unforgettable moments.

Awards and Rewards – Three Defining Days in the Career of Lewis Hamilton

'What are you going to do in the next few years?' the legendary sports presenter Steve Rider quipped to the ten-year-old standing beside him.

'Just win,' came the reply from the young Lewis Hamilton.

He wasn't wrong.

The *Autosport* magazine awards in 1995 saw Hamilton receive the McLaren rising star trophy, but his on-stage patter wasn't the only notable part of the evening – earlier he'd set the foundation stone for his career. The young boy approached McLaren team boss Ron Dennis, boldly telling him he wanted to race for McLaren in the future. Just 12 years later, remarkably, it had all come true. From the same ballroom in the same hotel stood Britain's new sporting superstar, once again standing next to Steve Rider. Even Hamilton seemed bowled over at the significance; turning raconteur, he told the sea of tables: 'I went up to Ron and said I wanted to race his car and be world champion. Colin McRae was there as well, he was such a character … I was ten years old and he was trying to get me a drink!'

The gist of Dennis' courteous reply was – do some more winning and then give him a call. Hamilton kept up his end of the bargain and was signed to the junior driver programme just three years later. While all the front-running teams have clear pathways through the motor racing ladder in 2025, things were less straightforward in the 1990s. Sponsors like Marlboro had a stable of young talent, but no one had a defined academy in the modern sense. A photo taken in 1997 tells the story well; McLaren's entire stable is pictured: their F1 drivers Mika Häkkinen and David Coulthard all the way down to their two go-karters, Wesley Graves and Lewis Hamilton.

McLaren had given Hamilton a clear roadmap, and the pressure to succeed created a simmering intensity in Hamilton. He knew the chance could disappear at the end of any season and feared poor results on a daily basis, despite the junior categories being designed to allow for learning. The approach at the time being: learn the championship, then win it the following season. But the Hamilton family knew the talent they had. 'My contract was ripped up with McLaren towards the end of the year [2004], I had to find sponsorship money for the last two. I was pushing to go to GP2 earlier.'

The often omitted detail from Hamilton's Cinderella story was a huge fallout between McLaren's chief operating officer, Martin Whitmarsh, and Lewis' father and manager, Anthony Hamilton. With the new GP2 series generating huge attention and racing on the undercard of an F1 weekend, all drivers with budget wanted to be on the grid for 2005. McLaren insisted Hamilton win European Formula Three and wait. The Hamiltons approached Williams co-owner and technical guru, Patrick Head. Head later recounted: 'They rang up and said, "Can we come and see you?" And they came in and said, "Ron Dennis has dropped us." Frank Williams rang up BMW who declined [to fund the signing of Hamilton]. So much to Frank's annoyance, he could have had Lewis in a Williams.'

Having shopped around only to find no buyers, Hamilton turned in an eye-catching performance at the Bahrain Super Prix, a one-off race at the end of the season for F3 drivers. Starting 11th on the grid, he produced multiple bold overtakes to win and remind McLaren what they'd lost. The relationship was quickly repaired for 2005, where Hamilton duly fulfilled his team's wish and won the European Formula Three Championship.

A year later, Hamilton was on the back foot in the flourishing GP2 series. He recounted to F1TV years later:

> I remember that year, in my mind, if I could win this in my first year maybe they'll give me a chance to be in F1 next year. So, I put an unbelievable amount of pressure on myself.
>
> In that race [in Turkey] there were multiple obstacles. I had that spin and I remember that feeling I had, holding the clutch, making sure I didn't finish, letting go and not hitting the car that came by. Then not just giving up, and pushing like never before, and coming second. What a moment. It was one of the pivotal moments in my career. People thought, 'He's the real deal.'

The result again transcended the junior motorsport ladder; it was realistically a title-saving performance in a season where McLaren had a senior team vacancy. McLaren traditionally didn't use rookies, and hadn't since 1993. Hamilton defied convention to be promoted to Formula One, four races later, having secured the 2006 GP2 title.

So 26 years on from the awards show, 17 from the Superprix and 15 from Istanbul, Lando Norris and Lewis Hamilton were separated by just a second and the battle for the lead was on. McLaren's straight-line speed turned out to be tricky to pass for the Mercedes, with Norris just able to stay out of the DRS zone. Even when Hamilton was in range, he still couldn't quite get close enough.

As ever with Formula One, the weather gods had different plans. Hamilton resisted calls to switch to intermediate until the final three laps, again emerging behind Norris who was still on slicks. McLaren had to gamble between pitting and losing track position or staying out and risking it to the end; his hopes that the dry areas of the circuit would stop the intermediate tyres from making up time failed. Norris chose the latter strategy with an emphatic 'no!' The gap between the leading pair shrunk as Norris began to lose time all over the track. With the rain coming down harder, his slicks just weren't up to it when Norris hit a wall of spray on the exit of turn 3. In what would have been his maiden victory, at the second to last lap of the race, Norris skidded off the track.

Mercedes and Hamilton's greater experience in leading races in wet conditions showed through. Hamilton took the lead and held it to achieve his 100th Grand Prix win; the first driver to achieve this landmark in the history of motorsport: 'Obviously the team made a great call right at the end. I didn't want to let Lando go and of course I didn't know what the weather was doing but I'm incredibly grateful to all these men and women that are here and back at the factory because, wow, one hundred.'

Even with a record-breaking number of race victories, it's hard to know how the path winds if a young kid doesn't cross the floor to clear his throat and ask one of the most powerful people in the history of the sport for a seat at the table.

43

Hill Gets Fired in the Press

It was the weekend of the German Grand Prix.

The Town of Hockenheim was hosting its huge annual sporting event. The brutalist concrete grandstands of the circuit's arena section were full of red-shirted Michael Schumacher fans. He was the reigning champion, but he had no chance of retaining his crown – that was going to be taken by Britain's Damon Hill. Things should have been jovial but there was a problem in the press. *Autosport* magazine had hit newsstands with one of the most sensational headlines in publication history: 'Has Hill been dumped?'

The headline somewhat undersold Andrew Benson's scoop. The article stated the World Championship leader would be dropped by his team at the end of the season and replaced by young German driver Heinz-Harald Frentzen. The British sporting hero, household name and World Championship leader had been fired by the team he was currently winning for.

It didn't make any competitive sense. Worst still, it was all happening publicly. Career death by headline ahead of phone call from the boss. A rush of denials poured out from drivers and team; both Hill and Frentzen said it was incorrect. Team boss Frank Williams denied Frentzen had been signed but ominously refused to confirm Damon for 1997: 'I honestly can't tell you who will be driving for the team next year,' he told a press conference.

Counter-rumours began to circulate that Damon and his management team wanted a big pay rise, having been made to suffer the comparatively meagre Williams wages for all four years of their Formula One career. Williams had a long history of believing the driver to be important but replaceable. Hill was set to be the fourth driver to win the Drivers' Championship and yet not be with the team the next year. Williams' recent history stood as:

- 1987: Piquet won and then left for Lotus

- 1992: Mansell won and then left for IndyCar

- 1993: Prost won and then retired

- 1996: Hill was leading the World Championship …

Williams' trading name was Williams Grand Prix Engineering – it summed up the approach. The team believed it needed good drivers but refused to pay top-line wages when the car would dictate who would be champion. It was hard to argue with this logic, especially when the team had the services of best-in-class designer Adrian Newey.

This was where the logic began to fall apart, because Adrian was unhappy. The driver line-up was directly linked to Newey's contract – he explicitly had to be consulted on any driver changes and inexplicably team management Frank Williams and Patrick Head had repeatedly ignored this clause. Newey had not been consulted when it came to the lack of renewal for Nigel Mansell, the hiring of Jacques Villeneuve and now the probable firing of Damon Hill. Newey's last straw would be the handling of the Hill saga.

But if Newey felt he was in the dark it was nothing compared to Hill. Despite a paddock full of disbelievers in the story, Damon knew something wasn't right. Many just couldn't believe the news as Hill was in the form of his life; why would the team choose to cause such bad publicity? The answer was found in 1995.

In the previous season, Hill had struggled in the World Championship, repeatedly crashing into his title rival, Michael Schumacher, or spinning off mid-race. Schumacher had retained his title with two races to spare and Williams had lost the Constructors' Championship where the money was made. Williams were so concerned at Hill's slump they sought out Frentzen and signed a pre-contract with him. Adrian Newey directly asked Patrick Head about the rumours and was told Frentzen had been signed; in contrast, when Damon Hill asked Head, he was told they had not signed anyone.

On the German Grand Prix media day, Frank Williams called the story 'news to me'. Heinz-Harald Frentzen said he would like to drive with Williams in the future. The mood was dark within Williams' hospitality – in those days little more than an awning by the side of a truck. The journalist who'd broken the story attempted to find Damon to explain himself. He managed one step inside the door before Damon Hill bellowed: 'Get Out Andrew. You've made yourself look very stupid.'

For Hill, a siege mentality was the only option; he'd been blindsided by the headline and was upset having won six of the nine races that had been held so far in 1996. Hill was now under a cloud when he should have been enjoying a year-long victory lap. The second and final blow came the month after, in the days before the Belgian Grand Prix. On 28 August, Frank Williams told Damon they'd be moving on and he had to think of the team's future. Damon called the process 'humiliating' as his professional standing had crumbled.

The blame game again began, with the main accusation being that Damon Hill's manager was asking for too much money, with an unearned swagger in his step. Huge sums of money were quoted – sums that Frank Williams wouldn't pay. Hill's camp denied such things, saying he wanted a championship bonus and the same deal as in 1996. But as Nigel Mansell had found after winning his title, Williams would look to the future, and since

1989 people had been talking up Heinz-Harald Frentzen. The German had been part of the Mercedes sports car programme and had even talked of as quicker than Schumacher. Giant-killing performances in the new Sauber team pressed his claim and many in the paddock believed he'd been an outstanding driver of the previous season.

On the eve of the Italian Grand Prix, all the talk was of the driver market. This was meant to be a race where the focus was on whether Damon Hill could achieve motorsport history as the first son of a world champion to win the title. Instead, Frentzen was confirmed, Hill was out, and he had to face the British press for over an hour, trying to answer the question of why he was fired. The circus took its toll, and Hill would retire from the race having clipped a tyre on the apex of a chicane – his crowning moment had been postponed.

The story had been true and scooped the confirmation by months; the implications for team and driver would be enormous. Hill was forced to choose between midfielder teams like Jordan or Jackie Stewart's brand-new entry – it was a loud thud to earth. Adrian Newey argued the team was breaching his contract by not consulting him when it came to the drivers' market and used this to leave for McLaren in 1998. Williams would only fight for the title on one further occasion after they stopped using his designs. Damon Hill would eventually confound F1 and choose Arrows, a team famous for having never won a Grand Prix.

44

Hill vs the World and the Washer

After his controversial dismissal from Williams, Damon Hill knew he'd arrived in trouble town from the first moment he left the garage driving the new Arrows.

It was simply dreadful and possessed no qualities of a quick Formula One car. It had no grip at speed, its pace on the straights was dismal. Hill knew things would be tough in the midfield, but he didn't expect it to be this bad.

How bad was it? The new lead designer John Barnard, who had inherited the design, said the first priority was to make the car safe! It was about as damning an indictment as you could hear in Formula One. Slow and unsafe. Hill had entered professional hell and the whole world was watching. It appeared things could hardly get worse for Hill, who described the situation he faced as 'ignominious and humiliating', but as the first qualifying session of the season dawned there was a real possibility Hill wouldn't qualify the car.

To stop chancers trying to make a quick buck, Formula One used a rule that said the lap time of the slowest car had to be within 107 per cent of the pole sitter. This usually equated to around seven seconds behind. With eight minutes to go in the qualifying hour, reigning world champion Damon Hill wasn't in the race, the trackside footage showing a flurry of activity in the car as the Brit attempted to control the machine. He cut the beam six seconds behind the pace of Jacques Villeneuve, a driver who he had beaten to the World Championship just five months previously. He was in the race, twenty-first on the grid, with no hope of a good result. Mercifully, Hill's car broke down on the formation lap and he could make a hasty exit after a humiliating weekend.

Things would barely improve and by the halfway stage of the 17-round championship, Hill had a single point to his name after a fighting drive to sixth at his beloved Silverstone. He was already turning his attention to which team he should transfer to when he arrived in Hungary 17th in the standings, with his old rival Michael Schumacher leading the championship by 10 points – the equivalent of a single Grand Prix victory at the time. Ferrari and Formula One had expected Williams to run away with the championship, but they had lost famed designer Adrian Newey after repeatedly leaving him out of big team decisions – such as firing the world champion. Newey had moved to McLaren, and Williams were struggling to understand how to develop his design. Ferrari had sensed an opportunity and brought a new lightweight chassis in their attempt to extend their championship lead. Williams, meanwhile, blamed their drivers for making a meal out of a championship they too expected to win at a canter.

At the Hungarian Grand Prix, qualifying saw the two title protagonists, Schumacher and Villeneuve, share the front row, with Hill a shock third on the grid – his best qualifying result of the season by a whole six places. It was only his second top 10 qualifying result of the season, but he had great form at the unrelenting Hungaroring having taken his first F1 victory there in 1993 and dominating the field at the circuit in 1995.

There was plenty of focus on the tyres, which had been the case throughout the 1997 season. Goodyear had all the established front-running teams and Bridgestone, the new upstarts, had produced a tyre that in hot races gave better wear. It meant unfancied teams like the new eponymous Prost team found themselves vaulting up the order unexpectedly in Spain, finishing second with Oliver Panis.

Hill's chances of points were helped by a rule that meant the drivers had to choose between a soft or hard compound for qualifying and the race straight after FP3. The majority of front runners chose the soft compound, which on race day suffered from the troublesome trait of falling apart immediately. Two key things happened on race day: Schumacher stuffed his lightweight Ferrari into the wall in the warm-up and the weather remained sunny.

Schumacher's heavy Ferrari led away from pole as Hill leapt to second position, and then the Goodyear tyres began to fall apart. Schumacher was soon lapping three seconds a lap down from his original early pace. Spectators and TV viewers were treated to the bizarre spectacle of a train of cars unable to pass around the twisty circuit. On lap 10, Hill produced one of the greatest overtakes of his career as Murray Walker revelled in another Schumacher vs Hill battle, 'Yes, Damon Hill looked like he almost nudged the Ferrari. Move over you can feel him saying in the cockpit … AND GOING THROUGH AND DAMON HILL LEADS. OH BOY! Damon Hill goes into the lead of the Hungarian Grand Prix.'

You could hear Walker's smile, and his astonishment at what he was watching. Arrows had the record for the most races without a victory. Hill had just slapped a move on a rival at a circuit where you can barely pass.

Damon was now driving away, but there were other threats in the field. Häkkinen's and Coulthard's McLarens both looked quick but would retire; Villeneuve had more pace in the Williams but struggled to lap cars and lost five seconds with a slow pit stop. Hill was eight seconds clear of his old teammate. The real problem for Hill was the driver who'd replaced him: Heinz-Harald Frentzen.

The German was the only front runner to choose the hard tyre and aim for one stop – he led by a mammoth 19 seconds, with both him and Hill having to make one more stop. Then on lap 29, a small piece of metal could be seen flying from a Williams; it was the Williams fuel tank connector. This meant that Hill's old team could not refuel Frentzen's car, and the threat from Williams appeared to diminish. Hill in the cockpit of his unwieldy Arrows began to believe. It was only 10 races ago that he'd struggled to even qualify in the slow but dangerous car. Now he was leading the race by 30 seconds! It amounted to one of the greatest turnarounds and shocks in F1 history; it would be an iconic win, a first for Arrows, utter vindication for Damon.

But with three laps to go Hill's car began to slow; a loss of hydraulic pressure meant he lost gears and throttle and was coasting around on the tick over of the engine. Nine seconds were lost. On the penultimate lap, 19 seconds fell away, and on the final lap towards the climb of turn 4, Villeneuve got past with two wheels on the grass. Hill tried to make his car as wide as possible, but it was done. A moment of joy robbed by a 50p hydraulic 'O Ring', a washer – one of the cheapest parts on a Formula One car costing a famous win. Damon Hill would still coast home in second, having delivered a performance to silence the doubters. Arrows would never win a Grand Prix.

Schumacher Wins in the Pit Lane

In July 1998, Michael Schumacher was driving through the rain, unopposed and untroubled.

The changing of gears and sweeping of the steering wheel all in one great symphony as the German swept past the chaos littered around the rest of the Silverstone circuit. But he'd missed something in the spray, amid one of many deluges of the day. The yellow flags by the side of the circuit waving – spelling danger – a non-negotiable instruction to reduce speed and stop any opportunity to pass, which is what he had done. He'd overtaken Alex Wurz's light-blue Benetton under waved yellows. It was one of motor racing's oldest rules. It spelt a penalty for certain, didn't it?

Two hours earlier, Formula One was hitting the halfway stage of the season with a trip to the venue where it had all begun, 48 years previously. Michael Schumacher bounded into the weekend on a roll, having taken victory in the two preceding races held in Canada and France. Leading Championship contender at McLaren, Mika Häkkinen seemed unperturbed. He'd stated in the Thursday press conference that he felt no increased pressure, despite his lead being drastically reduced by spinning mid-race in France.

Adrian Newey's first McLaren design had coincided with the new rules for 1998 and the team started the season brilliantly – lapping the entire field in Melbourne to recall their glory days of a decade previously where they won every race of the season bar one. While McLaren were on pole for every race, they were facing increasing resistance from Ferrari who based their entire operation around two-time champion Michael Schumacher. McLaren insisted they were happy and there were no team orders between their drivers, Häkkinen and David Coulthard, but despite outward appearances, Mercedes-Benz was actually pushing McLaren to sign Schumacher for the 1999 season.

Schumacher rejected the offer and signed an extension, with no performance clauses allowing him to exit like his original Ferrari deal from 1996. The press release included the quote, 'Everything is going in the right direction.' McLaren vs Schumacher was solidified as the era-defining battle.

In qualifying, Häkkinen continued McLaren's superb run of taking every pole for the season to finish a whopping four-tenths up on Schumacher by the end of the session. At the start of the race, Häkkinen led the field from the line as Schumacher began to struggle in the early stages. Ferrari had gambled on a lower downforce dry-weather set-up and Coulthard was able to hunt down the German and thrillingly pass into the Abbey chicane, to the delight of the home crowd. The timing of which tyre to be on and when would be crucial. Coulthard was kept on the intermediate tyres, while a few laps later, teammate and race leader Mika Häkkinen took on the full wet-weather tyre. Schumacher too took on the fully grooved rubber, and moments later Coulthard would aquaplane off the road and into the gravel at the same Abbey corner. Coulthard stormed back to the pits, demanding an explanation as to why the tyres for one McLaren had been different to another.

With the rain hammering down, cars headed in all directions. The leaders showed strong skills behind the wheel until Häkkinen aquaplaned through the rapid right-hand Bridge corner and damaged his front wing in the process, losing four seconds in the process. With driving near impossible, the safety car was called onto the circuit, resetting the race. As the rain relented, it became clear a late restart would be possible. Häkkinen feared it was a matter of time before Schumacher would get past. Sure enough, with less than 10 laps until the flag Häkkinen went deep at Beckett's corner allowing Schumacher through to take the lead.

With a handful of laps to go, an official handed Ferrari a piece of paper saying they'd been given a penalty for overtaking under yellow flags. There was confusion whether this was a time penalty or stop-go penalty – the difference between losing 10 seconds or 25. None of this was communicated to the wider TV audience as the procedure of the penalty put on the race control screen hadn't been followed.

Ferrari and the stewards were the only ones aware of the threat – only when Schumacher started pushing the car to qualifying levels of commitment did the watching world twig something was happening behind the scenes. Schumacher had overtaken Austrian Alex Wurz in his Benetton under yellow flags, but crucially in another break of procedure, the penalty was delivered after the 25-minute time allotted by the rule book. Then 31 minutes later, future Formula One CEO Stefano Domenicali, sitting on the Ferrari pit wall, was handed the piece of paper.

On the final lap, Schumacher peeled from the racetrack to the pit lane, crossing the line to win the race before serving the 10-second stop-go penalty. This was plainly farcical as the driver had already crossed the line to conclude the race without serving his penalty. To recap, the penalty was delivered too slowly, via an incorrect method, not displayed on the race control screen, the wrong penalty was told to Ferrari, and Ferrari took the wrong penalty after the race had concluded.

Murray Walker told viewers on ITV: 'I'm pretty sure Michael Schumacher has just won the British Grand Prix, but that is very, very unofficial.' Extraordinarily, the nonsense was not yet complete as Schumacher continued to race on the circuit long after the chequered flag had been displayed. The German driver and Ferrari team said they were covering themselves off by taking the flag, but in reality one of the greatest drivers ever was hammering round covering off an inadmissible penalty for a race that had long ended. He would keep the win.

McLaren naturally appealed the result but this was dismissed by the FIA, which stated the time limit, nature of the penalty administered and actual penalty itself were out of order. The stewards were summoned but resigned before the FIA hearing. No race has ever been won in the pit lane since. The closest we've come was Max Verstappen being crowned world champion in 2022 in parc fermé.

European Grand Prix 1999 – What Happens When the Lights Don't Go Out

We all know what happens when the five red lights go out – Formula One goes racing.

So, what happens when all the lights stay on? Well ... you know that you're in for a classic.

In 1999, F1 was headed for the European Grand Prix race at the Nürburgring. Mika Häkkinen of McLaren and Ferrari's Eddie Irvine were leading the World Championship, level on 60 points. Michael Schumacher (of Ferrari) was ruled out, having broken his leg earlier in the season at the British Grand Prix. On both of their tails was the unlikely challenger Heinz-Harald Frentzen of Jordan who had just won the race at Monza, his second of the season. With three rounds to go it was still anyone's title. On the starting grid at the Nürburgring, Heinz-Harald Frentzen was sat on pole next to David Coulthard on the front row, Häkkinen's partner at McLaren. The 1999 World Championship contender, Mika Häkkinen, was in third and his closest rival, Eddie Irvine, was mired in the midfield as Ferrari seemed to lose all momentum without Schumacher.

As the race started, the five red lights illuminated on as usual and then ... stayed on. The lights had never stuck on before, not since Formula One had adopted this way of starting a race in March 1996. Despite this, confusingly, the first four cars on the grid moved. Frentzen, Coulthard, then Häkkinen, and Ralf

Schumacher of Williams, all moved before the lights went out, effectively jumping the start.

The theory behind this is that the teams had been intercepting the signal that led to the lights being extinguished. If it was the FIA proving a point, then it had been clearly made. Thankfully, you can't jump an aborted start and so the grid reset.

Damon Hill, 1996 world champion, found himself in a bizarre quandary. He had wanted to retire at the 1999 British Grand Prix (six races before), but his team principal Eddie Jordan of Jordan racing fame wanted to fire him a race earlier at the French Grand Prix. Neither man got what they wanted, and Damon found himself in the horrible situation of trying to complete a Grand Prix career without really wanting to be in the car.

At the second start, all the cars successfully left the line, only for a key moment in the 1999 Championship to transpire. The Jordan had a bizarre starting system, which required a two-press button situation: one button for low speed and one button that had to be deactivated. Damon Hill failed to press the second button and his car ground to a halt on the exit of turn 1, causing a crash as Benetton's Alexander Wurz swerved to avoid the Jordan and clipped Sauber's Pedro Diniz. Diniz was pitched through the air and ended up upside down. Scarily, the rollover hoop – meant to protect the driver's neck – failed, and Pedro Diniz only managed to cheat death due to the incredibly wet nature of the Nürburgring, the wet ground giving way and ensuring his survival.

The reason for the Nürburgring construction was to attract people to the area who wouldn't normally visit – and the reason they wouldn't normally visit is because it often rains sideways. Bad news for a holiday; great news for a motor race. In the early stages, local hero Frentzen was disappearing into the distance in the lead and Häkkinen was in second place after overtaking his teammate, Coulthard. While a no-longer-in-the-shadow-of-his-brother Ralf Schumacher, meanwhile, was driving some of the best races of his entire career, and brilliantly moved his way past Coulthard in the rain, up to third position.

It was a case of guessing which way the weather would go and putting the right tyres on at the right time. Häkkinen came in for a fairly pedestrian stop, but it was nothing compared to the mess next door. Ferrari were in shambles; the team didn't have four wheels ready as Eddie Irvine pulled into the pit lane, and then the stop ground to a halt with the crew on the wheels not knowing whether to attach said tyres. The commentary from Martin Brundle said it all: 'Don't have a committee meeting about it. Stick it on and send him out.'

Race leader Frentzen came in for his first stop, but the two-button system had also been forgotten by their lead driver. Frentzen pressed one button, and then forgot the second. And again, the entire car shut down. Frentzen's chance of the most unlikely title victory in modern times was over. An independent team would never get as close as Jordan had to the title in 1999.

As the rain came down, the race broadcast became a series of jump cuts to cars spinning off the circuit in all directions, with Häkkinen out of contention having chosen the wrong strategy and Irvine way back, despite being lucky to escape the pits with four wheels on the car. It came down to Ralf Schumacher and David Coulthard to head the field. Coulthard was inspired, driving lap after lap on a wet track on slick tyres until he snatched a brake at the fifth turn and slithered off the road.

Out of this chaos, Ralf Schumacher had a chance to win his maiden Grand Prix. The crash eliminated Coulthard from championship contention and promoted the other Ferrari of Giancarlo Fisichella to the race lead. But moments later Fisichella spun off too, promoting Ralf Schumacher to the race lead.

The cameras joined Schumacher just as he went off into the gravel trap with a puncture. As Ralf limped back to the pits, out of nowhere, into the lead went British favourite Johnny Herbert in a Stewart Ford. Johnny's season so far had been reduced to a series of cutaways from the main broadcast as his car broke down time and time again.

His teammate, Rubens Barrichello, who was signing for Ferrari in 2000, had been making all the headlines earlier in the year, starting the French Grand Prix from pole position and brilliantly leading his home race to the acclaim of the crowd in São Paulo. But as the racing gods would have it, Johnny Herbert would be the man for the breakthrough victory.

Such was the attrition of Formula One in the late 1990s. Luca Badoer, a perennial backmarker for Minardi, retired from the points paying fourth place with a gearbox failure and promptly burst into tears. Meanwhile, further back, having been on the wrong strategy for the better part of 90 minutes, Eddie Irvine crumbled under the pressure of Mika Häkkinen's recovery drive and crucially Häkkinen was able to outscore him in the championship.

It would have lasting implications for the World Championship on a day where keeping the car pointing in the right direction in the rain was remarkably challenging. Murray yelled down the microphone, 'Johnny Herbert in the Stewart turns into corner 13 and takes the chequered flag to win. And there is Jackie Stewart. Well, oh, words fail me.'

Barrichello would eventually come third behind Prost's Trulli. Jackie Stewart had won in the nick of time, as he was selling his team's entry to the Ford Motor Company, realizing the budgets had risen way beyond what a private entrant could afford.

Ford, with all the money in their possession, would have an unremarkable run before again selling to a group that had far more success called Red Bull Racing. Jackie Stewart was a 27-time Grand Prix winner behind the wheel, and now a victorious team owner, all with three races remaining before he gave it up. There have been more consequential races, there have been more exciting races, but in terms of unpredictability, the European Grand Prix of 1999 set a standard that we've rarely seen since.

47

The Real Rules of the Game

In October 1999, Ferrari released a statement telling the world Michael Schumacher had notified the team he would not be taking part in the remaining races in the Formula One season, as he was not sufficiently fit.

Schumacher had broken his leg at Silverstone six races earlier and Ferrari had floundered in his absence. The team had won some races and qualified outside of the top 10 of others. The low point had come when they only had three wheels ready for a pit stop at the European Grand Prix. Plainly, the team needed its leader, but he appeared reluctant to return.

A few days later, at a press conference at the Mugello circuit near Florence, a prickly Schumacher repeatedly outlined why he couldn't drive at his normal level. He was driving himself mad going back and forth between thinking he was ready and getting frustrated at setbacks. He'd managed his usual standards for about five laps but that was it. On the defensive, at one point during the conference he'd even railed against the team's own statement for giving the false impression that there had even been a choice to make. He also hit back at questions claiming he'd abandoned his team. Insiders posited various theories why Schumacher was reluctant to return. Did he not want to look weak racing in a semi-injured state? Could he bear to play number two as a double champion especially if it was to hand his dream to another driver.

In 1996, Schumacher had given up the path of easy titles in order to chase the dream of returning Ferrari back to the front, all with a mammoth paycheque from Philip Morris cigarettes.

Schumacher was being paid one of the biggest salaries in sport, and with no title the sponsor wanted to know what they were paying for if the driver wasn't returning to the cockpit. Ferrari president Luca di Montezemolo phoned the Schumacher house to discuss things, only to be told: 'Michael is outside playing football.' The president reportedly hit the roof and just days later a second statement was released. Schumacher was back! In a twisted sporting conundrum, he'd be fighting for his number two, Eddie Irvine, to give Ferrari their dream – a first Drivers' title since 1979.

Schumacher had essentially been forced back, but he appeared to take the same obsessive approach to being a number two as he had as the number-one driver. At the first-ever Malaysian Grand Prix at the brand-new Sepang circuit, Schumacher had put the car on pole position by nearly a second. There was no doubt who the greatest driver in the world was, even if he wasn't fighting for the title. The race was run in sweltering humidity and would be a great test for legendary Schumacher fitness.

Ferrari controlled the race with ease; first Schumacher gave up the lead to Irvine, then Schumacher started to slow the pace against Häkkinen, placing his car in tricky places and ruining the race pace of the reigning world champion in the silver McLaren. Irvine crossed the line to win, calling it a depressing day with a smile on his face. Schumacher was not only the best number-one but also the best number-two driver as well.

Schumacher revelled in silencing the doubters who called into question his commitment to Ferrari. He summed up his performance with the simple, 'I knew what my job was.' Hours later, chaos reigned in the paddock as both Ferraris were disqualified after their bargeboards were found to be outside regulation parameters. Häkkinen was the race winner and world champion after all.

McLaren designer Adrian Newey had wanted a good look at the Ferrari bargeboards for a while. After surveying the part in parc fermé in Malaysia, he'd pointed out to the FIA that they were clearly illegal, with parts visible from underneath the car. Ferrari were furious and raged that they'd run the same part at the previous race, which had passed all scrutineering checks. Ferrari team boss Jean Todt and Eddie Irvine felt the penalty of disqualification was over the top.

Ferrari, in full panic, sent sporting director Ross Brawn out in the dark with a ruler to explain that if you measured in different places, you'd get different numbers. Brawn came to regret the impromptu lecture, as Ferrari hadn't yet constructed their argument – without one, for the first time the World Championship was settled by disqualification.

In the days that followed, the briefing became more refined. The offending parts offered no performance gain. A design engineer had simply made a mistake and quality checks had been missed. The appeal hearing at the FIA took place the Friday after the race. Ferrari had argued the bargeboards fell within the 5 mm tolerances outlined elsewhere in the technical regulations in relation to the flat floor. Then the point of measurement and mounting became clear.

FIA president Max Mosely announced five days after the race had finished that Ferrari had won, even if they'd needed a loophole. The title battle was back on.

McLaren team boss Ron Dennis called it 'a bad day for the sport' and made reference to the outcome suiting Formula One, who now had a last race winner-take-all decider on their hands. Many in the paddock felt McLaren had been dealt a tough hand. When Mika Häkkinen out-dragged Michael Schumacher off the line at the final race in Japan there was a huge cheer in the press room. Mika checked out and won his second World Championship title. Schumacher never had to play number two again and the bargeboards controversy was forgotten after there were huge TV ratings for the title decider across the world.

48

The Shootout that Made Jenson Button's Career

It would be hard to argue that the Circuit de Barcelona is anyone's favourite racetrack.

Built as part of the city's Olympic regeneration in 1990, it had become a Formula One testing favourite due to the short flight from the UK and relatively predictable weather. The order of play was cold mornings, warm afternoons and days of uninterrupted running. In the year 2000, this test would carry huge significance for two young drivers. In an almost mock gameshow, Williams were having a winner-take-all shootout for the final seat on the grid. This was a team with 16 world titles, incredible engineering pedigree, unlimited testing and cutting-edge data analysis.

There shouldn't have been a vacancy for the forthcoming season at all. Fan favourite Alex Zanardi had become the first ever Williams driver to be fired mid-contract, as the likeable Italian found adjusting to late 1990s Formula One incredibly difficult. He finished the 1999 season with 10 retirements and no points finishes. This was a big surprise as Zanardi who had competed in Formula One at the start of the decade boasted a strong US pedigree – winning the preeminent US CART title, and pulling off a dazzling array of bold, exciting overtakes.

Curiously, Williams had returned to the same source to sign his replacement; the punchy and aggressive Juan Pablo Montoya had a deal with Williams for 2001. However, his American CART team refused to release him a year early and a driver to keep the seat warm was required. Twenty-year-old Jenson Button had finished a creditable third in his rookie season of the British Formula Three championship, at the time the leading third tier championship in the motorsport pyramid. Bruno Junqueira had more experience; he was the reigning F3000 (the F2 of its day) champion. He had won the category in his third season of competition, with four assured wins along the way. He was also heavily backed by the Williams team's Brazilian oil sponsor, Petrobras.

Anticipation was high, many press were in attendance, and questions abounded. Who would put together the best race runs? Would anyone struggle moving from the slick tyres of the junior championship to the cursed grooved tyres of the era? Would there be a disparity between one-lap pace and high fuel between the two competitors? The answers to all these questions were unavailable as the new BMW engine proved unreliable and the fair fight Williams had desired was not possible.

But Williams refused to decide amid a healthy amount of publicity surrounding the shootout, so continued to commit to the idea. The team booked an extra day at the circuit but this was it – the successful driver would test, sign the contract in the evening and just 24 hours later be announced to the world at a press conference. Frank's reasoning for the shootout would point to Michael Schumacher turning up almost unknown in Spa in 1990 before stunning the whole paddock with his talent (*see* Chapter 38).

Over the winter, the team consensus had been to sign Junqueira, who was already a test driver and knew the team and its processes well. But first in a test at Jerez and then Barcelona the tide had begun to turn. Button's raw talent started to win key personnel over; when he tested one of Alain Prost's cars, the four-time world champion couldn't help but be reminded of his own talent behind the wheel. Button's smooth style was at odds with his limited experience.

As the sun set over the unremarkable industrial estate in Catalunya, the timing page displayed Button as faster than

Junqueira. In the end, it came down not to logic, not to data, but to childlike excitement at a raw talent. Jenson Button was announced to the mass ranks as an F1 driver at just twenty years of age. Defining himself as a champion of the future, he would drive just one season for the Williams team in his career, though not for the want of trying.

Bizarrely, after scoring 10 podiums with the BAR Honda team, in 2004 Button and his management stunned Formula One by announcing a move back to Williams for the next season. The Williams BMW engine team collaboration was well funded and the outright fastest power unit in the field. As ever, no matter previous success, a driver is always chasing the better car and engine package. Teams and driver engaged in a public war of words before lodging the contracts to the thrillingly titled 'Contract Recognition Board'. The sports court ruled: Button would remain with BAR Honda for 2005. Staggeringly, Button then signed again for Williams for the 2006 season, only for BMW to announce they were leaving the team and setting up their own entry.

In scenes of total farce, Button's newly installed management had to extricate the driver from a team he had signed for twice in two years. A deal would be struck but at a significant financial cost for Button, who was relieved to settle things and race for the newly acquired Honda Formula One team. He would win his first race with them in 2006. Button delivered on his promise of being a future world champion in 2009 (*see* Chapter 55). After Formula One retirement and becoming a respected TV analyst, in 2021 Button finally returned to Williams as a special adviser and ambassador – this time, mercifully, the contract stuck.

49

Mercedes' Disgruntled Employee Changes the Race

The Hockenheim circuit in Germany's Rhine Valley was a true outlier on the Formula One calendar.

The layout was the strangest combination the drivers would face all year. The first three-quarters were a series of flat-out blasts interrupted by a chicane on three occasions before a stadium section. A right-left-right section then brought the cars back to the line, surrounded by huge concrete grandstands. It meant that a large part of the track was unseen by spectators, with the flat-out sections lined by 30ft-high pine trees – out there it was just the drivers, the marshals, a few camera operators – and Robert!

Halfway between turn 1 and the first chicane, beyond the catch fencing and the barriers, was a man walking on the grass during the middle of the race. His leisurely pace gave an unreal nature to the unfolding scene. Cars were tearing past beyond 200 mph, metres away from a catastrophic accident. The protester then crossed the track and continued his stroll in front of the cameras.

Frenchman Robert Sehli had worked for Mercedes for 22 years at their Le Mans factory before being made redundant. The decision had been disputed, and Sehli hatched a plan to get the attention of his former employer at their home race, the German Grand Prix. He would break onto the racetrack, inform the world of the injustice done to him and then deal with the consequences. His protest message was completely illegible, but as for ruining Mercedes' day, that part worked perfectly.

The race was all but won for Mercedes at the start, who only supplied engines to McLaren at this point in their Formula One journey. All the pre-race talk had been of two-time champion and local hero Michael Schumacher's tactics, known as the 'Schumacher chop'. David Coulthard was Schumacher's nearest rival in a tight championship battle. The Scot was on pole for McLaren and led away from the line, trying his version of the dastardly chop, but his momentum was slow and teammate Häkkinen was able to bolt from fourth to first.

Schumacher drove to the left and made contact with Giancarlo Fisichella's bright blue Benetton. The home favourite was out, but Murray Walker identified the Ferrari as Barrichello and not Schumacher. The incident would have lasting implications for British viewers as a critical editorial piece in the next day's *Daily Mail* led to the broadcasting great setting his retirement in motion.

With Schumacher out, the opportunity for McLaren was clear. Ferrari had started the season in fine form, with Schumacher winning five out of seven races he'd finished. But, in a reversal to the championship momentum of previous seasons, McLaren were staging a comeback.

After the previous Austrian Grand Prix – where Häkkinen had won – in post-race scrutineering, McLaren were found to be missing a required seal on the engine control unit. Ferrari wrote to the FIA in an attempt to get McLaren thrown out of the result. Schumacher was coming off the back of two mechanical problems and being spun on the opening lap in Austria.

Things were so febrile in the Italian press that Schumacher was forced to deny Ferrari were in crisis. All while Michael Schumacher led the standings by six points in the Drivers' Championship, but the long championship win drought amplified everything. No drivers' title for Ferrari since 1979 meant the pressure kept building. Worse still, his teammate, Rubens Barrichello, was down in 18th after an interrupted qualifying left him on the ninth row. In the early stages of the race, Rubens tore through the field, climbing to third place on an aggressive two-stop strategy.

A McLaren win should have been a formality from here, but when the Mercedes protest unfolded, race control had no option but to deploy a safety car to slow the field and the McLaren advantage was wiped out instantly. Ron Dennis said the strategy didn't account for a spectator wandering on the circuit. Mercedes engine chief Norbert Haug called the protest a scandal after it transpired the intruder had unsuccessfully tried to get onto the track at turn 1 before the formation lap. Crucially, he hadn't been detained in the circuit cell, leaving him two hours to have another go.

On track, second-placed David Coulthard didn't hear the radio call to pit so had to do another lap behind the safety car, costing him five places. On the restart, Häkkinen was first, Jarno Trulli in a Jordan second and Barrichello third. The safety car was instantly required again after an enormous accident between Jean Alesi and Pedro Diniz in a Sauber, which pitched the Prost driver into a series of violent spins.

When the rain arrived, it hit the stadium section first, which would have been a relief to the drivers who were carrying huge speeds of up to 220 mph in the first part of the lap. Race leader Mika Häkkinen and second-placed Trulli pitted from the top two places, while Barrichello, Coulthard and Jordan's Heinz-Harald Frentzen stayed out on the slick dry-weather tyres. A few laps later, Coulthard bailed out for inters, not wanting to take any undue risks.

Frentzen then broke down to leave Rubens as the lone front runner on dry tyres, when at least a quarter of the circuit was wet and claiming cars from the points. Ferrari sporting director Ross Brawn called Rubens Barrichello in for wets. Time and time again, Rubens overruled the strategic genius, believing he could keep the car on track and, crucially, keep the tyres working in the temperature window: 123 starts without a victory must have played a part in his thinking.

Ross Brawn had given up arguing as Barrichello continued to keep tyre temperature and a 10-second buffer. Rubens always had a great feel in the wet, scoring a pole position for Jordan in 1994 and a second place for the new Stewart team in 1997 in the similar conditions. As he approached the final lap, he said it felt like the longest of his life. Tears of joy swelled as he crossed the line to win at last.

Afterwards, he said he was thinking of Ayrton Senna, who'd mentored him in his early Formula One days, and his dad, who'd worked so hard in order for him to head to Europe in search of the F1 dream. It was the first Brazilian F1 win since 1993 and the harrowing loss of their sporting icon Senna. The occasion allowed the Brazilian Globo TV channel to revive their legendary winners theme music. The pressure of following Senna had been immense in Brazil and with this breakthrough win, Rubens was just 10 points behind Schumacher in the championship. Ferrari instantly reiterated their desire to back one car. The protester was fined 90,000 francs for trespassing on the circuit. Only two Grands Prix in championship history have ever been won from further back on the grid.

As Murray Walker put it: 'Anything can happen in Formula One, and it usually does' in a sport where even employment law can change a race from nowhere.

50

The Greatest Overtake of All Time

In 2000, Mika Häkkinen was chasing his third World Championship in a row.

He'd fall short in this quest, betrayed by a failing engine at Indianapolis with three races to go, but he didn't leave the season empty-handed. In Belgium, at one of the greatest driving tests on the planet, the Finn claimed an accolade he may yet never lose. This is the greatest Formula One overtake of all time, told to me by the man who achieved it. It all began with him spinning, losing the lead of the race:

> I automatically realize I'm losing control of the car. You are maximizing all your talent to keep the car in position. That way you don't hit the wall plus keep the engine running. And then you're really pissed off after, when you do start going back, and start fighting your original position, which means when leading a race there is a little anger.
> So, this anger makes you drive much more aggressive. What that means is you have an hour and a half, whatever is left in the race, you don't give any mercy for the car, not for the tyres, not for the engine, not for the brakes, not for anything. You hit the kerbs and you just go flat out. And that's what happens, you see a good possibility to catch the leader and win the race, you just continue going flat out and you're taking a risk that way, something can break.
> So normally you leave a little in for the breaking. But

in that particular race I kicked some ass, man. It was an incredible moment because Michael saw in the mirrors that the speed I was approaching him at was huge. My overtaking in normal cases should be easy and there was quite a big number of laps still left in a race. So, I thought, he knows I come so fast, so I thought it's no way he's gonna start blocking me 'cause I was so bloody quick. But he did and he did very nastily.

I said, OK, if we have about 10 laps to go, he's gonna block me like this 10 times and if he gonna block me 10 times like this, we could have crashed. Michael was really heavy, blocking me. My [front wing] endplate has some marks from his rear tyre. When you're 200 mph and your wing is touching somebody's rear tyre, that means we were pretty close. It was very clear for me that this is it. This is the only place where I can overtake him. So, I will put all my energy for that straight line 'cause there was no chance to go anywhere else.

So, what I did in all the other areas on the racetrack ... I was, all the time, saving a little bit because then I was close to Michael ... I was not too close to Michael, not to heat up the brakes or the gearbox or engine, to leave all the energies from the car for that straight line. But there was only one problem. That means Eau Rouge, I need to go nearly flat. I mean full speed and qualification style. You can go through that corner very fast. Uh, but in a race it's different tactics. So, I need to put my own energy into really go, like in a qualification. When I decided that, my body prepared Eau Rouge differently than other laps.

I knew that anything could happen. If the car moves slightly in the middle of the corner, moves at the rear, I'm going to fly to Brussels. [Mika laughs for a while at this point].

I managed to go through Eau Rouge perfectly. Uh, and when I was top of the hill, I felt when the car was landing basically back to the four wheels, I was like impressed that way. Wow. The car was able to do this!

Uh, it's no way. If I would've done a second lap like that, then obviously my speed was again up. I see the red car there, I can see Michael there. He was waiting to block me again. I was thinking, here we go again. What's gonna happen this time?

But I see in the distance, I do see Riccardo Zonta in a very unusual situation. He was travelling in the middle of the racetrack, right in the middle of the straight, not on the left-hand side or not on the right-hand side as would normally be the situation. So, it was the middle of the track in a distance. This is my chance.

We were approaching and counting. And this was a difficult part because when I was all the time catching Michael closer and closer and closer, it comes to the point when I have to show Michael which way I gonna go. So, if I showed Michael a little bit too early, which side I'm going to overtake, he's gonna block me. So, the timing was very crucial. So luckily Michael chose a normal racing line and to go on the left.

So, adrenaline. Your heart rate comes up. All your reactions are absolutely sharp. It was a really incredible feeling. This racing moment, what we were going through.

When I overtook Michael, you put your mind back to normal. My body comes down in a mode that I am 100 per cent in control of the car then I can see Michael and my distance is not increasing purposely because I want to enjoy seeing him in my mirrors. I really enjoyed it. I don't want him to go too far. I got high pleasure out of that.

Mika won the race, celebrated, and told Michael not to block him at speed like that ever again. It was the landmark moment of their wonderful rivalry.

Ferrari's Team Order Farce in Austria

There's no such thing as a dull Formula One season, but the early stages of 2002 really pushed the limits of that statement.

Michael Schumacher was seemingly coasting his way to the title, having won four of the first five races. Three of the victories had been dominant to the point of no contest. Schumacher had won by margins of 18, 17 and 35 seconds, and the team was undefeated since introducing its new F2002 chassis at the third race of the season.

Admittedly, Williams had won in Malaysia. Ralf Schumacher led home a one–two for the team as Ferrari struggled in the stifling heat of Sepang, conditions that played to the Michelin runners' strengths. But for everywhere else it wasn't even a contest as F1's most famous team had turned the page from nearly-men to firm favourites for every Grand Prix.

Round six of the season was in the picturesque venue of Spielberg in Austria's Styrian hills. The championship stood with Michael Schumacher on 44 points (10 points for a win in this era), Juan Pablo Montoya on 23, and Ralf Schumacher had scored 20.

At the race before in Spain, Ferrari had qualified nine-tenths of a second faster than the closest competitor and the fears of F1 having a foregone conclusion of a season continued. Happily, for fans of racing, Rubens Barrichello qualified on pole with teammate Michael Schumacher in third. Schumacher would have to fight through; he passed his brother, Ralf, for second off the line. Ferrari began to comfortably pull away as a pair. McLaren and Williams simply didn't have the performance of the Ferraris, who were operating with a confident authority not seen from the team since the mid-1970s.

Within 20 laps, Ferrari were a full pit stop ahead already, 30 seconds clear of the nearest challenger, Ralf Schumacher in the Williams. Ferrari had placed both cars on a two-stop strategy and Barrichello pitted from the lead when Panis' BAR spun from engine failure on the main straight. On the restart, Nick Heidfeld had a huge lock up, spinning uphill at speed at the right hander at the top of the hill. He narrowly missed Juan Pablo Montoya's Williams and smashed into the side of Takuma Sato's yellow Jordan. The impact was so great, the chassis was damaged and the young Japanese driver was temporarily trapped in the car.

After being T-boned and parts of the suspension breaching the car, Sato could count himself very fortunate to escape the 47G accident without serious injury. Ferrari made a late second stop, having dominated the race throughout. First Barrichello then Schumacher came in to receive a final top-up of fuel and new Bridgestone tyres. They were a whopping 40 seconds ahead of the opposition. But the number-two driver led their golden boy. For Ferrari in the early 2000s this was a problem – despite a dominant weekend, the arguing began.

Notes on the Ferrari pit wall begin to be exchanged from the team principal to sporting director, Jean Todt and Ross Brawn barely making eye contact as the folded slips of small paper began to be passed about. A year ago, at the same venue, Barrichello had been asked to give up second position to teammate Schumacher, and while the Brazilian had been frustrated, he was given assurances by his boss, Jean Todt, that the team would never ask him to give up a win in similar circumstances.

Not for a year anyway.

Ferrari were asking Rubens Barrichello to move out of the way in a direct team order. Barrichello was steadfastly refusing.

Barrichello's new two-year contract extension had been announced on Thursday, the length of the deal surprising the paddock who expected Barrichello to have a single-year extension to maintain control over their driver. This was a tactic used by Mercedes with Valtteri Bottas in his time with the team, 15 years later. Such control did not appear to exist at Ferrari, as the leading car and sporting director continued to slug it out, all while Rubens drove the 10-turn circuit with speeds up to 180 mph.

Barrichello is reported to have told Ferrari: 'Get my lawyer on the phone.'

Ferrari were slightly frustrated as they'd discussed this exact scenario pre-race and believed Barrichello was onboard with a plan to move aside after the second stops if he was still ahead. Agreeing in the team strategy briefing is one thing; actually giving up a Grand Prix victory is another. As Barrichello rounded the final corner it looked as if such a contrived finish would be avoided. 'It doesn't look as though there's going to be any team orders here and nor should we have believed there would be,' said an audibly relieved James Allen in the commentary box.

Seconds later, Barrichello gave up what would have been just a second career victory. Schumacher won the race at slow speed by less than two-tenths of a second. The reaction from all broadcasters was astonishment: 'I do not believe it, WHAT IS GOING ON?' was the soundtrack on ITV; former F1 driver John Watson called it a 'disgrace' on F1's own digital channel.

The crowd of the main grandstand provided a highly unusual noise as the collectively disgusted booing thundered down, ferocious in its intensity. Ross Brawn could hear the reaction but didn't blink, telling a massed scrum of reporters that 'Rubens was managing the pace, Michael was managing the pace, you can't call that a race.'

Barrichello forced the issue all the way to the final corner, but he knew he could not refuse his team. 'What should I do? I have in the contract I have to obey orders ... if I disobey right now, at the beginning of my two and half years of contract ...' The implication was clear: lose today, and hope being with Ferrari would bring wins another day. Ferrari's super team had become so focused in operations, they didn't care how early in the season it was. Schumacher fought for the championships and nothing got in the way of that.

For watching fans, a dominant team manipulating a result so cynically was a step too far. The boos continued as the drivers stepped on the podium. Schumacher, unsure of how to handle the reaction, ushered Barrichello on top step, which only seemed to antagonize things further. By the time the Italian anthem played for Ferrari, both drivers were on the top step.

Ferrari had broken no racing rules. The 1950s and 1960s had seen drivers physically give up their cars to other competitors – three wins in F1 history are shared for that reason. But the FIA felt it needed to do something to punish Ferrari, and after Schumacher gave Barrichello his winner's trophy, the team were fined $1 million.

Perhaps most remarkably, the assembled press loudly booed the Ferrari drivers as they took their seats for the post-race press conference. Rubens, having already listened to booing for 15 minutes straight, tersely instructed: 'Don't do that.' In the press conference, again the drivers swapped positions. Sitting incorrectly in the second-placed position, Schumacher looked stunned as he took a series of aggressive questions. 'I'm not very pleased about it ... I'm thankful for the points but obviously I don't take a lot of joy from the victory,' he replied. Team Principal Jean Todt refused to give any ground, saying, 'There's even more people to face when there's no result.' He pointed to last-race heartbreak in 1997, 1998 and 1999 as reasons for his ruthlessness. The race proved so controversial, however, that it would see team orders banned for eight years until Ferrari again got themselves into a mess moving Felipe Massa out of the way of their team number one, Fernando Alonso, by coded message.

Rubens Barrichello would never make peace with his implied number-two status at Ferrari in the way his predecessor Eddie Irvine had. Irvine had managed to take a wider perspective and enjoy racing cars all over the world to the podium. Rubens' ambition for the title would never dim. There was a plan; he was in sight of Schumacher retiring and then he would lead the team. But eventually Barrichello's patience wore out, and he could take the number-two treatment no longer. He left for the Honda works team at the end of 2005. In 2006, Schumacher would leave Ferrari and retire.

Rossi and Surtees – From Two to Four Wheels

In the early 2000s, Valentino Rossi, the motorbike racing icon and seven-time MotoGP champion, flirted with the idea of becoming a Formula One driver.

The move from two wheels to four was not unprecedented and had been achieved by John Surtees in the 1950s. Rossi was the man who has been regularly described as the greatest rider of his generation rode his first motorbike at just five years old, with his talents apparent from his teenage years. As a successful sporting hero, he inspired his fans in a manner reminiscent of Ferrari's Tifosi in Formula One. The idea of the crossover of the Italian motorbiking legend with Formula One's iconic Italian team was too alluring for both parties involved not to at least consider the option.

Rossi first had a test in a Ferrari car in April 2004 at the Fiorano circuit, and ended up using Michael Schumacher's spare helmet. The Fiorano circuit is a private racetrack used by Ferrari for development and testing, near Maranello. Rossi described having to stay in Enzo's old house the night before to avoid the press for his tests given the interest! It was said that he took a bit of time getting used to racing in the car, with his four-wheel racing experience mainly being limited to karting, but by the end of day he was very impressive – even Schumacher said he didn't need any advice. This test was again repeated in 2005 at the same circuit.

The most serious test occurred in 2006, when he took part in a major pre-season group test in Valencia, Spain. The test included famous Formula One names, again including Ferrari drivers Schumacher and Felipe Massa but also Renault's Fernando Alonso and Honda's Jenson Button, among others. Rossi drove a detuned V10-engined car, while Schumacher and Massa drove different cars, making a direct comparison tricky. And yet, he managed to get his lap times to within 0.7 seconds of Michael Schumacher, much to the surprise and delight of everyone involved!

Did Formula One now beckon for Rossi? With Michael Schumacher's retirement on the cards at the end of 2006, Ferrari's chairman Luca di Montezemolo was keen enough to attempt to run a third Ferrari for Rossi, but sadly the rules prevented this. This wasn't the only time that a motorsport giant from a different stream was blocked; reportedly the FIA refused to grant the rally superstar Sebastien Loeb a super licence after his test with Toro Roso in 2007. Whatever the discussions were behind closed doors, Rossi ended up re-signing for his MotoGP team, Yamaha, in June 2006.

Another opportunity arose when Felipe Massa was badly injured by a loose spring at the Hungarian Grand Prix in 2009. Massa's replacement, Luca Badoer, struggled in the next two races, opening the door for a bored and relatively newly retired Schumacher to make his return. Then Schumacher, with supreme irony, injured himself by coming off a motorbike, with his doctor reportedly stating that if it was anyone else, he wouldn't have survived. With Schumacher's recovery preventing a return to racing, the seat was once again open for Rossi. However, by 2009, unlimited testing had been banned and an intensive preparation period wasn't possible. And so, the tantalizing prospect of Rossi at Ferrari racing Lewis Hamilton was sadly not to be.

Further paddock gossip suggested that a move to a Ferrari-supported team was possible in 2008–09, with a move to Ferrari planned for a few years later once Rossi had enough experience. However, Valentino didn't appear to want to spend a few seasons in a feeder team as a backmarker when his MotoGP career was still going strong. In an interview later recounting this experience, he said he went with his heart, despite his mother's advice to go with Ferrari.

Rossi's father stated that Valentino was 'very very close' to making the switch in 2006–07 after the Valencia test. Rossi continued to have test days with Ferrari but they didn't appear to be as serious.

With Valentino Rossi flirting but never quite committing to Formula One, John Surtees maintains his reputation as the only world champion on both two and four wheels. Surtees' father, Jack, a former British motorcycle sidecar champion, ran a motorcycle shop in London in the 1930s and '40s. At the age of eleven, John was capable of riding and repairing his own bike. At seventeen, he competed and won his first race, and by twenty-one (in 1955) he was a member of the Norton motorcycle works team, where he won 67 of his 78 races. He was approached by the famous Italian MV Agusta team, with whom he won seven World Championships. Surtees then sought contract flexibility and went looking for other opportunities to race on four wheels rather than two.

By 1959, Surtees was given test drives by talent hunters eager to find the next single-seater racer. He went on to debut in April 1960 in four-wheel racing at Goodwood, driving a Cooper-Austin entered by Ken Tyrrell. His close finish in second behind Jim Clark in a Lotus brought Surtees to the attention of the F1 paddock. The founder of Lotus, Colin Chapman, hired Surtees to race in the last four races of the 1960 Formula One season, which turned out to be an astute move. Surtees came second in his first Grand Prix at Silverstone; he followed this up with a pole at the next race in Portugal at a tricky circuit, which included tramlines and cobbled streets, but failed to finish the race. With a strong work ethic and a great deal of hard work, Surtees made the leap from bikes to cars look easy.

After those four races, Surtees switched full time from

motorcycles to Formula One, where he considered several offers. He rejected Chapman at Lotus and drove a Cooper in 1961 and a Lola in 1962 but without the success of his first two races. His fortunes were to change with another giant of Italian motorsport, Enzo Ferrari. With Enzo having managed a motorcycle team in the 1930s, Ferrari was aware of Surtees' reputation in motorcycling and admired his passion and fighting spirit. Surtees was hired as the number-one driver at Ferrari in 1963. That year, he went up against Jim Clark in the Lotus and Graham Hill in a BRM – two giants of the sport. His first win, and Ferrari's first in two years, came at the notoriously difficult Nürburgring, where he punished the previously untouchable Clark for his Lotus engine trouble. By 1964, he was in contention for the World Championship, where he won again in Germany and Italy. He secured the World Championship at the very last race in Mexico, beating Graham Hill by a point and Jim Clark by eight.

The first and only world champion on both two and four wheels was known for his forthright attitude, which proved his undoing when it came to more World Championships. At Le Mans 24-hour race, he fell out with Ferrari team manager Eugenio Dragoni; Surtees simply walked out and never returned. After a few frustrating years with three further wins in Formula One, he decided to set up his own team in 1969. Team Surtees never quite reached the heights of the others like Brabham, McLaren and Williams. He retired from driving in 1973 to concentrate on managing the team. Alongside Clark's perfect score, Hill's triple crown and Brabham's win in a car of his own construction, Surtees legacy is one of the great motor racing achievements.

Kimi Rips the Tyre Off and Everyone Ignores It

In 2005, a new tyre rule had been implemented to try to halt Ferrari's domination of the championship.

Ferrari's run now stretched to five straight years, including the 2002 and 2004 seasons, where the titles were complete formalities and viewership numbers had drastically dropped. It meant for the first time since 1996 that Michael Schumacher was not a viable candidate for the World Championship as Ferrari could not get their Bridgestone tyres to work within the new parameters of the rules. There were a few race day exceptions like in Imola, where Schumacher had charged through from outside the top 10 to the brink of the lead.

The driver who thwarted Schumacher that day had filled the void at the top of F1. Fernando Alonso of Renault had won three out of the four races to take an early lead in the championship but that wasn't the full picture. Alonso was worried; with 13 of 19 Grands Prix to go, his blue and yellow Renault was no longer the best driver and car combination. Kimi Räikkönen and McLaren had emerged as the strongest package, and the standard of Kimi's driving wowed all those who witnessed the car trackside. Earlier that year at a Silverstone test day, I watched the speed that he carried with the widest possible lines into fast corners. It is commonly agreed this was the best version of Räikkönen in his Formula One career. Ferrari used that time to look to the future, signing a pre-contract agreement with Räikkönen to lure him from the McLaren team for the start of 2007.

On pole position at the Nürburgring was a home favourite: light fuelled Nick Heidfeld had taken his first Formula One pole position. He was proposing to attack the Grand Prix with a three-stop strategy, preferring to play to the car strengths, which didn't include running the car heavy.

Kimi built a lead of 16 seconds. This should have been race won, but the advantage was not quite big enough to pit and re-emerge in front of title rival Alonso. This was something that really wasn't required but McLaren instructed their driver to try to do it anyway. In trying to build the luxury gap, Kimi went wide at one point, damaging a bargeboard on the sweeping McLaren design, and so began the first pulling of the threads. When lapping the Sauber of Jacques Villeneuve, Räikkönen locked up and created a severe flat spot on the front-left tyre. In most other seasons this would have been monitored and Räikkönen would almost certainly have pitted within a few laps, as the McLaren easily had the pace to catch and pass Fernando Alonso for the win. But McLaren couldn't change the tyre as it had been banned, so the team and driver were stuck trying to nurse a tyre to the finish.

The race would end either with McLaren taking a huge risk and failing – or they would pull off an audacious win. Alonso immediately began pushing hard, his metronomic pace seeing the gap whittled from 16 seconds to under two by the time both cars crossed the line for the last lap. It had set up a grandstand finish between Formula One's two new stars – the leader a monosyllabic Finn, and the other an intense Spaniard.

At the turn-one hairpin, Räikkönen applied the brake and the front suspension exploded. This pitched the silver McLaren into a spin and out of the race – the certain victory had been thrown away. The vibration from the misshapen tyre had rattled the suspension assembly to breaking point; breaking downhill, it made for a huge high-speed snap, which nearly collected the BAR of Jenson Button, who was nearly a lap down minding his own business on the apex. Fernando Alonso glided through to take the win and extend his lead to 32 points in the era of 10 for a win, as paddock scrutiny fell on McLaren.

Team boss Ron Dennis said no one at McLaren had any regrets about trying to hang on for the win and the strategy had been followed because of the 'need to claw back ground on Alonso'. Their main reasoning was an expected dispute over whether it was in the rules to change the tyre that hadn't failed. The rule book only allowed for a precautionary change for safety, which could only happen if race officials felt there was a risk to the car. The points system of the day only gave a two-point advantage for the winner, but when put to Kimi he wanted to go for it. Alonso told the press conference it had been 'a lucky win'.

The tyre rule changes had been officially adopted for 'cost reasons', as it was tricky to write 'we desperately need to stop Ferrari' in a press release. What was striking was how completely against the culture of the time it was. FIA president Max Mosley had made safety the cornerstone of his time in charge; he was constantly trying to slow the speeds of the cars. Post-race, he stressed that safety needed to be the priority and reminded the team of their responsibilities.

The balance between show and spectacle would grow uncomfortable across the season. Montoya risked a failure in Monza in similar circumstances. It seemed a bizarre position to be taking a decade on from F1's existential crisis post Ayrton Senna's death. Less than a month later, the obvious lessons about tyres would have disastrous consequences …

Top: Damon Hill with Adrian Newey in the Williams garage at the Portuguese Grand Prix in 1996.

Bottom: Former world champion Michael Schumacher leads Jacques Villeneuve during the 1997 European Grand Prix – not long after, the pair would collide in a moment that showed Schumacher's dark arts.

Top: Eddie Irvine leads, ahead of teammate Michael Schumacher during the 1999 Malaysian Grand Prix. Irvine won the race to take the lead in the Drivers' World Championship.

Middle: Michael Schumacher and Mika Häkkinen race around a corner at the 2000 Belgium Grand Prix.

Bottom: Kimi Räikkönen wowed all those who saw him drive in 2005, but he would lose the European Grand Prix on the last lap.

Top: Alexandre Premat battles with teammate Lewis Hamilton in the GP2 support race at the 2006 Turkish Grand Prix.

Middle: Spanish McLaren driver Fernando Alonso chases his British teammate Lewis Hamilton during the 2007 Hungarian Grand Prix.

Bottom: Sebastian Vettel drives at Monza in 2008 in the Italian Grand Prix, where he won the race ahead of McLaren Mercedes' Heikki Kovalainen and BMW Sauber's Robert Kubica.

Top: The Red Bull Racing F1 team unveil their new car, the RB5, at the Circuito de Jerez in 2009.

Middle: At the 2009 Brazilian Grand Prix, Jenson Button claimed the drivers' title as Brawn GP became the first constructor to win the title in their first year of competition.

Bottom: Lewis Hamilton leads at the start of the 2010 Canadian Grand Prix while, behind him, Renault's Vitaly Petrov and BMW Sauber's Pedro de la Rosa crash.

Top: Renault's Robert Kubica qualifying for the Japanese Grand Prix in 2010 with a mighty lap.

Middle: At the second race of the season in 2013, Mark Webber leads Sebastian Vettel at the Malaysian Grand Prix.

Bottom: Lewis Hamilton and Nico Rosberg celebrate finishing in first and second place respectively at the 2014 Bahrain Grand Prix.

Top: Max Verstappen celebrates his first Formula One win at the 2016 Spanish Grand Prix.

Bottom: The Bahrain International Circuit was considered one of the safest circuits in the world, but Romain Grosjean's crash at the 2020 Grand Prix reminded everyone of the risks drivers are always taking.

Top: Lewis Hamilton and Max Verstappen lead the field into turn one at the start of the 2021 British Grand Prix.

Bottom: Lewis Hamilton and Max Verstappen battle for the World Championship on the final lap of the 2021 Abu Dhabi Grand Prix.

Top: Race winner Charles Leclerc celebrates in parc fermé during the 2024 Monaco Grand Prix.

Bottom: The sport shows no sign of slowing down as the McLarens have dominated the 75th season. Team rivalries are as present in the sport as ever, with Piastri and Norris fighting it out between them for the top spot on the score sheet. Here they are in Austria in June 2025.

Politics in Indianapolis Overwhelm the Sport, Setting Up Years of Change

Moments before the US Grand Prix of 2005 was due to begin, 14 cars of the 20-car field slowly peeled into the pit lane to deliberately retire from the race.

The sight was barely credible. Formula One's greatest own goal was complete: 72 hours of political rancour had finally taken the sport to a place of complete farce where internal and sporting politics overwhelmed all else – even actually going racing.

At the legendary Indianapolis Motor Speedway, the actual problem appeared minor the first time it manifested at the track. For the second year in a row, Ralf Schumacher hit the wall at the banked final corner. A year previously, Schumacher had struck a concrete wall and injured his back, missing six races in the process. Thankfully, barrier changes meant he was able to climb clear without serious injury when he hit in the same place during a practice session a year later, but the hit was still hard enough to affect his vision and the six-time Grand Prix winner was stood down by the FIA for the rest of the weekend.

When the second of three Toyotas in the session spun off at turn 5, few in the paddock linked the two events. When the red-and-white machine was recovered back to the garage, Zonta's car displayed similar issues with the left-rear tyre. Surveying the damage in FP2 and having a whopping four practice sessions in the weekend, Toyota stopped running and the whispers began.

In 2005, the new technical regulations had changed the load on the tyres through the unique banked final turn. The car was being compressed into the tarmac in a repeated way, creating more stress on the left-rear tyre. This information would not be known until long after the race. In most years, the tyre problem, though serious, could have been worked around by restricting stint lengths, but in 2005 mid-race tyre changes were banned. Despite evidence less than a month before in Germany that this rule was plainly dangerous, no changes had been suggested.

Heading into Saturday, Michelin was still unable to diagnose the problem and suggested technical changes not just to Toyota but to all their runners. It was the first moment of the weekend when the race was in doubt. In FP3, Juan Pablo Montoya and David Coulthard were the only Michelin runners to set a lap time after their crews at McLaren and Red Bull were the only ones to complete the changes in time. The other 12 cars simply completed system check laps and pitted again without setting a time or stressing the tyres.

After four laps for Montoya and seven laps for Coulthard, Michelin still couldn't locate the exact issue and sent for reinforcements. They suggested bringing a new compound of tyre that could withstand the load. FIA race director Charlie Whiting warned this was against the written rules. There was now a publicly known threat to the race on safety grounds, and a list of solutions was drawn up. These included stop-and-go penalties for Michelin runners if a chicane could be built (and thus banking avoided) at the final turn; the loss of 30 seconds was intended to compensate the Bridgestone runners, who had brought tyres that worked on the banking. The idea wasn't outlandish: a raft of temporary chicanes had been crudely installed in numerous fast corners in the aftermath of the Senna and Ratzenberger fatal accidents.

The final final practice session began with teams trying to reduce loads; this meant the Michelin runners were running low downforce on the rear wing, increasing tyre pressures and looking for setups nowhere near the optimum, all in an attempt to protect the rear tyres. Then, a dramatic move. On the record, Renault team boss Flavio Briatore said they would not compete in the race unless Michelin's Spanish specification of tyres were used for the race.

This was now a technical problem being played out publicly, with control of Formula One at the heart of the matter. On Saturday afternoon, the seven teams and Michelin met before the crucial qualifying hour. It was agreed that all teams would take part in qualifying, with the teams saying they still needed a full explanation for the failures. By the time Michelin's new tyre compound landed, it was clear the problem lay in the physical construction, not in the durability of the compound; the Spanish Grand Prix specification tyres were no longer an answer. The qualifying hour took place with all cars pushing to the limit, with the circuit unaltered. The tyres could survive three laps. Under rules that required the cars to qualify with race fuel in the car, Jarno Trulli took Toyota's first-ever pole in Formula One. Believing there would be no race, the team had placed a splash of fuel in the car in order to top the session and generate good headlines.

Sunday arrived with no answers in place. The Michelin runners were told that safety could not be guaranteed unless the speed of the final corner was reduced. The new tyre batch was unusable because of the failure of the rear-left tyre being structural. An alteration to the circuit was looking like the only solution. Frantic suggestions began flying about again: some proposed a speed limit on the banking for the Michelin runners, but this was deemed too difficult to police. The fact that the term 'speed limit' was being used showed the depths F1 had reached over this issue.

Another pretty desperate idea was that Michelin runners could take to the pit lane on every lap, which would cost them 30 seconds 71 times and leave the 14 cars scrapping over seventh to eighth places, while the Bridgestone runners contested the top six. There was a suggestion that teams could change the stressed tyre on safety grounds, but even then, there was a maximum tyre allocation given to teams. Having to change every 10 laps would clearly go beyond what was permitted in the rules. Everything suggested was instantly called a breach of the rules by the FIA, who expressed surprise that Michelin didn't have the right equipment for its competitors.

The FIA and Bridgestone were also firmly against the chicane idea, but the FIA were not the only sheriffs in town. Head of Formula One Management, Bernie Ecclestone, got nine out of 10 teams to agree to a chicane and even instructed the circuit to start building it. With two of the Bridgestone teams prepared to back the only method of holding a race, it all came down to the holdouts.

Ferrari hadn't won a race all season and felt the 'no tyre change' rule had been aimed not at cost-cutting but purely at stopping them winning for a sixth year in a row. The team were uninterested in creating a united front and declared the whole scandal nothing to do with them; it was up to the FIA to decide. With one hour to go, panic was setting in. Teams were still pushing for a chicane, but there were mere minutes left on the clock. Bridgestone-shod Minardi boss Paul Stoddart said: 'This is the time for F1 to come together as a sport and leave politics behind.'

For the seven teams, the situation was clear; they couldn't safely race without a chicane before turn 13. When attempts to construct one were made, FIA race director Charlie Whiting, taking orders from FIA president Max Mosley, who was in his back garden in England, instructed the circuit staff to stand down. The clock had run out. The instruction was given: all Michelin runners would have to enter the pit lane once the formation lap had ended.

F1 would be left with a six-car farce of a race.

David Coulthard said on the radio: 'If it comes down to my choice, I want to race.' He was overruled. The two Minardis, Jordans and Ferraris would battle for victory. The booing was the loudest Indianapolis had ever heard. Beer cans were launched onto the circuit. The atmosphere in the famous grandstands, which had been rebuilt for Formula One's arrival in 2000, was mutinous. After a minor battle with his team mate, Schumacher won the race, and later commented:

> This was a strange Grand Prix and it was odd seeing the other cars go into the pit lane at the start. The situation we had today was out of our hands and I don't know all the details of the problems the others had. But I do know that we left at home tyres that had more performance and less durability, but we and Bridgestone made our choice knowing how much stress there is here on the tyres.

It had nearly been a two-car race, but Jordan backed down from a deal to join the Michelin runners, and given both teams were fighting to avoid last place, Minardi had no choice but to join them. Tiago Monteiro for Jordan won the four-car battle for the season's most unlikely podium finisher, finishing 31 seconds ahead of his teammate, Narain Karthikeyan. Briefed behind the podium not to celebrate in front of the crowd, the Portuguese driver managed to contain himself for a few moments before the occasion overcame him, and he celebrated to a chorus of boos. Despite the fan reaction, he was forever able to call himself a Formula One podium finisher.

The headlines the next day were unsparing: 'Day of Shame for Formula One', 'Fans Outraged at Depleted Field', 'US Grand Prix Never Gets into Gear'. Afterwards, the FIA continued to bring the world's attention to the matter summoning the seven Michelin teams for not having suitable tyres for the race. A verdict was issued that if compensation was not agreed by September, severe penalties would be imposed. Michelin agreed compensation and 20,000 free tickets for 2006's race.

Not everyone was miserable. Someone in the media centre had seen the whole debacle coming and placed a bet on a Minardi or Jordan podium, and made a huge amount of money. The paddock accused Max Mosley of overplaying his hand.

F1 at this time faced a near constant breakaway threat from the manufacturers, and Mosley was determined to show F1 could continue without them. It was the fans who paid the price; tickets were refunded but accommodation was not, and the Indianapolis circuit had pulled the plug on its Formula One deal within two years of the debacle. It would take 15 years, and the timing of a global pandemic and docudrama series, to bring F1 into the American consciousness again.

The Rebirth of the Second Tier

In the early 2000s, the motorsports community was beginning to lose faith in junior motor racing.

After nearly two decades as the final stage before Formula One, it was time for it to stop being routinely ignored. Jenson Button's promotion to Formula One from third place in Formula Three had been a real warning sign. Button had bypassed Bruno Junqueira, proven in the second tier, straight to an F1 race seat for the 2000 season. Frank Williams had explained in 2000 that such was the collective embarrassment in the paddock of being caught unaware by Michael Schumacher's electrifying debut and talent, they never wanted the situation repeated. Schumacher had found his way to the grid by happenstance (*see* Chapter 38), and then gone on to beat the Williams team to two championships in 1994 and 1995.

If Button's promotion was notable, Sauber's elevation of Kimi Räikkönen straight out of Formula Renault seemed to threaten the whole fabric of junior motor racing. Kimi was dominating the championship. His manager persuaded Peter Sauber to run a full three-day test at the glorious Mugello circuit, and he quickly outpaced the team's current driver. Rather than offer Kimi a test drive, as had been expected, a race deal was drawn up. Peter Sauber assembled his team and informed them of his decision: 'We're going to hire the Eskimo.'

With this move, the junior ladder had fallen apart in the traditional sense and fears grew that F1 teams, desperate to beat each other to the next big name, could punt on talent that simply wasn't ready. Bernie Ecclestone knew F1 needed a new junior series in 2003, after watching drivers get hired from F3, Formula Renault and Formula Nippon (now Superformula). A replacement championship had to be created or the quality on the grid could not be guaranteed. Ecclestone turned to Renault F1 team principal Flavio Briatore and Bruno Michel.

The idea was a series far closer to what the drivers raced in Formula One, sold to teams and drivers as an F1 support race, as well as a feeder series; all events were to be on the F1 weekend in full view of the team principals. The new championship sprung into life in 2004, with Dallara commissioned to build the chassis for a car that could overtake easily and not suffer from dirty air from the car in front – something that blighted Formula One at the time. The engine would be from Renault, and the specification of a V8 power unit showed the intent of making the championship much closer to F1 in terms of lap time.

There were myriad ideas about the race format, but the idea of no qualifying seemed a classic ruse to generate headlines rather than anything under serious consideration. The announcement that F3000 would be replaced by a new series called GP2 came in 2004. But the final test session before the first race in the championship in April 2005 was pandemonium. There were problems with the gearboxes and electronics, and most worryingly the brakes kept failing. No one had completed a single race distance before the brakes 'exploded'.

First practice for the first race began with trepidation in the air. The electronics on the cars went crazy, and no representative running could be done by nine cars. It wasn't the best start, but things were rectified for qualifying – only for the brakes to start looking troublesome once again.

The first race was to be held in Imola. The calendar comprised 12 rounds, including a Feature and a Sprint race (apart from Monaco, which just ran a Feature race). The new GP2 era began with a rolling start due to fears over the clutches. It was a flimsy beginning, but the race was underway with a very talented field, including Nico Rosberg, son of Keke, the 1982 world champion, as well as Heikki Kovalainen, who was fresh from beating Michael Schumacher at the Race of Champions.

Then the brakes fell apart. Six cars retired, and Giorgio Pantano had to make two stops in order to finish. Heikki Kovalainen won by six seconds, but his drive had been overshadowed. The online reaction was brutal and the GP2 paddock was ablaze in rows. Championships can die very quickly if perceived to be implausible; despite the heavy hitters backing the Series, instant change was required.

Italian brake supplier Brembo thought this might happen and had a truck of replacements ready for the right price. Overnight, the brakes were changed for the entire field. Once the farce of Imola had been overcome, GP2's prominent place on the support bill, multiple races and highly raceable car, meant the championship would rapidly become the default final option before Formula One, in addition to enhancing the Grand Prix weekend for promoters, spectators and TV audiences. Paddock insiders believed the first race's very public troubles bound the personnel in the paddock together. Williams promoted the first champion, Nico Rosberg, to their race team for 2006.

Lewis Hamilton's arrival on the grid and spellbinding drives at Silverstone (where the whole grandstand at Stowe corner stood and applauded him after his double pass at Becketts) and Turkey enhanced the standing of the championship. Both Hamilton and the driver he beat to the title, Nelson Piquet Jr, were promoted. Within two seasons, GP2 had reestablished the natural order of the junior ladder. Many brilliant racers and races would follow, and every champion of the series would get a chance in a Formula One session, apart from 2012 champion Davide Valsecchi. He had to settle for the dubious runner-up prize of commentating with me in the championships' final season of 2016 before it was rebranded Formula Two.

Adrian Newey Goes for Dinner on the King's Road

The table had been booked for three – a meal that would change the destiny of nine drivers' titles in a single sitting.

Unbelievably, design genius Adrian Newey was back on the market. Well, possibly. With McLaren team bosses not providing Newey with enough ownership and space for innovation, Jaguar had nearly tempted him to leave in 2001. Four years later, the paddock knew there were frustrations barely hidden from the surface. Self-styled rock 'n' roll upstarts Red Bull Racing decided to test his resolve.

The new team really needed his signature. The UK-based, Austrian-owned outfit had been told to get their act together by the founder Dietrich Mateschitz. They'd had a ton of fun since they'd joined the sport, but budgets were high and, on track, they were downright uncompetitive. There were two routes to success in F1: hire a champion driver, or hire a design genius. With the key drivers under contract, they made their pitch.

Following advice from his driver David Coulthard, young Team Principal Christian Horner arranged a dinner for his driver and potential designer at the Bluebird restaurant on the famous King's Road in Chelsea, London. Horner had wisely delegated a potential hire to a driver with a greater standing in the sport, who had a previous working relationship with Newey from their seven years as colleagues at McLaren. The pitch: come and have fun; we'll let you design with total free rein.

It was a huge risk, but Newey was tempted. He'd enjoyed seeing Red Bull's less restrictive corporate atmosphere in the paddock and pit lane; it was as far from Ron Dennis' McLaren as you could get. Newey asked for a salary bigger than both the men finishing their desserts; he knew his worth and priced in the possibility that joining this start-up wouldn't work. It was so large a number that Horner had to take the request directly to Mateschitz. The Austrian couldn't believe the figure, but he wanted to win and he knew they may never have the chance to sign a designer of this calibre again.

Adrian Newey left the second most successful team in F1 history for a drink manufacturer that had never made a road car. It would prove a brilliant decision ... eventually.

Later, Newey admitted to expecting too much too soon from the young team that was still developing its infrastructure. No winning was done in the first three years, although Newey's design did win the Italian Grand Prix with the junior team, Toro Rosso.

The target was 2009, which provided another opportunity for Newey and his current team. But by then Honda and Brawn aerodynamicists had discovered a loophole that Newey had investigated but discarded because it appeared illegal – the double diffuser. Brawn dominated in the opening races of the year, but accusations of cheating led to an FIA investigation. Red Bull was the best of the cars without the double diffuser and would have benefited the most if it had been deemed illegal. Adrian Newey was not immune to studying other cars' approaches where necessary, and Red Bull went on to challenge Brawn GP. In the end, Jenson Button and Brawn went on to win both the drivers' and team championships in a remarkable debut, with young Red Bull driver Sebastian Vettel and his team in second place for both. While they may not have won, Red Bull had shown they could run at the front, and they'd made enough of a mark to be considered serious contenders for the first time, all because of the Bluebird dinner.

With a new exhaust-blown diffuser added to the car for 2010, and a young rookie superstar in the making in Sebastian Vettel, that was to be Red Bull's year – or years, as it turned out. The exhaust-blown diffuser blew exhaust gases into the diffuser as the throttle was pressed, with a feedback loop that the more throttle, the greater the downforce generated. The diffuser required a slightly different, almost counter-intuitive, style of driving that Vettel excelled at. Red Bull embarked on an era of dominance with four consecutive double title wins with Vettel.

'Let Newey be Newey' was the pitch; the entire trophy wall at their factory in Milton Keynes was the result.

Budapest – McLaren at War

It was a scene of total farce.

Ron Dennis, team boss of McLaren, slammed his headset down and put his head in his hands on the pit wall at the Hungaroring. His two drivers were openly warring.

Frustratingly, the problem was all of Dennis's own making. Back in 2005, behind the São Paulo podium, moments after Alonso had let fly the roar of a newly crowned world champion, Ron Dennis had enquired whether Fernando ever wanted to drive for McLaren. He was surprised in the moment of the championship triumph that the answer was an emphatic yes. What had started as a casual fish for information quickly turned into full negotiations for a three-year contract starting in 2007. Alonso would leave Renault for his childhood dream.

The team of Prost and Senna, who had inspired a generation, would welcome Fernando Alonso as its number one to lead the team to more championships. Unfortunately, in the year that followed, two things transpired that would cause the team to be run at a white-hot temperature. First, Alonso, still at Renault, won a second title in a superbly close championship with Michael Schumacher. Secondly, Lewis Hamilton's name started being linked to the other McLaren race seat. Hamilton had not even started GP2 when Dennis attempted to recruit Alonso, but soon he was the first rookie in a McLaren seat since Michael Andretti in 1993. Ron Dennis had inadvertently paired two of the greatest drivers in the history of the World Championship together again. No F1 fan needed reminding how the last pairing of titans had ended in 1989 (*see* Chapters 34 and 35). Dennis strode up the pit lane to the Hungaroring's parc fermé, where the cars that had qualified first and second were parked, and walked along with his arm resting on Alonso's trainer's shoulder, like an off-duty policeman who had caught a minor criminal. It was genteel and daft, but Dennis was caught in a storm.

Incredibly, this was only his second biggest problem. His biggest issue had been dubbed 'Spygate' by the press. McLaren's chief designer had been sent 780 pages of Ferrari car information by disgruntled senior staffer at the Scuderia. The World Motor Sport Council said there was 'insufficient evidence' that the material had been used on the McLaren's design; it was a perilous situation for McLaren, but they received no punishment from the FIA.

Ferrari were completely outraged, releasing a statement saying there was 'no logic' to the outcome. The matter would worsen considerably for McLaren after they lost control of their drivers in Budapest. At the start of the third part of qualifying, Hamilton had leapt to the front of the queue, ahead of Alonso, who was meant to be at the front as per McLaren's policy of alternating who left the pits first. Hamilton's engineer instructed him to let Alonso through as the latter furiously ranted on the radio to get the cars back into the agreed order.

Formula One had adopted a strange rule that required the cars to burn off fuel before getting whatever fuel was used back for the start of the race. This reads like complete madness because it was. The upshot was, if you went first in Q3, you could dictate the pace, burn off most of your fuel to make your car as light and quick as possible for the timed lap on Saturday, all while getting the fuel back for the race so you could run a longer first stint. It was best for the drivers to go first in qualifying, which is why McLaren alternated. But that was a policy, not a hard-and-fast rule, and Hamilton took matters into his own hands.

Ron Dennis radioed Hamilton, but the 2007 rookie ignored him too. This was part of a battle over Alonso demanding number-one status, having been signed as the champion. Hamilton was fighting for his right to be equal number one and was forcing the issue by deliberately ignoring team orders. Hamilton's tactic worked. He was the fastest on first flying laps, with a 1:19:781, but with the fuel-burning-off gimmick, the last lap would always be fastest. Alonso slowed on track, and when he pitted for a new set of tyres he was ahead of Hamilton at the McLaren pit. McLaren planned to hold Alonso for 20 seconds for optimum placement on track for the flying laps.

But when Alonso's countdown ended, he sat there with the lollipop pit signal raised to tell him to go. He was deploying tactics of his own. Rather than accept second and argue it later, Alonso continued to sit there, questioning whether he had the right tyres. Having bought time, he then drove off out of the pits to begin his final lap. Hamilton no longer had enough time to get round and start a second flying lap, and initially thought the team was punishing him, especially when Dennis barked on the radio: 'That's what happens when you don't do as you're told!'

Alonso had calculated in real-time the exact number of seconds needed to get out so he could set a lap, and then produced a standard of driving good enough to take pole; it was a remarkable display of mental and physical sporting and tactical ability.

After an argument with Hamilton, Dennis began his march to parc fermé to speak to the Alonso team. McLaren were now in crisis management as they faced the entire world's media, ready to grill the three men about the farce that had taken place. Ron Dennis began his explanation: 'We are trying our hardest to balance these pressures.' Hamilton questioned the time Alonso waited, but it was clear the younger driver's disobedience towards the team had stemmed from the Monaco Grand Prix, where he'd been issued with a team order to hold fire and finish second to Alonso.

At the Monaco press conference, Hamilton acknowledged his position: 'It is something I have to live with. I've number two on my car and I am the number two driver.' Alonso had taken pole and controlled the race and was furious that a narrative was being constructed that he'd only won because of team orders. When Dennis told him he'd had to handle things from the pit wall, Alonso became enraged that his win was being publicly tarnished. At that moment, Alonso was at war not with his teammate but with the CEO of McLaren.

Back in Budapest, race day brought chaos. First, Alonso was given a five-place grid penalty for impeding Hamilton; next, McLaren was barred from scoring any constructors' points due to the ongoing Spygate scandal. Alonso called the penalty for impeding 'funny' and accused the stewards of determining the race result.

Behind the scenes, Dennis and Alonso were arguing with unprecedented ferocity. Alonso wanted a team punishment towards Hamilton, and it is widely accepted that the disgruntled driver mentioned the Spygate scandal during this argument. Ron Dennis called in Martin Whitmarsh, his number two, and asked Alonso to repeat his statement. Next, Alonso was benched – McLaren couldn't allow the driver to race for them given his mindset. FIA president Mosley insisted Alonso race, however, given not allowing him to drive could decide the nature of the Formula One World Championship via politics rather than on track. With tensions at fever pitch, Alonso backed down and apologized, finishing fourth as Hamilton cruised to an easy win. But the damage done to all parties was immense.

The relationship between McLaren's star drivers had fallen apart in just 11 races. Alonso would lose the 2007 championship by one point. He would have to leave the team and return to an uncompetitive Renault, losing his shot at the 2008 World Championship – which would become Lewis Hamilton's first. In 2009, neither McLaren nor Renault had the car to fight for the title, but other teams appeared to be extremely wary of signing Alonso. McLaren were later fined an enormous $100 million at a second hearing in the Spygate scandal. Dennis and Mosley's decade-long animosity towards each other added another dramatic chapter, as the fine was accompanied with Mosley's outrageous one-liner: 'It's $5 million for the offence and $95 million for being a ****.'

Kubica – The Man Who Could Have Challenged Alonso and Hamilton

In June 2007, Robert Kubica, suffered a horrifying crash at the Circuit Gilles Villeneuve in Montreal with BMW Sauber.

It was an accident in which the first Polish driver to race in Formula One was lucky to emerge relatively unscathed, let alone return from it a few weeks later. A junior racing contemporary of Lewis Hamilton and Nico Rosberg, Kubica had started his karting career in Italy and gone on to race in Formula Renault and Formula Three. He took up the reserve driver position at BMW Sauber before replacing 1997 world champion Jacques Villeneuve in a full-time seat halfway through 2006.

On lap 27, Kubica's awful accident occurred. The cameras cut to the smash mid-hit, the car exploding off a concrete wall and shunting to the other side of the circuit so quickly it was reduced to its survival cell, with Kubica's feet protruding from the end of the car's monocoque.

The man from Poland was only in his second year as a Formula One driver when he suffered his massive crash. At the kink just before the turn 10 hairpin, Kubica had clipped the back of Jarno Trulli's Toyota. This lost him downforce and sent him onto the grass, where the car became airborne. So serious was the impact, the world waited with bated breath for the announcement that Kubica was alive, as he was stretchered away from the crash.

Remarkably, this would not be the defining crash of Robert Kubica's F1 career. After missing one race in Indianapolis, he returned to complete the season, as rapid as ever. A year later and redemption at the St Lawrence River awaited. After Lewis Hamilton had hit Kimi Räikkönen at the end of the pit lane under a red light, Kubica controlled the race from the front to give Poland, Sauber, BMW and the Kubica family their landmark breakthrough win. Improbably, he had gone from the medical centre to the top of the World Championship in one calendar year.

Sadly, for Kubica and his ever-present army of Polish fans at the circuit, BMW would simply call the shots wrong in the following weeks, the board deciding resources should be diverted not to winning that year's championship but focusing on the following year's set of regulations. It was a decision that dismayed Kubica who knew that chances at the championship were never given and easily squandered. BMW were soundly beaten to the best 2009 car design, and after the worldwide financial crisis of 2008 the famous brand withdrew from the sport just 13 months after leading the World Championship. It left Kubica shuffled into the pack playing glorious cameos in a sport where he should have been a protagonist.

Kubica transferred to the ailing Renault team, who had been champions four years previously but had struggled since. Without a car to compete regularly, he was still able to stand out. His qualifying 2010 lap in Monaco placed a car that really had no right to contend at the front in the battle for pole position. Later in the season, his qualifying performance in Japan was astounding. He couldn't talk after Suzuka as he was so moved by what he'd done with a limited car; it was only fourth place but he'd found access to 'the zone'. This is the place that Niki Lauda said left him shaking at Monaco in the 1970s, the vein of form that caused Lewis Hamilton to drop to his haunches at Silverstone in 2018, the realm that Senna called 'the tunnel', where the road feels like one straight line. The state they can go to because of their ability.

The drivers knew Kubica could access that ability. Two-time champion Fernando Alonso said, 'I'll think [he's the best] because he won all the smaller categories.' Lewis Hamilton called him 'One of the most talented drivers that I had the pleasure of racing against.'

But despite the ferocity of his crash in 2007, the crash that defined Robert Kubica's career was, in fact, on a rally stage. At the opening stage of the Ronde di Andora rally held in February 2011, Kubica suffered life-changing injuries. He lost control of his Skoda Fabia and once again hit a wall at high speed. This caused the car to smash into a guardrail that ended up piercing the car's cockpit. While his co-driver walked away, Kubica had severe injuries all the way down his right side from his toes up, with his right forearm nearly severed. Rescuers worked for an hour to free him before he was taken to hospital for his first of 18 operations. The first operation took 12 hours, he suffered 42 fractures and lost three-quarters of his blood. It took Kubica six to seven months to recover feeling on the right side of his body.

The bitter irony of that event: Kubica had not even been sure he should compete. He had initially accepted and then got cold feet. Once he had been told Pirelli was arranging tyres and the roads were blocked for testing, it became difficult to keep saying no, despite the risk to his Formula One career. In the end, he took the gamble, hoping this would improve his driving overall. A great driver through and through, he was inspired by a compulsion to constantly improve.

In rallying, drivers are expected to contend with difficult driving conditions such as rain and snow and simply persevere through with going sideways – this allows drivers to hone an incredible feel at the wheel in challenging conditions, which Kubica believed would help him in Formula One.

The recovery was as intense as it was brutal. It took two years for Kubica to return to any form of racing after the accident, starting with the discipline that had caused the crash: rallying. In later years, it emerged that Kubica had signed with Ferrari for 2012. It would have been his first stint with a legendary established front runner, and he would have partnered with the great Fernando Alonso – it would have been an incredible driver pairing. It wasn't to be, and it is fair to say Formula One had lost a probable champion to injury for the first time since the 1980s.

In the following seasons, Robert had recovered the use of his arm, but the movement was severely restricted for what a racing driver requires from the flexibility of the wrist, forearm and hand. Incredibly, after years of rumours, in 2019 he joined Williams back on the Formula One grid. But sadly the car was a long way off the back of the pack, and he scored the team's single point of the season at Hockenheim. To even make it back on track with a backmarker team, however, is a testament to his grit, determination and talent as a driver.

While the tight confines of a single-seater proved troublesome to Kubica, a sports car offered slightly more space to operate. He finally joined Ferrari in the World Endurance Championship in 2024, seeking to close the 'open wound' that the missed chance with the Scuderia represented to him.

A year later, Robert Kubica, who watched others win while he was operated upon, began the final lap of the Le Mans 24 hours in the lead. He let no emotion creep in, for he'd lost a LMP2 win on the final tour in 2021 which had only added more heartbreak, but three minutes later he could revel in the moment. He took his Number 83 Ferrari through the famous final corners having driven 44 per cent of the race distance, in one final act of heroism. He had dreamed of F1 victory in Ferrari red, but his comeback for the ages, was won in Modena yellow, the colour of the badge, the home colours of the founder. The completion of a journey, Enzo would have tipped his hat to.

59

Vettel Becomes the Youngest Winner ... With the B Team

It hadn't rained at Monza for decades on a Grand Prix Sunday.

The traditional dappled light of autumn in the former royal park was snuffed out by the dreadful weather that was set for the weekend. After sodden conditions for practice and qualifying, race day again was gloomily grey and damp. What would follow would confuse and astound as Sebastian Vettel rewrote the record books.

Crucially, the race started behind the safety car, removing the risk of any manic first-lap accidents, which Monza had a long and sometimes dangerous history of. After two laps, the pack was released with Vettel leading pre-race favourite, Heikki Kovalainen of McLaren, who had started in second place. Toro Rosso had been showing real glimmers of progress in recent times and looking out for Vettel's giant-killing qualifying performances had become a fun subplot in the middle of a championship battle between Kimi Räikkönen, Felipe Massa and Lewis Hamilton.

The engineers had been joking about going for pole, and it was a joke because Toro Rosso was effectively a customer team. They ran tech from senior team Red Bull with a customer old Ferrari engine and no one had fought at the front with one of those. Ever. In the entire history of the sport no one had ever won a Grand Prix with a customer Ferrari engine. The Toro Rosso was just one of those cars that came alive in wet conditions, as the previous week's results in Belgium showed. Fifth for Vettel and seventh place for Sebastian Bourdais, who had again underlined the car's speed in the rain by placing fourth in qualifying. Vettel had stunned the pack with a time good enough for pole by seven-hundredths of a second.

Vettel was a highly rated prospect. Originally a young BMW driver, the German marque had released him from a contract when a race seat had materialized in the middle of 2007, after Toro Rosso team boss Franz Tost and then driver Scott Speed extraordinarily had a physical fight in the garage and the American had been sacked with immediate effect.

Out front, the young German driver's strong start had been converted into a commanding 12-second lead. The Toro Rosso team began looking for threats on a one-stop strategy, as the two stoppers had no answer to his lap times. It was all so muted from the championship contenders: Massa would finish sixth, Hamilton only seventh from 15th on the grid to maintain his championship lead. The rain finally eased by lap 36, when it was time for Vettel to face the final hurdle in his bid to make history. Would the different tyre change the picture drastically? Kovalainen was finally able to fire up his brakes and tyre temperature but it was too late, the gap was too big; he could only match Vettel's times but not beat them.

Vettel's greater command of the fully wet conditions had built him a vital buffer. Kubica would complete the podium with a well-judged strategy and drive. But to the general bewilderment of Formula One, Vettel's win was never in doubt; he'd completed a near faultless 53 laps with only a trip over the run-off at the Roggia. Vettel crossed the line a full 12 seconds ahead to become Formula One's youngest ever race winner at twenty-three years and 134 days old, giving the small Toro Rosso team a maiden victory. The achievement was a truly astonishing result considering the teams former guise of Minardi, known for always being at the back. The team had never set foot on the podium, let alone the top step.

Now the crucial caveat: Adrian Newey had designed the chassis. Back in 2008, the rules were slightly more open then for what could be bought and sold, leaving the A team (Red Bull) to watch on as the former backmarkers entered a dreamland.

Vettel himself was a hugely popular winner, and the post-race podium was delayed as every driver congratulated him. Vettel exclaimed, 'It's the best day of my life. These emotions I will never forget. It's so much better than you might imagine it is. I must say a big, big thank-you to all the guys working in the team – we never thought about this at the beginning of the season.'

The 'guys in the team' were in disbelief; some had spent two decades going racing where a point would be celebrated like a title. Luca Badoer had wept like a child after retiring from a would-be fourth place at the Nürburgring in 1999 – that result would have caused a riot in the garage – and the win seemed almost too much. Massimo Rivola, the team manager, who had also been at Minardi, summed it up: 'It's just unbelievable, Sebastian wrote something into Formula One history today. We always dream of a podium and the first podium is P1 in Monza – the most amazing racetrack in the world.'

The raw emotion poured out in a dream day for the Faenza-based team who could now call themselves winners. Awkwardly, they could do this before the senior Red Bull squad had managed it. Vettel would sort that statistic out seven races later, again in the rain, with a first Red Bull victory in China, having graduated for the 2009 season. The Italian breakthrough win would place Vettel's confidence sky-high for his Red Bull years. He'd go on to win four of the next six World Championships before leaving for Ferrari, where the same ironclad confidence in his performance never quite matched that damp, delirious day at the Temple of Speed.

Brawn's Two Titles – Won in Translation

Junior aerodynamicist Masayuki Minagawa was certain he'd found the most prized possession for an engineer in Formula One: a loophole.

For 2009, new sweeping technical regulations were introduced with the aim to clean up the dirty air generated by the cars' increasingly impressive F1 performance. The newfound speed was coming at the cost of the car being able to overtake and a new blank sheet of paper aimed to reduce aerodynamic performance. The engineer's job was to circumvent this. For the Honda team, the new rule book could not come soon enough. Having achieved a breakthrough win in 2006 with Jenson Button, the 2007 and 2008 seasons had been miserable. The team had only avoided back-to-back ninth place finishes in the championship after McLaren were disqualified in 2007.

All efforts turned to the rules reset in 2009. It was crucial the team found answers or Honda's funding of the outfit would be called into question – people's jobs were on the line. Early in 2008, all the engineering knowledge in the team was focused on the newly written technical regulations.

Despite being owned outright by Honda for three years, the design and build of the car was conducted from the Brackley factory in the UK. Japanese-based Honda engineers worked on a campus in Tochigi, Japan, where Honda's research and development centre was based. It left the Japanese engineers making long trips to the glamour of Northamptonshire at crucial moments of the season. There was a feeling at Honda that their ideas were ignored by the UK arm of the team. UK-based Honda head of aerodynamics, Atsushi Ogawa, sent a plea to his staff in Japan: 'Send me your ideas, handwritten or anything. I want to show them Tochigi's presence,' he later recalled.

Amid the avalanche of ideas sent, one stood above the rest. It claimed to increase downforce generated from the floor of the car by up to five times that of a single-decker diffuser. The hand-drawn designs attracted buzz back at Brackley, with every possible innovation needed to try to catch the teams at the front. Minagawa was flown to the UK in the summer of 2008 to explain his concept further. With promising signs for the 2009 car, the move was made permanent from November, where Honda had just concluded the 2008 season without scoring points in the final nine races. Worryingly, even competitive big factory teams like BMW, who at one point in June had led the championship, had elected to ignore their chance at the 2008 championship and focus development on the new generation of rules.

Mere weeks later, the future of Honda was thrown into disarray despite hugely promising wind tunnel numbers and the real possibility of a Honda car fighting at the front once again. The Honda board had withdrawn from the Formula One World Championship on 5 December 2008, with immediate effect. The company could not be seen to be spending $300 million a year on motor racing, not when the organization would need to go through many thousands of redundancies in response to the world financial crisis. While other manufacturers knew they would have to withdraw for similar reasons in the coming years, the speed of Honda's withdrawal stunned Formula One and the 750 staff employed by the project.

In the factory, there was a cruelty to the uncertainty as CEO Nick Fry and Team Principal Ross Brawn searched for buyers and backers for the team to no avail. There was a real chance Masayuki Minagawa's idea might never see the light of day, but until they were told there was no hope, they would have to continue work as normal. The original hand-drawn idea had evolved and adapted.

The first pre-season test was in Bahrain on 16 February. Still without any backers, Fry and Brawn began to consider a management buyout of the team. They pitched to Honda that instead of spending $90 million on closedown costs, they hand that budget directly to them and go racing for one more season, buying time to facilitate a sale. Honda agreed, as some internally wondered if they had been hasty in instantly withdrawing, given both Toyota and BMW remained for 2009.

Overnight, the team had gone from the luxury of massive numbers to an independent team with a budget a third of the size of all front runners. Wrappers were saved, parts that were normally thrown away kept and refurbished. The culture shock of penny-pinching created a renewed team spirit, but despite Honda's hospitable approach in their business dealings, they drew the line at selling the engine. The independent team would need a new power unit, for a car that was designed around an entirely different one.

With Toyota and BMW openly considering quitting at the end of 2009, Formula One needed every team it could get, especially during a time of political power struggle. The teams had grouped together to form the Formula One Teams Association with the aim of gaining a greater revenue share from Formula One. With the FIA potentially losing three teams, this could mean a total disbanding of the resistance movement and the end of any hopes for a new deal. The upshot of this was McLaren was prepared to waive its exclusive rights to Mercedes engines; this was especially useful as the Mercedes was closest in size to the original Honda design and this meant minimal redesigns.

When the car hit the track at the Stowe Circuit at Silverstone, a tiny ribbon of tarmac used as a car park on British Grand Prix weekend, the question was: would the car work with the new engine? After the system checks, the most basic fears were allayed.

The car worked, the team would continue and the double diffuser would see the light of day. The team even had a name! Brawn GP began life on 6 March 2009 and was heading to Barcelona for testing.

When Brawn in a striking white and luminous yellow livery rolled onto the track, the paddock noted it was the third team to use a double diffuser. Williams and Toyota had also spotted the loophole – angry noises began to emanate from the seven teams without the design innovation. The grumpiness was not helped when Brawn's suspected light fuel running in testing turned out to be nothing of the sort. The doubted data of the three wind tunnels was accurate. Brawn GP would start their first race from first and second on the grid, with Jenson Button aiming for just a second career victory.

Button controlled the race from start to finish, with Robert Kubica's charging BMW colliding with Sebastian Vettel with just a few laps remaining. It meant Brawn started life in F1 with a one–two finish. Brawn had won, but would they keep it? Seven teams appealed the results.

Inter-team relations were not helped by Jenson Button winning in Malaysia, opening up a commanding championship lead over the rest. A hearing was set for 14 April. The diffuser innovation, which as part of a strong overall package had created a Formula One fairytale the like of which was thought to have been consigned to the past, was on the line. If the appeal was successful, Brawn would not only lose the wins but would face another season in the doldrums with the entire car concept designed around a banned part and chances of selling the team severely diminished.

Far from the usual stuffy affairs of the appeal court hearings, Ferrari's lawyer went for the jugular immediately. Nigel Tozzi accused Brawn of being 'a person of supreme arrogance', which was a slight departure from Ferrari's opinion from 1997–2007 when he helped them win 11 championships as sporting director. Fireworks aside, the appeal looked unlikely to succeed because the grey area in the rules had first been discussed by teams in 2008 but, unable to get agreement from all 10 teams, the design offices had had to make a judgment call on the legality of the part.

Ferrari's lawyer returned to argue: 'The position of the FIA is baffling ... Anyone with a command of English will tell you it's a hole ... The appeal is not because we have not made the most of an opportunity, but because Brawn, Toyota and Williams have not acted within the regulations.'

The judges disagreed: the Brawn was declared legal. They kept the wins and their championship dream was on. The other seven teams scrambled to redesign their floors and gain back the ground.

Brawn would win six of the first seven races. Just six months after the ruling, in a day of delirium in São Paulo, Jenson Button claimed the drivers title as Brawn became the first constructor to win the title in their first year of competition. Ferrari's lawyer wasn't completely off the mark, though. The Japanese version of the FIA rules was believed to be behind the original discovery of the idea. For Brawn GP it meant two titles won in translation.

A Crazy Bridgestone Race Defines an Entire Era

In 2010, a brilliant Grand Prix at the Circuit Gilles Villeneuve led to a change of tyre philosophy.

The change continues to have ramifications for how the drivers operate in races to this day.

Formula One returned to Canada after a year's absence after a dispute over money left the event off the calendar for the first time since 1987. One year on, with new funding secured, the teams and drivers convened in Montreal in the middle of a hugely competitive season.

The year 2010 had seen a return to form for McLaren and Ferrari, but Red Bull continued to keep pace with their Newey-designed car at the front. The Brawn GP had been bought by Mercedes but a lack of development in 2009 saw them drop into the mid-pack. The rule book was also vastly different. Refuelling was banned for the first time since 1993. That meant racing from lights to chequered flag on one tank. The car got quicker as the fuel burned off throughout the race; it also made tyre life and tyre management key. Strategy became far more uniform – gone were the bold three-stop strategies with flat-out attacking laps throughout. One-stops became the norm as the teams tried to minimize the time lost in the pit lane.

The lack of a race in Montreal in 2009 had given the opportunity for the circuit to be resurfaced in areas where the tarmac had shown signs of breaking up in both the 2007 and 2008 races. The circuit was subject to brutal Quebec winters, and the nature of the short and slow corners meant traction areas always took punishment. The new surface was in place for 2010.

The Red Bull vs Ferrari vs McLaren title battle continued as the first non-Red Bull pole of the year was taken by Lewis Hamilton in a McLaren. But the result wasn't completely straightforward as the tyres were behaving erratically. Practice on Friday had shown signs of extreme tyre wear, with a huge pace performance drop of six to seven seconds after just a few laps of pushing the super soft tyre. Red Bull had played it safe and put both cars, Sebastian Vettel and Mark Webber, on medium tyres, sacrificing their one-lap performance for more durable rubber.

The qualifying rules of the day required you to start the race on the set you achieved your best time on. Everyone else knew there would be trouble if you started on the super softs but considered that a pesky Sunday problem and qualified on the grippy tyre anyway. It left a grid of Lewis Hamilton in pole, with Sebastian Vettel next to him on the front, followed by Fernando Alonso in a Ferrari and Jenson Button in the other McLaren, with Mark Webber in seventh after taking a five-place gearbox penalty. The resurfacing of the track combined with harder compounds brought by Bridgestone and cool early weekend temperatures meant there was plenty of relief when Sunday turned out to be sunny.

The early stages saw Hamilton lead away before the inevitable tyre drop-off began for the super soft runners. Drivers on that tyre began pitting for new rubber as early as lap 5, which was around when Hamilton stopped looking out of the front of his car and drove on his mirrors, with Vettel on the much better tyre just a few minutes into the race. On lap 7, Hamilton pitted from the lead with Alonso right behind him as Vettel was promoted to an expected lead with Red Bull teammate Webber in second. Then the twist of the race as medium-shod Robert Kubica's Renault peeled into the pits on lap 9, barely going longer into the race than super soft runners. Both Bridgestone compounds were working well below operating temperature. The surface tread of the tyre was tearing apart in a handful of laps.

Which created happy racing chaos. Out front, Vettel and Webber soon hit the end of the tyre life and the drop-off was so severe the pack of Alonso, Hamilton and Button caught them rapidly, negating the early stop. Vettel took his tyres to lap 13; Webber to lap 14. Re-emerging on track, Vettel had been somewhat confused about the competitive picture. He asked his engineer, Rocky, 'Do I have to overtake Button on track for the win?' 'Yes, Button and the three cars ahead of him,' came the reply, to Vettel's unfiltered fury.

Webber was lumped onto the mediums as Vettel was put on the racing super softs, like those ahead of him. Alonso had brilliantly jumped Hamilton at the first round of stops but found himself shuffled off the racing line, trying to get past the Toro Rosso of Buemi who'd gone super long on his tyres. Hamilton pounced, taking a crucial lead of the race. Hamilton, Alonso, Button and Vettel all pitted on lap 28. This promoted Webber from seventh on the grid to the race lead, the fourth different leader of the race as he attempted to keep his medium tyres working.

On lap 50, his efforts were for nothing as Hamilton retook the lead on track, and Webber's long stint ended with new rubber in the pit lane. Old teammates and rivals, Hamilton and Alonso pushed each other as far as they dared – trying to balance tyre life with track position. Alonso then again found himself blocked by a backmarker as Jenson Button used the chance to try to take the victory. In the end, Hamilton took the win, revelling, as he told the post-race press conference:

> It was an incredibly challenging afternoon, especially in the last 20 laps, when I was trying to look after my tyres while also keeping Jenson and Fernando behind me. It wasn't easy, I can tell you that! This track is unique; you really have to look after your tyres, and it's so hard to

know how long you can make them last. Fernando put a lot of pressure on me. We had a really good battle. It was such a sensational feeling to cross the line.

That sensational feeling was shared by spectators both at the circuit and watching on TV. So popular was the race, F1 bosses set about trying to recreate it. Bernie Ecclestone asked incoming tyre supplier, Pirelli, if it could engineer a tyre that could recreate the type of race seen in Canada 2010. Pirelli Head of Motorsport Paul Hembrey said later in the year, 'We can happily make a tyre that would last the whole race and not degrade, but we need to balance that with a good show.'

The product created was unlike anything Formula One had seen in the single-tyre era bar one race. Less durable by design, the first race of 2011 saw every car forced into at least two stops aside from Sergio Perez, who would build his early career on making the Pirelli rubber last longer than seemingly anyone else could. With the advent of DRS, the number of overtakes exploded, doubling from 2010 to 2011. Few drivers were happy, complaining of the dreaded 'cliff edge'.

For three years, the conversation often centred around the durability of the Pirelli tyres but the tyre manufacturer pointed to the brief they were given. The legacy continues to the present day with drivers still reminded on the radio to slowly bring the rubber up to temperature after a pit stop, and out-and-out pushing is rarely possible unless a certain combination of track and low temperature combine. It was a total fluke of timing, temperature and brilliant racing that decided the direction of Formula One for a decade and a half.

Lewis and Niki Chat in Singapore

In 2012, the one-time F1 world champion Lewis Hamilton was mulling over his racing future.

Having spent his entire racing life with the front-running McLaren Formula One team through their junior programme, he was now considering which team would give him the best opportunity to try to win his second title.

It was a decision that weighed heavily, and he couldn't afford to get it wrong. With a looming rule change, multiple titles were at stake. Hamilton had watched Fernando Alonso fail to add a title in the six years that followed his second triumph. He had seen Alonso's ability first-hand and was acutely aware that a switch to the wrong team could cost you dearly, regardless of talent behind the wheel. Hamilton was computing this weighty decision while contending for the 2012 World Championship.

Hamilton had instructed his management to scope out where was available for the forthcoming seasons. When it became clear that Red Bull had no interest in paying him the salary his standing required, choosing instead to promote internally from junior team Toro Rosso, it left Hamilton with two front-running contract options. He could remain with McLaren, who had guided his entire career, or move to Mercedes. The German manufacturer had failed to recreate the title-winning heights of the fairytale 2009 Brawn GP season after purchasing the team's facilities at the end of that season. In fact, since Mercedes had taken over, the team had won just once, in China with Nico Rosberg.

Leading the charge to sign Hamilton for Mercedes was a Formula One giant. Niki Lauda was a three-time F1 world champion who had redefined what a human being was capable of behind the wheel of a racing car, defying both odds and logic to return so quickly after his sickening fiery accident at the Nürburgring in 1976. He recovered to win a second championship in 1977, and after a short retirement won his third title against the quickest driver at the time. So far, he is the only driver in history to win the title for both McLaren and Ferrari.

Lauda had nothing to prove after his era-defining driving career, but objectively he had failed as a team executive. In his second stint with Ferrari in 1992–5, he had fallen out spectacularly with Team Principal Jean Todt before losing a political power struggle for control of the famous F1 team. When ousted, he declared to Austrian television, 'Ferrari will never be successful with Todt in charge.' Lauda could only watch as Todt-led Ferrari then dominated the sport, claiming the Drivers' and Constructors' Championships from 1999–2004 in an unprecedented run of success. In 2001, Lauda was appointed the team principal of the Ford-owned Jaguar team, only to be fired 16 months later. Here was another missed opportunity at team management level.

With 44-year-old Michael Schumacher uncertain about continuing, Mercedes dared to dream big. An all-German line-up was discussed, potentially elevating the highly rated Nico Hulkenberg to a team of super Nicos, but Lauda believed if Mercedes could sign a driver of Hamilton's calibre, success would finally be assured at executive level. Asking Hamilton to leave McLaren would have to be a truly compelling offer pitched by a heavyweight – there were few people in F1 who fitted the bill.

Hamilton was initially sceptical when he was informed Lauda wanted to pitch to him. He believed the Austrian didn't have a very high opinion of him and was uncertain around Lauda, given comments he'd made as TV pundit for the German RTL channel. Another big F1 beast, Ross Brawn had started the overtures to get

Hamilton on board, as Brawn sensed his long-time collaborator Michael Schumacher losing motivation to compete at the highest level as he approached his mid-forties. Hamilton headed into the Singapore weekend tempted by the new start. But McLaren still had those engines, and having spent his career with the team as early as go-karts, he was leaning towards staying.

The five lights went out in Singapore and Hamilton needed the win. He'd retired from two of the last four Grands Prix leaving him 37 points adrift of Fernando Alonso, with 25 points for a win. With Alonso's points advantage and Red Bull's strength at developing the car deep into a season, Hamilton had to convert any race he started on pole from. Then at lap 23, while leading, the sickening crunch of a gearbox failure and retirement could be heard. Another victory had slipped away: 52 points back with just six races to go. The 2012 title was gone; thoughts about his future intensified.

Ross Brawn had impressed the Hamiltons by visiting Lewis' mother's house for tea. There he had outlined the plan he was implementing, underscoring what he had achieved during the last regulation reset and sharing Mercedes' belief they had mastered the complex power unit regulations for the 2014 season. Brawn spoke to Hamilton's head, Lauda to Hamilton's heart. To the astonishment of the 2012 paddock, it was announced Hamilton would join Mercedes in a multi-year deal. The prevailing opinion was he'd made a mistake.

Hamilton later reflected on his move. When paying tribute to Lauda, he stated, 'Probably the fondest memories I have are from my first conversations. We started talking some time in 2012 and I just remember being home during the day, having a call from Niki and he is trying to convince me to come to the team.'

With Lauda's and Brawn's input, Lewis escaped McLaren's decade of decline. Lauda had finally succeeded in the executive role at the third attempt, and Mercedes would dominate from 2014 to 2021.

By the time Hamilton left Mercedes at the end of the 2024 season, he had redefined what was possible with a team, setting the single team records for most wins (84), most poles (78), most podium finishes (153), most laps led (4,210) and most championships (6). In the first race after Lauda's passing, Hamilton stood on the streets of Monaco victorious, pointing to Niki's name on his crash helmet repainted in the colours of the great champion. Unlikely friends who won because of each other.

'Multi 21, Seb ... Multi 21'

In Malaysia, at the second race of the season in 2013, the on-track racing action strangely took a back seat to the drama on the team radio.

This is the story of 'Multi 21', Red Bull's code for 'Hold station and do not race each other.' It was terminology clearly known to both their drivers, Sebastian Vettel and Mark Webber, and the firmest instruction the team could issue.

Formula One arrived in Malaysia off the back of a thrilling season opener in Australia. The race had been won by 2007 world champion Kimi Räikkönen after making a one-stop strategy work when other teams and drivers had chewed through their tyres. It was a fine victory, his second since leaving Ferrari in 2009. Naturally, the rest of the paddock had responded to this Lotus victory by furiously complaining about the state of the Pirelli tyres. It then rained in Q3, giving everyone a break from the tyre chat and a grid of Vettel on pole ahead of Massa, Alonso, Hamilton and Webber. The start was wet as well, with the whole field on intermediate tyres. Alonso tagged the back of Sebastian Vettel into turn 2, leaving Vettel's car undamaged but breaking the front wing of the Ferrari. With the track expected to dry in around five minutes' time, Ferrari took the unusual decision to keep Alonso out with a clearly broken front wing. It didn't pay off – at the start of lap 2, it shattered, lodging underneath the car and sending Alonso deep into the gravel and out of the race.

The rain did relent as expected a few laps later. Vettel had gone for slicks a lap too soon, whereas teammate Webber timed things perfectly and took the lead on track. Something Vettel was not happy about on the radio: 'Mark is too slow, get him out of the way.' This was the beginning of an uncomfortable insight into the mentality required to win repeated championships. It was a dismissive remark born of an uneasy long-term rivalry with Webber. It had begun even before they were at the same team in 2007, when Vettel had hit Webber behind the safety car when the Australian was chasing his first win. Lewis Hamilton and Nico Rosberg in the Mercedes were close behind; Red Bull had no intention of seeing a big fight between its cars.

After Vettel had cleared Hamilton for second place, he set about closing the gap to Webber before the leader's final pit stop. But Webber emerged from the pits marginally ahead on his out lap and the two Red Bulls ran side by side for five corners, brilliantly fighting fairly for the lead. On lap 45, the team then issued the instruction 'Multi 21' to Vettel – code to hold position and call off his overtake attempts as Webber was ahead of Vettel. With the team's horrible tyre wear in Australia still front and centre of team consciousness, the decision was made to bank the points and ease away from Mercedes, who were also suffering from intense tyre degradation. They had to manage fuel after aggressively pursuing light cars for the start of the race.

Webber was then given the same message. When the call came, Webber was surprised because team orders had rarely worked in his favour. This included when he was the team's lead contender in 2010: Vettel was allowed to win the Brazilian Grand Prix, rather than supporting Webber's championship challenge against Ferrari's Fernando Alonso. Webber studied his teammate in his mirror, concluding he didn't look like a driver who had accepted the team order to settle for second. He wrote in his autobiography, 'I knew within two laps Vettel was going to take matters into his own hands.' Panic ensued on the Red Bull pit wall with Team Principal Horner directly intervening rather than leaving it to race engineer Guillaume Rocquelin. Horner tried to reason with his three-time champion: 'Come on Seb, we need to give him space. Hold position.'

This was roundly ignored, resulting in 'This is silly Seb, come on' being broadcast on the F1 world feed. In the mania, Webber had forgotten to turn his engine back up, allowing Vettel DRS and superior power. 'Yep, that's good teamwork,' Webber said as he was passed. 'He was told,' came the reply from the team. Vettel built a four-second gap to the flag, and huge anticipation built about how the two teammates would address the nonsense. It is the only time I can ever remember watching a Grand Prix hoping the race would hurry up and finish so we could get to the arguing.

When Vettel tried to approach Webber, Webber simply repeated 'Multi 21, Seb, Multi 21' with a venomous look. The podium interviews saw Vettel use his media training to avoid creating any more news. Webber, meanwhile, was customarily more straightforward telling the world the full story, which hadn't been immediately obvious with the team radio messages in the way it would be in a modern broadcast. The team had called the fight off but he expected nothing would happen as Vettel 'would have protection, as usual' – a less than subtle message for senior adviser Helmut Marko, who stood beneath the podium.

The backlash dawned on Vettel by the time he sat in the press conference. Sebastian was suddenly very uncomfortable with how everything had played out, calling it a 'big mistake' and saying he wanted to apologize: 'If I had the chance to do it again I would do it differently.' Webber sat listening in a cold fury and was directly questioned about his future in Formula One: 'My mind was thinking many things,' he said.

At the next Grand Prix, Vettel further inflamed matters by performing a complete about-turn on his previous position, saying the comments Webber had made on the podium had made him 'lose respect for him as a man'. When asked now if he would do it again, he said he would, as he felt Mark didn't deserve the win. Behind the scenes, it emerged Vettel saw Malaysia as his payback for the season decider in Brazil the previous year. Vettel felt Webber hadn't played the team game by squeezing him at the start before he was spun at turn 4, in a moment that could have cost him the World Championship. His approach was unpopular – Vettel would be booed on podiums for the rest of the year even as he claimed his fourth consecutive Drivers' Championship – winning the last nine races in a row.

Both drivers were paid a win bonus at the behest of CEO and owner Deitrich Materschitz, who was unimpressed with the whole debacle. The incident set a train of events in motion leading to Webber's retirement from F1, with his replacement and fellow Australian, Daniel Ricciardo, soundly beating Vettel in 2014. This led to Vettel leaving Red Bull for Ferrari where his career would never hit the same heights. Ignoring 'Multi 21' would have decade-long repercussions.

64

Claire Takes Over Williams

**Frank Williams set up his second
racing team in 1977 alongside engineer
and designer Patrick Head.**

Two years later, the team won their first Grand Prix in 1979 at the British Grand Prix. They have gone on to be the second-tied most successful Formula One team, only behind Ferrari, having won nine Constructors' and seven Drivers' titles. The success came with its own share of heartache such as Frank's serious car accident in 1986 that left him wheelchair bound and the death of Ayrton Senna in 1994. By 2012, Frank stepped down from managing the team day to day. His daughter Claire Williams took over running the team with the title of deputy team principal in March 2013. Frank retained the title of team principal. Following in the footsteps of Monisha Kaltenborn at Sauber, Claire is one of only two women to have run a Formula One team.

The Williams team had always been something of a family affair. Claire's mother Ginny was known to have funded her husband's racing career if money was ever in short supply and was pivotal to the survival of the team after Frank's accident (*see* Chapter 32). Claire had spent summer holidays working for Williams, even booking flight tickets for the mechanics. She officially joined in 2002 as the communication officer, then worked her way to becoming the team's commercial director, leading marketing, communications and sponsorship. On her appointment, her father said: 'I know the future of Williams is in extremely safe hands.' The plan was for Frank to mentor Claire over those first few years. Claire's brother Johnny was passed over and went to run the Williams heritage business.

In those early years of her tenure, the team enjoyed success with Felipe Massa and Valtteri Bottas. The team went from ninth in 2013 to securing back-to-back third-placed finishes in the Constructors' standings in 2014 and 2015, behind Red Bull and Mercedes. What's more, in the era of Mercedes dominance, Williams secured 15 podiums. Claire looked to be the saviour Williams needed to get the team back to the glory days of the 1980s and 1990s. However, this promising start was not to continue, and by 2016 Williams was falling down the Constructors' table, going from fifth to last by 2019. Claire faced a great deal of personal criticism for this; inexplicably, pregnancy and early motherhood were blamed, and it was suggested her brother should have become team deputy principal.

So, what went wrong? It can be argued that Williams' issues began before Claire became team principal. Williams' last World Championship was Jacques Villeneuve's 1997 Drivers' title. That was also the last year of Williams' lucrative relationship with Renault over their engine, and when renowned engineer and designer Adrian Newey left for McLaren. Williams struggled to regain form with different engines, but by 2003, 10 years before Claire's time, the team signed a deal with BMW. The team came close to winning the F1 Constructors' Championship that year, with Juan Pablo Montoya and Ralf Schumacher, but BMW was unhappy with the results. Believing they could do better, BMW set up their own team, which proved to be a washout.

At the end of 2004, the engineering and design maestro, and fellow founder, Patrick Head, began to hand over his reins to Sam Michael. There was also ill-fated succession plans made with Chris Chapple and Adam Parr – neither of whom lasted long in their CEO roles. Toto Wolff's decision to leave Williams for Mercedes in 2012, despite having invested in the team, was another lost chance.

Claire Williams' promotion to deputy team principal came in the context of these earlier team difficulties. Alongside her promotion in 2013, new technical director Pat Symonds also joined the team. Symonds returned the team to first engineering principles, and under both his and Claire's leadership Williams returned to scoring those podiums in 2014 and 2015. It wasn't to last; the Williams board appeared unable or unwilling to make the investments needed to remain competitive, and Pat Symonds left. And so the team started its descent down the rankings.

Claire's experience was on the commercial and logistical side of running a Formula One team. But this is not unusual; the success of many team principals' careers has been symbiotic with those of their technical leaders, such as Christian Horner and Adrian Newey. Indeed, Claire's father's name was above the garage, but Patrick Head as team designer was equally crucial to Williams' earlier success. When Claire was supported by the technically able and well-respected Symonds, the team looked to be returning to form.

The other key part of Williams' decline was down to money. In Frank's time, Formula One was composed of a mixture of manufactured sponsored teams and what could be called 'Garageistas'. It was much easier to fund an individually owned Formula One team, in the days of Big Tobacco money. In contrast, in the 2010s, the cost of running and developing Formula One cars was extremely prohibitive, with car manufacturers dominant in the space. Williams was racing in Formula One on budgets of around £150 million in comparison to title winners Mercedes' £300 million. When Covid hit in 2020, all teams' revenue streams were hit, as races were cancelled or postponed. With Williams' costs regularly exceeding their income in prize money and sponsorship and solely reliant on Formula One derived revenue, the team struggled. Williams' determination to stay independent meant it just could not compete in the big-spending, pre-cost cap days, and Covid was the final straw that broke the camel's back. By August 2020, Williams and its board announced the sale of the F1 team to US investment company Dorilton Capital. Retaining the name of the team was a stipulation of the sale.

The sale of Williams and the severing of the 40-year relationship between the family and the team marked the end of a Formula One era. Claire Williams faced many challenges in her time as team leader. Tough financials and the lack of consistent technical leadership at the team made it an incredibly challenging time. To save the team, the family name and accompanying heritage during Covid without letting the team go into administration is a testament to her. To do this in the face of severe criticism shows her strength and steel.

Claire is rightly proud of her father's achievements as one of the Garage-istas:

> What Frank achieved with Patrick by his side over many years is nothing short of incredible. My dad came from nothing in F1. He had nothing except a dream and he managed to create this extraordinary team that so many people around the world love, not least the people within it.

For all who compete in F1, the music stops eventually. The team was sold but with the strict proviso the great name remained.

The Battle that Saved Mercedes' Engine Advantage

Ahead of the Bahrain Grand Prix 2014, incredible unrest swirled in Formula One.

Leading figures queued up to trash the newest incarnation of the sport. Legendary designer Adrian Newey said the new engine rules were brought in 'without proper thought'. Ferrari launched an online survey that generated 50,000 responses – 83 per cent of which were negative. In response, FIA president Jean Todt, F1's CEO Bernie Ecclestone and Ferrari chairman Luca di Montezemolo met to try to contain the crisis amid the real possibility that everyone else's engines were years behind Mercedes. The screaming V8s had departed at the end of 2013, replaced with a far more complex and efficient 1.6-litre V6 turbo.

Mercedes had created the finest power unit by far and the early paddock whispers that started years before about their package dominating proved to be true. CEO Toto Wolff immediately defended their advantage; he told a press conference: 'The rules are the rules, were implemented a long time ago, and if you want to change them then do it for next year, but I don't see that happening.'

There was a genuine feeling of uncertainty approaching the race, which was further whipped up as Bernie Ecclestone publicly railed against the lack of noise and slower speeds on show:

> I don't think the way things are at the moment are acceptable to the public. People buying tickets to come here expect to see what Formula One used to be. What is

wrong is these fantastic engines, the engines are without doubt incredible ... But I don't think it is F1 business. They should do it in touring cars or something – not in F1.

The Mercedes era needed to prove it could still excite while being fast. Such was the Mercedes dominance that the title fight was an inter-team affair between Nico Rosberg and Lewis Hamilton. The season started with one race win a piece for Rosberg (in Australia) and Hamilton (Malaysia). As the cars lined up in Bahrain for the third race, Rosberg was on pole ahead of Hamilton. While Hamilton had dominated free practice, Rosberg had been slightly faster in qualifying and had taken the leading position by 0.3 seconds. The Mercedes cars were dominant – over 0.9 seconds clear of the competition.

Ahead of the race start, the sun began to set over the desert, helping to cool the track. As the floodlights illuminated the circuit, the cars lined up and the five red lights were extinguished. Hamilton got off to the better start and squeezed between Rosberg and the pit wall to take the lead. Hamilton swerved to the right side of the track when exiting turn 3; he defended hard against Rosberg into turn 4. Rosberg tried to tough it out on the outside, but Hamilton was having none of it. The pair were well clear of the competition and pulling clear at 0.5 seconds per lap.

With Rosberg's start not quite as intended, plans were rearranged to focus on having a stronger end to the race. Pre-race strategy calls had been made that whoever lost the start would be given mediums for the middle of the race, offering the option for faster tyres while the leader was on primes. It was deemed the fairest approach. Saving fuel at this early stage meant potentially being able to generate more power at that crucial final stage of the race.

One lap away from the first scheduled stop, Rosberg got more desperate to get in first and try to leapfrog Hamilton during his pit stop. He made a feisty late-breaking move into turn 1 using DRS. It worked for a bit, but he was forced to go wide and Lewis maintained his lead. This was repeated on the start of lap 19, just before the pits – Rosberg got ahead, but once again Hamilton hung on. Hamilton blocked Rosberg to stop any proper run into turn 4. Despite being slower, the close wheel-to-wheel fighting was a crucial moment in helping Hamilton retain the lead – even if the Mercedes pit wall looked on nervously. Lewis was called in first for fresh tyres.

Rosberg stayed out for a couple more laps, returning to the race on fresh primes. Hamilton had the faster tyre type with a six second advantage, but he still needed a good middle stint ahead of the all-out race in the final laps. Ten laps later, the gap was now nine seconds and he kept pushing. With 17 laps to go, the gap widened to 10 seconds – but wasn't to last. Pastor Maldonado's Lotus collided with Esteban Gutierrez's Sauber, flipping the car and leaving it stranded on the first turn. The safety car was deployed at lap 41, erasing Lewis' lead. Both Mercedes cars pitted for new tyres, and now Rosberg was on the faster rubber.

It looked like the race was Rosberg's to win, but Hamilton wasn't out of options yet. Hamilton's car was lighter due to less fuel. Executive Director Paddy Lowe went on the radio to remind both drivers that a clean finish was needed. The safety car pitted, and racing was on.

Rosberg had a better line after Hamilton's defence of turn 1. At turn 4, Rosberg went to the outside again, but Hamilton continued the fight and kept Rosberg wide. Rosberg pulled back and focused on storing energy for a late DRS-enabled attempt. He kept up, and at the start of lap 52, Rosberg sliced to the inside late and went wide into the first turn: Hamilton got his opportunity to retake the lead. The wheel-to-wheel ballet between the pair continued into the next lap, with Rosberg trying again and Lewis holding him back into turn 4. With five laps of holding Rosberg up, it was beginning to look like Hamilton's race. At least nine different times, Rosberg thought he had Hamilton, but the best from Rosberg's tyres was gone, and by the last lap he knew he was beat.

Hamilton roared down to the finish line, equalling Juan Manuel Fangio's 24 Grand Prix victories. Later, Rosberg reflected, 'So many times, I didn't know where he was and then he'd suddenly reappear again … it was definitely the most exciting race I've ever done in my whole career. Today was a day for the sport.'

'It was fantastic,' said a thrilled Lewis, adding:

> I haven't had a race like that since 2007. To have a real racer's race and to be able to use whatever skills I've acquired over the years since karting, pulling them all out the bag and using them again just feels fantastic, one of the greatest feelings you can have.

F1 had witnessed some of the most thrilling wheel-to-wheel racing seen in years, it recalled the glory battling of old, with instant comparison to Villeneuve vs Arnoux in 1979 (*see* Chapter 25). The battle in Bahrain meant the power unit dissent relented and Mercedes kept their advantage. They would go on to win every Constructors' title and all but one Drivers' title for the next eight seasons.

66

Marko Promotes Max Straight into F1 at Seventeen

On 11 August 2014, Red Bull announced they had signed teenage Max Verstappen to their driving programme.

'Effective immediately, the sixteen-year-old Dutchman will continue his FIA Formula Three European Championship campaign at the Nürburgring this weekend as a Red Bull Junior in the Van Amersfoort Racing team and additionally will compete at the Macau Grand Prix in November.' Newly introduced to the world, Max was the son of Sophie Kumpen, a former successful go-karter, and Jos Verstappen, a Formula One driver from 1994 to 2003. Jos had resisted the overtures of all the leading Formula One teams' junior driver programmes, keen to manage his son's career to the last possible moment when collaboration was inevitable.

That moment had now arrived, but the first statement had omitted the price for Verstappen Senior ceding control. One week later, the truth was revealed – a second statement dropped into journalists' inboxes to widespread disbelief. The statement began: 'Max Verstappen to drive for Toro Rosso in 2015. The Dutchman is set to make history and become the youngest ever F1 driver when he debuts next year.'

Helmut Marko, the head of the junior driver programme, and Red Bull had shredded the form book. No one had ever put so much faith in a driver so young. Anticipating the backlash, Marko was punchy in his quotes at the bottom of the bombshell press release: 'He is an exceptional talent that comes along only once in decades … you must not look at his age. He has been talking with people who are experts when it comes to the development of youngsters and they all say that [in terms of] his mind he is more like twenty-two than sixteen.'

One year after becoming the karting world champion and just 27 car races into his career, all at Formula Three level, Verstappen would line up on the grid in Melbourne, shattering all previous precedent. Analysing the list of the 10 youngest F1 debutants at the time, three had been given a chance by the Red Bull junior programme: Sebastian Vettel, 19 years, 349 days old (Indianapolis, 2007); Daniil Kvyat, 19 years, 324 days old (Melbourne, 2014) who'd been promoted straight from the third tier in GP3; and the previous record holder Jaime Alguersuari, 19 years, 125 days old (Hungaroring, 2009). Alguersuari had competed in four years of single-seater racing before reaching Formula One.

Ferrari had broken the mould first in 1961 when they promoted Ricardo Rodríguez to a guest drive at the Italian Grand Prix. Enzo Ferrari had the confidence after Rodríguez had stood on the Le Mans 24 Hours podium in one of his customer cars at just eighteen years of age. Now, 53 years later, Red Bull were taking it even further.

Many in the paddock thought the move was rash and Verstappen was simply too young. When I questioned him at pre-season testing in 2015, I read him the list of motorsport heavyweights who didn't think he should be on the grid:

- Mika Häkkinen, two-time world champion: 'It's too young because in F1, the risk is high. In F1 you don't go to learn, you have to be ready. F1 doesn't allow you to do too much learning.'

- Felipe Massa, Grand Prix winner: 'Seventeen is a little bit young!'

- Jean Todt, FIA president: 'Personally, I do think he is too young.'

- Jacques Villeneuve, 1997 world champion: 'He is still a boy so it is very risky.'

After reading the heavy famous rollcall to him, I added: 'They don't think you should be here.' He smiled, shrugged and said, 'Look, we'll see. I can only focus on myself.' What else could he say? No one truly had any idea whether it would work. The long queue for his services featured the biggest names in the sport – Ferrari, Red Bull and Mercedes – each giving the Verstappen camp all the cards in negotiating.

This wasn't without risk for Jos Verstappen and Helmut Marko; Jos Verstappen had watched his Formula One career get relegated to the midfield after early promotion to a race-winning team went awry. Marko was dealing with serious questions about adequately protecting a teenager from the danger of elite motor racing, but he'd been convinced by what he'd seen in Formula Three.

Verstappen had made a fast start with a Van Amersfort team not used to being championship contenders in European Formula Three, winning in the second weekend of his car racing career by dominating the field. Further notice was taken to his clean sweep of all three races in Spa-Francorchamps. But his performance at the Norisring really sealed things. In a wet-dry race of constantly evolving weather and strategy, Verstappen had mastered a drying track. He'd torn away from his competitors, who included future F1 race winner Esteban Ocon. Helmut Marko was left with no doubts that a rare talent was available to be signed. 'It was a surprise how quickly he adapted to Formula Three. The moment I thought [he was] something really special was at the Norisring. In mixed conditions – it was more wet than dry – he was per lap two seconds faster than anyone else.'

Toto Wolff had also followed Verstappen's career closely and believed there was a future champion on the market. Wolff and Mercedes' offer to the Verstappens was for Max to do GP2 (now Formula Two) and look to promotion to Formula One in 2016. None of the Mercedes-powered teams had vacancies, meaning Wolff would have had to drop multiple race winner Nico Rosberg for an eighteen-year-old, all in just his second year as team boss and owner. It just didn't work. Mercedes was snookered by the Red Bull junior team, Toro Rosso, who could offer an immediate F1 seat. Wolff would have had to negotiate with other team principals who had Mercedes engines – not quite the same level of control.

Marko had been openly judged for his Old Testament-style management of teenage talent. The junior programme and ownership of Toro Rosso would be his route to Verstappen. Only Sebastian Vettel and Daniel Ricciardo had passed the test in the seven years since the junior team Toro Rosso had been established; everyone else had been fired, some mid-season. The Austrian who owed his position of power to long-term consultation for Red Bull owner Dietrich Mateschitz on motorsport matters had insisted on a junior team. A team that now won the race to sign Verstappen: 'We are not playing the lottery – we know what we are doing. And success proves us right.'

Toto Wolff would cite the loss of Verstappen to Red Bull as a key reason he was determined to promote Andrea Kimi Antonelli to the Mercedes race team at eighteen years of age a decade on from missing out on Verstappen – a move precipitated by Lewis Hamilton's switch to Ferrari. It was a driver transfer only possible after the seven-time world champion had been offered a contract with a break clause after one year, such was Wolff's fear of losing the possibility of another teenage driving talent.

In early 2024, just under 10 years after the original announcement Red Bull and Marko had been completely vindicated. Verstappen was now a three-time world champion, and in 2023 was the first driver to win 10 races back to back. At the second round of the season in Saudi Arabia, Red Bull were now at war internally. Senior figures battling for control and survival within the team and parent company structure. Verstappen's appreciation towards Helmut Marko was notable amid this period of infighting.

When news broke from Marko, suggesting he was about to be suspended by the team, Verstappen did not attempt to evade the subject. Instead, he chose to stake his future on the issue. He stated if Helmut Marko left the team, he would too. It was a stunning claim for a driver who had won the last seven races in a row and three consecutive titles:

> If such an important pillar falls away, it is not good for my situation and I have told the team that. He is an important part in my decision-making for the future. For me, Helmut has to stay. I have a lot of respect for him and what we have achieved together.

Max believed that none of his success in F1 was inevitable and Marko's gamble would always be remembered as crucial to his story. He would close the season as a four-time world champion.

Verstappen and Son – The Road to Becoming F1's Youngest Winner

Former F1 driver Jos Verstappen doesn't like the story of the most infamous speed bump in the super close father–son relationship.

The story tells of the time the driver's father is reported to have left his teenage son at a petrol station when a go-kart race didn't go as planned. As ever, the reality is a bit more complicated. Verstappen Senior tightly managed every aspect of his son's racing education. He took the knowledge from his own time as a Formula One driver and twinned it with key lessons and insights learnt. Max Verstappen's journey to Formula One started early at an unremarkable pay-to-drive go-kart track in Genk, Belgium – he was just four-and-a-half years old.

With rules prohibiting competition until seven years old, Max finally got the chance to race after two-and-a-half years of practice. He won on debut in a category with drivers as old as 10. Jos immersed himself in the preparation, setting up the kart chassis and calibrating the engine. Verstappen Sr had been aggressive behind the wheel and he sought to dial that style out of his son, demanding more finesse and detailing where improvements would be required.

Max was given a mechanical education, and on track seemed completely at ease winning the European Championship and the KZ World Championship. Father and son would drive to the races in a van, with the journey taking eight to ten hours. For a decade, they would drive up to 100,000 km a year. Max was so naturally gifted, his father started introducing hurdles, and Jos would send Max out in a kart that was poorly set up to see if he could correctly diagnose what the problem was. Such was young Max's dominance in races, Jos would ban corners at which he could overtake to increase the difficulty.

When others would pack up and go home, Max would be told to get back out there – in every weather, in every temperature. If he complained of the cold, he was told to warm his hands on the exhaust such were the extreme temperatures in which he would practice. His father was bluntly imparting information – he wanted to add conscious thought to an obvious natural talent. Jos was hugely demanding in his standards but he exacted engaged driving from his son.

The infamous story has taken root in the public consciousness because it is so unusual, but is it true? At a World Karting Championship race in 2012, Max Verstappen was so fast, victory was assured ... until it wasn't. Max tried to repass a rival and crashed! Jos' reaction was total fury that his son had blown a World Championship race he should have coasted to. Max had to retrieve his crashed kart with a friend, and it got worse – in the car, while Max wanted to discuss what had happened, Jos sat in silence, kicking his son out at the fuel station.

Max's mother, Sophie Kumpen, an excellent former go-karter, was a few miles back. Jos returned to the petrol station a few moments later, afterwards clarifying that he didn't actually leave Max at the station, he just didn't speak to him *for a week*. Less than four years after being left behind at a petrol station, Max sat in second place of a Formula One Grand Prix. Red Bull had been elevated to the first two places after Mercedes had imploded in one of the most dramatic opening-lap crashes in F1 history. Going into the fifth race of the season, Mercedes had won all four preceding races. However, it was Nico Rosberg who was leading the Drivers' Championship by 43 points and not the reigning world champion, Lewis Hamilton.

The team that led the race, Red Bull, had made the early headlines that weekend. The team had acted with characteristic ruthlessness demoting Red Bull senior driver Daniil Kvyat back to the junior Toro Rosso team, after the Russian driver had started his season involved in multiple accidents. In the Thursday press conference, Kvyat revealed he'd been watching *Game of Thrones* when he received the news. It was an inescapably painful way for a frontline career to end. Verstappen, who had believed his promotion was a joke when it was first mentioned, made all the right noises in the media and now had a car capable of scoring podiums. In qualifying, it was Hamilton who beat Rosberg to pole, with Verstappen in fourth behind teammate Daniel Ricciardo. Verstappen had qualified ahead of both Ferraris on senior team debut, including former world champion and Red Bull driver, Sebastian Vettel.

Rosberg lined up for the start of the race in second on the grid next to Hamilton, but there was a problem. His engine was still on the formation lap setting and he was meant to change it for the race start but forgot. With team radio limited, it wasn't a mistake that could be easily rectified. The car had a third setting, launch mode, which initially hid the error. He got off to a start that was better than Hamilton's. Lewis tried to cut across up to turn 1 but Rosberg slipstreamed tight behind him on the long run, darted out to the left and cut clean across the outside to take the lead. Both drivers hit the buttons to disengage launch mode as they raced through turns 2 and 3, Rosberg's engine still in formation lap mode and Hamilton behind correctly in race mode.

The discrepancy in power was obvious, and Rosberg went to get a power boost by hitting the overtake button while turning sharply to the right to block the inside line of turn 4. So did Hamilton, but he was also travelling faster than Rosberg; he thought he could get his car inside his teammate's before being closed off. Rosberg, not believing that Lewis would hold that line, kept turning right. Hamilton tried to avoid an incident by going on the grass but spun out of control and into the other Mercedes, and Rosberg braked into turn 4. The badly damaged Mercedes pirouetted into the gravel bed. With the dominant cars having taken themselves out, the opportunity arose for the rest of the grid to take an unlikely victory.

Ricciardo had taken the lead with Verstappen second. Ferrari had a more work to do to get three–four with Carlos Sainz in a Toro Rosso, with last year's Ferrari engine holding them up. By lap 4, both cars passed and the fight between Red Bull and Ferrari was on. The data was showing that the Ferraris were slightly faster so the race would come down to pit stop strategy – three stops and racing on fresh tyres or two stops with no loss of time but a lot of work required to maintain the tyres. Red Bull had given themselves enough bandwidth to shoot for a two-stop strategy, but they were going to react to what Ferrari did. To share the risk, Ferrari split the difference: three for Vettel and two for Kimi Räikkönen.

With Vettel behind Verstappen and ready to pass, the only option for the young driver was a two stopper; otherwise, he was guaranteed to lose his position. Red Bull also decided to split the difference and Ricciardo, out in front, was given the three-stop strategy, the idea being he could use his fresh tyres to head off the threat from Vettel. In the end, it was the two-stop strategy that won the day.

Ricciardo and Vettel were brought in for their second stop of three, leaving Verstappen and Räikkönen out in front to wait for the fresh onslaught from the third-stoppers. But with Räikkönen fast closing, Verstappen was brought in and switched to mediums, which had to last for the remaining 32 laps. Verstappen was 15 seconds off Ricciardo and Vettel's race pace, with both set to pit for the third time, costing each around 22 seconds. Verstappen and Räikkönen went back into the lead; with less than a second between them, it was close. But Räikkönen couldn't get close, with the Red Bull having better traction through the chicane at the end of the lap. Despite managing to take good care of the tyres, Verstappen described racing on the worn tyres as racing on ice for the last eight laps.

I watched the race by the side of the track. The crowd were in conversation, it was more akin to a theatre audience at the interval trying to make sense of what they were seeing. Clearly, Verstappen wasn't totally at ease with the car, but he was keeping a world champion at bay. The crowd, eager to witness history, began encouraging the young Dutchman, who held on to win his maiden Grand Prix in his 24th F1 race at only eighteen years of age – the youngest Formula One race winner ever. It is a record unlikely to be broken and the scenes in the paddock afterwards drew enthusiasm from even the most grizzled veteran. It was just thirteen-and-a-half years between a first go-kart drive and F1 victory.

Rosberg Retires at Thirty-One

The sight was so thrilling, the situation so extraordinary.

I took a rare moment to look at it with my own eyes. So much commentary is performed in front of a sea of monitors. Leaning forward, peering beyond the screens of the commentary box where we were recording a pilot for what would become the Pitlane Channel on F1TV. I saw two Mercedes, a Ferrari and a Red Bull glued together – four eventual world champions stuck in a tactical game being played by Lewis Hamilton, who led Nico Rosberg, Sebastian Vettel and Max Verstappen. Four cars under the floodlights of Abu Dhabi, nose to tail. Second in the train was Nico Rosberg, who would survive the remaining laps and claim the Formula One World Championship for the first time, after Hamilton had slowed his pace dramatically in the hope Verstappen or Vettel would overtake Rosberg.

Only three of the drivers from the battle would return for the next race, because on the day of his World Championship trophy presentation Nico Rosberg dropped a bombshell. The new world champion was retiring at just thirty-one years of age, in the process turning down millions of dollars and the use of the best-in-class Formula One car. It was unexpected and left fans and insiders astonished. Rosberg set about explaining himself:

> Since 25 years in racing, it has been my dream, my 'one thing', to become Formula One world champion. Through

the hard work, the pain, the sacrifices, this has been my target. And now I've made it. I have climbed my mountain, I am on the peak, so this feels right. My strongest emotion right now is deep gratitude to everybody who supported me to make that dream happen.

Rosberg had a reputation of being a smart but very difficult operator. He'd won nine Grands Prix on the way to his championship – only the second son of a previous world champion to achieve this after Damon Hill in 1996. Hill's triumph had been sealed in Suzuka, where the idea of giving up years earlier than he needed to came to Rosberg: 'When I won the race in Suzuka, from the moment when the destiny of the title was in my own hands, the big pressure started and I began to think about ending my racing career if I became world champion.'

Having been beaten to the title in 2014 and 2015, Rosberg threw the number-two cap Hamilton had passed to him in the Austin cooldown room. From a moment of extreme petulance came an on-track response. Rosberg won the final three races of 2015 and first four races in 2016: 'I pushed like crazy in every area after the disappointments of the last two years; they fuelled my motivation to levels I had never experienced before.'

Increasingly, Rosberg had pushed the boundaries of what was possible within a team. Twice in 2016, he had collided with Hamilton when battling for the lead: in Spain, which eliminated both cars, and in Austria, where a clunky attempt at defensive driving only succeeded in ripping off the front wing. He was forced to personally pay for it by team boss Toto Wolff. The bruising battles that had often featured extreme moves towards teammates in the opening corners of a Grand Prix were unsustainable. Someone would have to leave the team: either Hamilton to Ferrari or Rosberg, as it would turn out, to ride off into the sunset.

Hamilton had lost the title in 2016 after a season defined by poor starts. An engine failure while leading in Malaysia swung the championship momentum towards Rosberg but the decision to leave the sport would prove crucial. From 2017, Ferrari would sustain a championship challenge led by Sebastian Vettel. Bottas was a strong replacement and race winner, but he never pushed Hamilton in the same way both on and off track. Had Rosberg remained with the team, the split points between Hamilton and Rosberg would almost certainly have enabled Ferrari to win across the season in much the same way Prost triumphed in 1986 and Räikkönen snuck in to beat the two McLarens in 2007.

Drive to Survive

In March 2019, a new sports docudrama dropped on Netflix, showcasing the relationships and human side of a sport once seen as elitist, cold and technical.

With Netflix billboards scattered in and around Federation Square in Melbourne, Australia in time for the first Grand Prix, it wasn't obvious what *Formula One: Drive to Survive* was to become. On its seventh season as of 2025, it's not hard to argue that it is a cultural lynchpin that has underpinned the growth of Formula One. The show has brought the sport to new audiences, helped to create Formula One's current social media landscape and grow awareness and attendance at US races. Not to mention making the drivers and team principals stars and household names.

Liberty Media, a US-based corporation that owns assets in media, entertainment and sports, acquired Formula One in 2017, effectively ending the reign of Formula One giant Bernie Ecclestone. While Bernie had revolutionized the sport over his 40 years of leadership, his approach to Formula One was quite different to Liberty Media's.

As with any acquisition, the new owners needed to look for growth; television audiences had been declining and there wasn't an obvious social media strategy. To broaden access, a behind-the-scenes documentary was pitched to Netflix. With Netflix's main audience being in the US, this had the potential to provide an opportunity to access a market F1 had always found elusive. The director of non-fiction series at Netflix, Nat Grouille, contacted the British production company Box To Box Films, who were already looking at putting together a documentary on Red Bull. They were able to negotiate pretty much all-access terms with Formula One, which includes race-day footage and the say on the final cut. Now the teams needed to be convinced about *Drive to Survive*. There were concerns over what this could mean; the success of the sport runs on a team's ability to keep their technical knowledge secret and ahead of their competitors. Ferrari and Mercedes were reluctant and didn't sign up for season one – although Mercedes' reluctance was attributed in part to their deal with Amazon for their own documentary. This quirk of season one helped to shape the direction of the show. In an interview, lead producer of the series James Gay-Rees described the focus of the show as being more on 'how the sport works and less about who won'. The choice of show runner for series one must have also impacted its direction; Sophie Todd was an experienced BBC producer of docudramas that focused on the people involved. The production company has chosen to focus on fundamental emotional arcs, not the technical details, which were left up to the traditional broadcasters on race day.

The first season led to solid reviews, but it was the later seasons that really took off. *Drive to Survive* came into its own in the pandemic, when live sport just wasn't available. Viewers connected with the human side of the sport and the access to the closed-off world of the paddock it provided. With only 20 drivers and 10 teams, the viewers got to know the drivers, team principals and engineers. *Drive to Survive* tapped into the zeitgeist of that pandemic era, which brought new viewers to the sport. This, coupled with the sports ever expanding social media presence, turned drivers like Danny Ricciardo and team principals like Guenther Steiner into household names. Formula One was able to build on this pandemic success by being one of the first sports to resume on live TV, first via virtual sim racing and then via actual races in July 2020.

The approach of focusing on the human side of Formula One

has paid off. This isn't easy to do, as some of the viewers have never seen a race before and this needs to be balanced with those that have. There is also the sheer logistics involved in covering a sport that now flies to 24 different locations around the world: Box To Box shoots between 20 and 40 times too much coverage to end up making ten 30–45-minute episodes. It leads to some heavy lifting in post-production to create the story arcs that the viewers love to see.

The series, helmed from season two by Tom Rogers, is reported to have had a cumulative audience of 800 million across its first six seasons. Formula One is one of the fastest growing sports in a world where viewership is fracturing and reaching younger and more diverse audiences is difficult. *Drive to Survive* has managed the rare feat of opening the sport up to new demographics, with the average age of viewers falling and the number of women watching doubling. Most importantly, this has translated into an effect where casual fans have become live race-day viewers. This effect has most notably been seen in the US, where viewership is reported to have grown significantly. Not only that, race attendance at the original US race in Austin Texas doubled and two new races in Miami and Las Vegas have been added to the calendar. This now means, twenty years on from the farce in Indianapolis that seemed to end F1's chances in the United States, the US has the most Formula One races out of any country.

The Cost Cap and the Pandemic

To mark the start of a new decade in Formula One, an unprecedented new rule was announced.

That's right, a whole chapter about finance. Buckle up. In October 2019, Formula One announced new rules and regulations for the 2021 season, one of which was the cost cap, set at $175 million per team, per year. Its aim was to curtail runaway spending to try to make the sport fairer and sustainable. It was an attempt to essentially level the playing field, and the gulf between the biggest spending teams and the backmarkers narrowed. It applied to anything that was involved in on-track performance. Marketing costs, driver and top-three personnel salaries were all excluded, as was travel and the cost of an engine supply deal. The aim was to make F1 an ultra competitive sports league.

Prior to its introduction, the biggest teams were reported to spend upwards of $400 million per year, while other teams got nowhere close. Putting together the number required a lot of consultation and the services of the accounting firm, Deloitte. The cap was based on 21 Grands Prix, with an extra $1 million allowed for every additional race. A Cost Cap Administration was set up to monitor compliance with the rules. The teams were to have a soft implementation period in 2020 with no sanctions if they did not comply. From 2021, the teams were to submit interim accounts for their spending between January and April, with full accounts reported the following March.

Penalties were planned for future breaches based on three

categories. The first were to be known as procedural, and the least serious for things like late accounts or mistakes in reporting. The second breach would be for 'minor overspends', defined to be less than 5 per cent of the cost cap. The third and most serious were named 'material overspends', with the cap being exceeded by more than 5 per cent. The penalties for any of these breaches were also set out and included a public reprimand, loss of Constructors' or Drivers' points, race bans, limits on testing or future reductions in cost caps. The most severe penalty was to be known as a 'material sporting penalty', leading to exclusion from Formula One.

Back in 2019, the cost cap was not universally popular with the teams. The backmarkers wanted to press ahead with publication of the new rules in June 2019 rather than wait until October 2019 and face dilution of the cap. The number had already risen by $25 million at this point. In contrast, Mercedes, Red Bull and Ferrari were reported to find the rules 'immature'. This is perhaps unsurprising given the different financial positions of the teams. In the end, the regulations were adopted and published four months later. Then the 2020 season turned out to be like nothing anyone had expected.

On 13 March 2020, that first race of the season in Melbourne was cancelled. A McLaren team member had tested positive for Covid-19. Formula One packed up and flew home. Italy was already facing a lockdown by this date and the British Government's measures to contain virus transmission began to be implemented three days later on 16 March, with a full national lockdown by 23 March.

With most of the teams and the Formula One offices based in the UK, Grand Prix racing was on pause and race after race was either cancelled or postponed. Measures still had to be taken to secure the sport's future. Zak Brown, the CEO of McLaren Racing, later described how the team nearly went bankrupt in 2020, with 1,000 jobs lost. A £300 million cash injection from its majority owner, the Bahrain Sovereign Wealth Fund, helped to shore up the wider McLaren group. Ultimately, the family-owned Williams team went up for sale in May 2020 and was sold to US investment firm Dorilton Capital by August of that year.

Formula One's first step to secure its financial future, while adhering to the travel bans and lockdowns globally, was to move the August summer break to cover the first lockdown period in March and April. This allowed the teams to save on overheads and freed up August in case races could be held. Technical regulation updates allowed the 2020 cars to be used in 2021 and delays to the introduction of the new regulations to 2022 helpfully reduced development costs. While these choices were being made, Formula One's engineers went to support the British Government's Project Pitlane to scale up and build much-needed respiratory devices. The drivers competed in Formula One sim racing from their homes, while providing a much-needed distraction to those in lockdown.

The other key financial measure taken to secure the sport was announced in May 2020; the new financial regulations including the cost cap were still to be implemented in 2021 as planned, but the thresholds were to change. The $175 million figure was reduced to $145 million for 2021, and then further reduced to $140 million in 2022 and $135 million in 2023. The sliding reduction was chosen to balance the need for the larger teams such as Mercedes, Ferrari and Red Bull to assess the size of their workforces while ensuring the financial long-term sustainability of the sport. The regulations once described as 'immature' were now considered key to the future of the sport. The regulations retained the right to increase the cost cap from 2024 if necessary.

Ultimately, the Formula One season was able to restart in July 2020 while under strict quarantine and social distancing rules. Of an original 22 races planned, 17 were able to run, admittedly in slightly different locations than originally set out. The new financial regulations continue to be implemented, with the cost cap planned to increase to $215 million per team per year in 2026.

There have been breaches, such as Red Bull's $7 million overspend that led to a £1.9 million fine and a 10 per cent reduction in their aerodynamic testing allowance in 2022. Williams and Aston Martin also had procedural breaches where the accounts were either late or inaccurate in 2022, as did Alpine in 2023. The sport has survived and continued to grow. While the financial regulations are not the sole reason for this, the teams do appear to be more competitive; seven different drivers from four teams won in 2024. And McLaren, went from nearly bankrupt in 2020 to being the FIA F1 Constructors' world champion in 2024.

Grosjean Cheats Death

Romain Grosjean's car was in two pieces, his survival cell surrounded by 100 litres of racing-grade petrol.

Instantly catching flames, the fire spread rapidly towards the driver. Worst still, the whole world was watching. On a long shot looking back from the fourth turn, it was inescapable. A car had hit the wall and burst into a fireball. What the TV gallery could see but the world could not – Grosjean was trapped in the car. It is no exaggeration to say Formula One sat on a precipice on 29 November 2020. Three eras had converged, a fire-filled past long thought to be forgotten, a critical minute in the entire future of the sport hinged on what happened next.

Grosjean had seconds to save his life and escape. He could not break loose immediately; his boot was trapped in the footwell of the car, wedged between the throttle pedal and the cockpit wall. It had been a huge impact, and he knew he was on his side, but the adrenaline and strangeness of the angle made it hard to ascertain exactly where he was. The colour, the heat, what was that? Fire had become so rare in Formula One it wasn't a natural fear post-accident.

To find something comparable, you had to rewind 26 years to the German Grand Prix, where a huge fireball engulfed Jos Verstappen's Benetton for a few seconds at a pit stop. So horrific was the risk caused from fire, it had always been at the top of the FIA's list of safety priorities. The 1970s had featured so many fatalities from fire – a cruel and gruesome reality that had been aggressively stamped out in the remainder of the decade.

A few seconds after the struggle to free himself began, Grosjean accepted the severity of the moment. 'My body starts to relax, I'm at peace with myself and I'm going to die,' he told a press conference. He thought about where he'd feel the pain first, how much pain there would be, then a jolt, a refusal. Thoughts of his three young children repowered him to rip and tear at the walls of the car and the struggle recommenced.

Then a breakthrough as his foot slips out of the shoe. Stage one complete, but was there room between the three elements of the Armco barrier? There was a route to the right but Grosjean had no momentum to haul himself downwards. He had to go up and left, behind the twisted strip of metal. He hauled himself up by grappling at the front of the halo, which had prevented him being instantly killed on impact 20 seconds earlier. Twisting his shoulders, he knows there's a chance. He finds the gap and passes his upper body through. The elation is short-lived, as he looks down and watches his gloves turn black in the flames.

Then help. His trial no longer endured alone. The fire decreases in front of him for a second, he places his left foot up on the barrier, his left arm is grabbed by Dr Ian Roberts. He places his right hand on the barrier and is hauled away. The crash helmet melted; the driver suit smouldering; six hobbled steps away, each one seeming to reaffirm the hell he'd been trapped in. He tried to shake the pain from his hands as he stumbled away. The pain was swelling but he was safe. Romain Grosjean had been exposed to fire in the worst Formula One accident for years – and had lived.

Bahrain International Circuit was one of the safest circuits in the world. In fact, it was so safety focused when the Grand Prix was first introduced in the country in 2004 that the drivers complained about the car-park-sized run-off areas. That such an accident could happen at Bahrain's facility was a reminder of the risk drivers are always taking. The extraordinary circumstances had begun when Grosjean had cut across Daniil Kvyat's Alpha Tauri car and pitched on into the angled Armco barrier. It was a very unusual place to go off, especially at speed, and with the car heavy with a full race distance weight of fuel. The resulting impact was devastating; 67G pierced directly into a metal barrier, not tyres or tech pro, which would be found at other high-risk parts of the circuit.

The first turn of Bahrain International narrows past the apex but visually the first three corners and the climb up the hill to turn 4 is unobstructed if you look to the right into turn 1. What Dr Ian Roberts saw ahead of him in the front seat of the car was beyond any training exercise they'd practised for in their time in the job. Medical car driver Alan Van De Merwe cut the first turn and 11 seconds later they confronted the fire:

'We saw a massive flame and as we arrived, a very odd scene where you've got half a car pointing in the wrong direction and just across the barrier, a massive heat,' he told me on the F1 Nation podcast in the days which followed.

> I could see Romain trying to get up. We needed some way of getting to him. We've got the marshal there with an extinguisher and the extinguisher was just enough to push the flame away as Romain got high enough to then reach over and pull himself over the barrier.
>
> I could see obviously he was very shaky and his visor was completely opaque and melted. It was a matter of getting his helmet off just to check that everything else was OK. He'd got some pain in his foot and on his hands, so from that point, we knew that it was safe enough then to move him around into the car, just a little bit more protection, get some gel onto his burns and then get him into the ambulance and off to the Medical Centre.

Dr Ian Roberts later quipped he'd 'got a good tan' from getting as close as he did to the fireball, but his improvised bravery was key to guiding the fire marshal and then aiding Grosjean out of the flames. His quick thinking under pressure undoubtedly improved Grosjean's chances. Grosjean had been saved by his intervention and benefited from recent changes to Formula One safety. Earlier the same year, the mandatory fire suits' resistance had been increased by 20 per cent, outperforming what was required by protecting Grosjean beyond the 20 seconds mark.

Grosjean was able to walk away from that crash due to decades of iterative safety improvements and a heavy dose of good fortune. On reflection, death was cheated three times that day: first, by surviving the hit with a metal barrier; second, by the halo that helped to wedge the car and stop it from moving; and third, by Grosjean escaping the fire within a minute. The crash once again highlighted the life-saving effects of the halo, which had been hugely unpopular after its introduction in 2018.

The near-miss was inescapably pivotal for the future of Formula One. Grizzly 1970s safety standards could not be accepted by fans who had come to love the sport based on its personalities and human drama. A driver simply could not burn to death live on television in the modern era. It would have meant the cancellation of the rest of the season and caused a safety reckoning on the scale of Senna's fatal crash in 1994. It would also have caused an existential crisis at an already financially critical time.

Instead, Grosjean's miracle escape made headlines across the world with the image of him fleeing the flames running in every newspaper and across social media. *Drive to Survive* turned the 27-second sequence into a four-minute epic which only increased the prominence of the series. The FIA released a report with 26 areas of investigation to improve safety standards, not just for Formula One but for all motorsport. The burned-out remnants of Grosjean's Haas car now tour the world as part of the Formula One Exhibition, a permanent reminder of the risks taken every time a driver sits in a car at any circuit across the world.

Silverstone Ignites a Battle for the Ages

In July 2021, the world was finally creaking back to something resembling normality.

Albeit this was taking place with a lingering legacy of the year before, with social distancing, repeated Covid tests and individual quarantine after any travel abroad all still in place.

Seven of the teams were finally on home soil. On track Mercedes' dominance of the sport since 2014 was finally being challenged by Red Bull. Ahead of the tenth Grand Prix of the season at Silverstone, Red Bull were emerging from the shadow of Mercedes. The team were having their best season since their title-winning days, with six victories to Mercedes' three. Both championships were in the balance, and the best part – 140,000 F1 fans returned to watch the sport live. For the first time since the pandemic began, the full spectacle would return in all its vivid glory.

Ahead of the main race on Sunday, the inaugural Formula One sprint race was held. In a hint of what was to come, Verstappen and Hamilton shadow-boxed their way through a thrilling opening lap. Verstappen fought off Hamilton's aggressive intent, including a daring attempt on the outside of Copse. Hamilton had started in P1 but Verstappen had a more incisive start, even with flames licking his front-wheel on the grid as the brakes begged for the cooling breeze provided by a car travelling at 180 mph. Verstappen managed to drag out the gap with Hamilton to 1.4 seconds by the end of the 30-minute race. The Mercedes struggled for a response, despite Hamilton's messages to race engineer Pete Bonnington asking for more power. Ultimately, Verstappen won the F1 Sprint, gained three valuable championship points and pole for the 2021 British Grand Prix.

Race day at Silverstone felt like a full restoration of the sport, although there were still signs of restriction with commentary boxes in car parks instead of overlooking the track, and all those working at the event had to detour to a portacabin for a Covid test. But there was no escaping the atmosphere, the crackle of anticipation had returned around the circuit in the hour before the race. The grid lined up with Max Verstappen on pole, next to Lewis Hamilton, with the Mercedes of Valtteri Bottas in third and Charles Leclerc of Ferrari in fourth. As the cars on the back row lined into place, it felt like Formula One had awoken.

In the commentary box, I excitedly counted on the lights for my first British Grand Prix on Channel 4, but what followed was beyond anyone's expectation: Silverstone lap 1 2021 produced one of the most intense minutes in Formula One history. Lewis Hamilton made the better start, but Max Verstappen would not yield. There was a silent shared acknowledgement that the Red Bull driver's commitment signalled an utter refusal to back down. They battled it out, sweeping, heavy with fuel, through Abbey corner. Verstappen measured his braking well to keep position into the first braking zone of the race at Village corner. Hamilton immediately placed his car on an alternative line.

Then the moment you knew we had entered a special sporting minute: driving down the Wellington straight, the drivers were staggering close to each other, the cars were swarming each other, minor changes of direction, with no safe space between them. This was truly gladiatorial. They were so close to banging wheels at 180 mph, the crowd noise absent from my headphones for 18 long months electrified the battle further.

Hamilton continued to try another move on the outside of

Brooklands but Verstappen cut him off by sweeping across Hamilton's front wing. Luffield corner was telling; Hamilton sacrificed the corner entry for greater speed on exit. It meant Hamilton tore through Woodcote, consuming the tarmac between him and Verstappen. This was the corner that decided the lead, possibly the whole race. Next was Copse corner, which has always been thrillingly fast and committed, a righthander to show you all the aerodynamic performance of a Formula One car.

At Copse corner, Hamilton went for the inside. Verstappen again refused to relent – both were all-in. They roared into the corner and made contact; the leader's right rear collided with the front left of the challenger. Verstappen spun hard and ended up in the barriers. For a second there was uncertainty as the TV pictures froze, the Red Bull slammed hard into the barriers and out of the race. It was the most intense collision between title rivals since Senna and Prost in 1990.

The race was quickly red flagged and only once Verstappen, winded and bruised, emerged from the massive 51G impact did Silverstone collectively draw breath again. The sport had returned with a staggering moment for the ages; it now had a title battle with true edge. A 10-second penalty was quickly doled out to Hamilton for the collision. Verstappen was taken to the medical centre and the race was red flagged after half a lap. 'It was a desperate move,' Christian Horner, team principal of Red Bull, seethed. 'Copse is one of the fastest corners in the world, you don't stick a wheel up the inside, that's just dirty driving,' he told us live on Channel 4, the adrenaline fuelling a normally calm media operator into a flustered accusation.

In the midst of this chaos, Charles Leclerc had passed Valtteri Bottas in the Village and loop corners. Avoiding any entanglement in the battle ahead, he took the lead, sliding past Hamilton and Verstappen after their contact. With the race briefly red flagged, Hamilton returned to the pits to get his front wing and wheel fixed.

The race restarted on lap 4. Leclerc took off ahead of Hamilton, while Lando Norris in the McLaren also managed to get the slip on Valtteri Bottas to move into P3. On lap 16 of 52, radio comms between Leclerc and his engineer reported that the Ferrari was having engine cut-outs – an intermittently recurring issue. By halfway, at lap 26, Leclerc was still ahead of Hamilton by 2.3 seconds, with Carlos Sainz's Ferrari behind them both. The next lap, Hamilton switched to hards and served his 10-second penalty in the pits; after which he rejoined the race in P5 behind Lando. He was 35 seconds back behind Leclerc, with the Ferrari's quick pit stop in the next lap giving the Scuderia real hope of a first win of the season.

Leclerc rejoined and dominated in the lead. But Hamilton wasn't done yet and fought to make up the time gap caused by the penalty. He passed Norris for P3 at Copse. By lap 40, Hamilton was up to P2, with his teammate, Bottas, following team orders to move aside. Hamilton drove his heart out to narrow Leclerc's 7.3-second lead, with a few laps to go, all buoyed on by the partisan crowd. At lap 50, the difference was only a second, despite Ferrari having given Leclerc all engine power possible. It was Copse again, not a traditional overtaking place, where Hamilton went down the inside of Leclerc and was forced onto the run-off. Hamilton swept into the lead with two laps remaining.

Hamilton brought the win home across the finish line at the strait that bears his name, with the crowd going wild. The reigning champion had reduced the title race to just an eight-point difference and achieved his 99th victory but the first lap remained controversial. It was a shame they didn't make it through Copse; the next sequence of corners would have naturally produced a single-file moment. But for 70 seconds, a capacity crowd had witnessed two of the all-time greats brawl. Two drivers, completely unwilling to yield – the stuff of Hollywood cliche made real, as two-time British Grand Prix winner David Coulthard remarked in commentary, 'It was always going to happen.'

Hamilton defended his first lap in the press conference:

> We're in a battle and I think this year he [Verstappen] has been very aggressive and most times I've had to concede and avoid incidents with him and live to fight on later in the race ... when an opportunity comes, I've got to take it, that's what we're out here doing, racing

Mercedes later admitted to regretting their celebrations with Verstappen watching on being checked over in hospital, something the team only learnt of after the exuberance on track before the podium. Red Bull used the option within the rules to call for a right of review, incredibly sending test driver Alex Albon onto the circuit to recreate the lines taken in the incident. The review was dismissed and the Mercedes statement following the review underlines how inflamed things had become: 'We hope that this decision will mark the end of a concerted attempt by the senior management of Red Bull Racing to tarnish the good name and sporting integrity of Lewis Hamilton.'

F1 had a new battle for the ages.

Abu Dhabi – Hamilton vs Verstappen

It really was winner take all – the final race of the 2021 Formula One season in Abu Dhabi Grand Prix had turned into a tense single-race showdown.

Who would take both the Drivers' and Constructors' World Championships?

In the head-to-head battle, Lewis Hamilton of Mercedes was fighting it out for a record eighth Drivers' World Championship, while Max Verstappen of Red Bull was seeking his first. The Drivers' title had swung back and forth between the two of them, with notable flashpoints in the middle of the year at Silverstone and Monza. At the start of the race, both drivers were on equal points, heightening the tension between the pair. The world was watching.

Going into the race, Verstappen had taken pole with Hamilton in second after locking up at the hairpin in his qualifying lap. With both cars on the front row, the epic finale to a dramatic season was about to begin. Once the five red lights had gone out, Hamilton managed to jump Verstappen at the start of the race. Verstappen attempted to come back into turn 6 and managed to push Lewis wide over the run-off, but Hamilton drove through and kept the lead. The decision was met with some disbelief in the Red Bull camp, with Verstappen reported to have described the incident as 'incredible'.

Michael Masi, the FIA race director, had started in the role in 2019 after the tragic passing of Charlie Whiting, long-time race director and Formula One giant. Charlie, as he was known in the paddock, had started in Formula One as a mechanic with Hesketh in 1977. He went on to join the FIA under Max Mosley in 1988 as technical director, which turned into race director, where he ended up having all responsibility for F1 at the FIA. Charlie Whiting's role of race director was all-encompassing and expansive in recognition of his expertise and experience in the paddock. He combined this with a calm and warm manner which made him popular with the drivers. With a background in Australian motorsport, Michael Massi unexpectedly stepped up to fill Charlie's position after only a year as deputy director of racing for Formula One, Two and Three.

Back to the action on track, Verstappen switched from soft to hard tyres at the end of lap 13, and rejoined the track in fifth. Mercedes and Hamilton responded on lap 14, with Hamilton also switching his mediums to hard tyres and rejoining in second behind Red Bull's Sergio Perez. Ever the good teammate, Perez was asked to hold off Hamilton to give Verstappen time to climb through the ranks, leading to some exciting racing between Hamilton and Perez in laps 20 and 21. With Hamilton finally in the DRS range of Perez, he managed to get past on turn 6, but Perez maintained the racing line and led into the corner. Hamilton then utilized his better exit to lead into the next corner. Perez overtook Hamilton again on turn 9 and led into lap 21. However, Perez was not able to hold off the Brit forever; Hamilton got the better of Perez in turn 5 with a better exit into turn 6, giving Hamilton P1. By about 16 laps later, Hamilton's lead over Verstappen was up to 17 seconds and it looked like he would cruise home to his eighth World Championship title – a feat never achieved before.

In a moment that would turn the championship on its head, however, on lap 53 the backmarker, Nicholas Latifi driving for Williams, crashed at the exit of turn 14 and went into the barrier. With the car and debris littered across the track, the race was neutralized. As the safety car was deployed, Verstappen pitted and changed his hard tyres for softs, while Hamilton chose to stay on the hard tyres behind the safety car. With only five more laps to run, the Williams recovery took longer than expected, hampered in part by the brakes catching fire. By lap 56, the marshals were still clearing debris when the drivers were shown a message that lapped cars would not be allowed to overtake. This wasn't how things were normally done, and it caused confusion on the track and on the pit walls. Perez, who had been in third place, retired, with Hamilton in first and Verstappen in second, with four lapped cars between them.

By lap 57, and with the race nearly over, it was looking like it might finish under a safety car. The track was finally cleared and, in contradiction to the earlier message, the four lapped cars between Hamilton and Verstappen – but not the three lapped cars behind Verstappen – were told to overtake. As this was ongoing, both Red Bull and Mercedes were in conversation with Michael Masi. Race control then issued the order for the safety car to return to the pits at the end of the lap. At the start of lap 58, further messages were shared that the track was cleared, allowing green-flag racing conditions on the final lap. Michael Masi's decision to let only four unlapped cars pass the safety car led to an unprecedented single-lap shootout for the title.

On the final lap of the Grand Prix, with Verstappen on his fresher and faster soft tyres, he boldly overtook Hamilton on turn 5 to take race lead, launching his attack one corner before the traditional racing logic dictated. Hamilton attempted to fight back. After Verstappen went deep at turn 6, the battle continued. Within a mile of the championship to go, the top two were separated by three-thousandths of a second. Into turn 9 the title was sealed, Verstappen managed to maintain the lead and crossed the finish line ahead of Hamilton, winning his first World Championship in the process, to become the 34th World Champion.

The race was over, the recriminations started. Mercedes filed two protests to the race stewards over the interpretation of the

FIA rules. First, it was argued that Verstappen overtook Hamilton when the safety car was out on track, something that is strictly prohibited. The second protest focused on a break of 'Article 48.12 of the F1 Sporting Regulations'. This directly relates to the restart of a Grand Prix under green-flag racing conditions after a safety car. Article 48.12 states that, if safe, lapped cars 'can overtake the safety car and once the last lapped car has passed the leader, the safety car will return to pits at the end of the following lap.' Mercedes felt the rule had not been properly applied and that another lap was needed by the safety car to safely unlap all the cars and restart green-flag racing. This would have ended the race under the safety car. They sought an amendment to the race classification, with the idea that the race should be considered having ended at lap 57 as the green-flag racing at lap 58 should not have taken place.

Both teams were summoned to the stewards; the overtake under yellow flags was dismissed outright – Hamilton was still in P1 once racing had been green flagged. The second protest, more controversially, was also dismissed. This decision was based on a different article in the same F1 Sporting Regulations – in Article 15.3, it states that 'the Race Director controls the use of the safety car including its deployment and withdrawal'. In addition, the stewards argued that 48.12 had been applied fully as the safety car had returned to the pits with a clear message that 'Safety car in this lap' was fully shown to the drivers as mandated – as it was at the end of lap 57. The race result was maintained with Mercedes then going on to choose to appeal the results with a deadline of 16 December 2021, four days after the race. On 16 December, Mercedes chose to withdraw their appeal and the race results again were maintained.

With so much controversy over the interpretation of the FIA rules and the impact on the 2021 World Championship, the FIA chose to launch an investigation with three main findings.

The first key finding evaluated the roles and responsibilities of race director Michael Masi. The conclusion was that essentially the job encompassed too many varied roles and responsibilities that Charlie Whiting had taken up over the years. It was recommended that the high-pressured job be split and some responsibilities assigned to others to reduce the race director's workload. The aim was to allow them to focus on their key functions of managing and controlling the race.

The second finding focused on radio communications between the teams and the race director. Just prior to the restart of green-flag racing on the last lap, both the team principals of Red Bull and Mercedes spoke directly to Michael Masi. Only some of the conversations were broadcast live to the audience. This change to broadcasting the conversations was a new feature brought in for the 2021 season. In particular, the conversation between Christian Horner of Red Bull and Masi created significant public debate as Horner encouraged the race to be finished under green-flag racing, which would give his team a chance to overtake Hamilton's lead. However, in the findings, conversations between Mercedes and Masi, and Red Bull and Masi, were considered to have negatively impacted the final laps and distracted the race director during a time-pressured situation. Communications between the race director and the F1 teams were recommended to be restricted to allow the race director to perform their role without unnecessary disruption and distractions.

The final recommendation focused on the safety car and unlapping procedures to clarify this position for future races, as it was clear that the rules or articles involved were open to different interpretations. As part of the review, early meetings within Formula One had shown that the team preferred to end races under green-flag racing conditions if it was safe. Ultimately, it was decided that *all* cars had to unlap rather than *any*.

The investigation into the race found that the 'results were valid, final and could not be changed'. Michael Masi was found to have acted in 'good faith', but 'human error' played a part in not all the cars unlapping themselves as they should have been. While Red Bull won the Drivers' World Championship, Valtteri Bottas' sixth-place finish and Segio Perez's unseen DNF ensured Mercedes retained the Constructors' Championship for a record eighth year.

The 2021 Abu Dhabi race marked the end of Mercedes dominance of Formula One and ushered in another period of Red Bull dominance with Max Verstappen, who at the end of the 2024 season sits on four World Championships. With Mercedes struggling with the 2022 regulation changes over the preceding years, Lewis Hamilton announced a move to Ferrari for the start of the 2025 season to seek that elusive eighth World Championship. Michael Masi left the role at the FIA ahead of the start of the 2022 season and returned to Australian motor racing. The FIA race director role was split between two people: Niels Wittich and Eduardo Freitas; neither remain in post just three years later. Since Charlie Whiting's death in 2019 until time of writing in 2025, there have been four race directors.

74

Charles, Herve and Jules

His career was finished without the intervention of the late Jules Bianchi who said to Ferrari, 'You've got to take this guy, you've got to make sure he gets to Formula One.'

And what a gift that was to give. In 2017, Charles Leclerc lost his father, and in his final days he told his father a white lie. That he'd made it to Formula One; that he'd signed the contract.

It wasn't true then, but his driving has made it true now, and look what he's done with the opportunity. The grandstands he saw built as a kid growing up now rise for him, and for the first time in 93 years this fabled race is won by one of their own.

'Charles Leclerc wins the Monaco Grand Prix to achieve his dream!'

'Well done, Charles Leclerc! it's mission accomplished, destiny fulfilled, you've got that one for ever.'

On the final lap of the 2024 Monaco Grand Prix, I watched as a driver who I'd commentated on from the third tier achieved his childhood dream in the first. This is the long version of that last lap commentary.

Charles' father, Herve, had raced in Formula Three, finishing eighth in the Grand Prix support race before focusing on his family and in later years his son's junior racing career. While Monégasque citizenship tends to come with associations of great wealth and privilege, that is not Charles Leclerc's story. In a more unusual parenting choice, Herve had first taken his son go-karting at his very good friend's track after Charles had complained that he was too ill to go to school. That track was owned by Philippe Bianchi, the father of Jules Bianchi – Formula One driver and Charles' godfather.

Bianchi was a member of the young Ferrari Driver Academy and the rising star of French motorsport. He was expected to eventually drive for Ferrari and compete for World Championships. Only two seasons into his career, Bianchi suffered a devastating crash at the 2014 Japanese Grand Prix. He later died from head injuries sustained in the crash, dying at just twenty-five – the last Formula One driver to lose his life due to a Formula One accident. This had a significant impact on Charles and his peers in that cohort of young French/Monégasque drivers moving up the ranks. He was a hero to Esteban Ocon, Pierre Gasly and the late Anthoine Hubert.

For Charles, Jules was so instrumental to his future career. It was he who brought Charles Leclerc to his manager's attention while Charles was still in karts. That manager, Nicolas Todt, was the son of Jean Todt, who at various points in his career had been FIA president and Ferrari team principal. When Leclerc's family ran out of money to fund his career, Ferrari stepped in with Nicolas Todt to support. He later paid tribute to Jules on the 10-year anniversary of the accident by wearing a helmet in his godfather's team colours at the 2024 Japanese Grand Prix.

Just two years after Bianchi's death, tragedy struck the family again when Charles lost his father to illness in 2017. Just four days later, Leclerc was back in the car in Formula Two for the Azerbaijan Grand Prix. He put on an exhibition of driving that would have been impressive under any circumstances. Leclerc took pole position and won both races, including a reverse grid. In the sprint race, he came second due to a daft technicality around a yellow flag infringement in sector two.

But there was no denying what he'd produced in the face of heart-rending adversity, and the paddock knew it. The Sauber contract was signed a month later. Leclerc had made it happen. In a touching story, Charles admitted to telling his father a white lie before his death: that the contract was already signed and he was already a Formula One driver.

The mental fortitude and maturity Leclerc has consistently demonstrated in the face of tragedy is staggering but hard earnt: 'My mental strength was definitely a weakness back in the karting days, and I've worked hard on that to be as ready as possible for whenever I had the chance in F1. I feel like now it's probably my strength.' He further demonstrated this mental fortitude after winning his first Grand Prix the day after Anthoine Hubert died at the Belgium Grand Prix in 2019. Anthoine was a close friend of his – Leclerc earned pole and led the race from the start . He went on to lose track position to his teammate at Ferrari, Sebastian Vettel, during pit stops, but team orders reversed this, and Leclerc continued to lead the race, although he was challenged by Mercedes' Lewis Hamilton at the end. He held Hamilton off to secure his maiden victory at twenty-one, which he dedicated to Anthoine.

Given the tragedies that Leclerc has experienced, winning the fabled Monaco Grand Prix in a scarlet car with a prancing horse was the career goal – for himself, for Monaco, but also for his father, a long-time Ferrari fan. Leclerc came close, achieving poles in 2021 and 2022, but they had not translated to podiums, let alone wins. In 2024, Charles Leclerc achieved his third pole at Monaco, with McLaren's Oscar Piastri in P2 and teammate Carlos Sainz in P3.

The 2024 Monaco Grand Prix race day dawned, partly sunny with a light sea breeze. Charles Leclerc lined up on the grid and got a smooth getaway as the red lights went out. While Leclerc cleanly led from the front, Sergio Perez in his Red Bull was tapped by Kevin Magnussen and then ricocheted across the tight street circuit managing to hit Magnussen's Haas teammate, Nico Hulkenberg. Both Alpines also collided and the race was red flagged. The race was restarted and Leclerc once again avoided danger by getting his second clean getaway and holding the lead from Piastri, Sainz and McLaren's Lando Norris.

What unfolded was one of the dullest Monaco Grands Prix in the history of this great race. With the strategic element removed, Leclerc had a clear path to the destiny he always chased. In the commentary box, it had been such a muted race, I pondered not telling the full story. But after eight years of covering the journey and knowing that many casual fans would write off the man from Monaco as a son of privilege, I waited for the TV director Phil to show us the Ferrari. In the immediate aftermath of the race, speaking on the streets where he'd claimed victory, Leclerc spoke of welling up with a few laps to go. Even the winner was caught by surprise at the raw emotion of having fulfilled his family's dream.

Peering through tears to take a victory which meant so much.

75

Hamilton Moves to Ferrari

**Lewis Hamilton's McLaren slowly
understeered at Juncao, the final real corner
at the Autodrome in São Paulo.**

The wet weather genius scrubbed wide of the apex and watched on as Sebastian Vettel's Toro Rosso powered through to fifth place. Hamilton was about to lose the World Championship – if he finished sixth or lower, Ferrari's Felipe Massa would win the Drivers' Championship.

Hamilton had spent the whole 2008 Brazilian Grand Prix cautiously avoiding everyone, happily trundling around alone in fourth position, aiming to convert the year's hard work into the points he needed for the crown. Then the rain fell. With just nine laps remaining, this could change everything. At first it was light rain, then heavier, then enough to force a tyre change. The tension was rising to nauseating levels in the McLaren and Ferrari garages as they could only wait to see the outcome of the fight for the title.

Hamilton, the overnight superstar who had electrified F1 since his debut in Melbourne 2007, faced three long laps in the gloom. The headlines would read: 'Another title lost in São Paulo' – exactly what had happened at the same venue the year before. Tough to take, tough to explain. And then, when heartbreak seemed assured, he caught up with the car in front. It was a Toyota! A strategic gamble from the Japanese team had failed; they were on the wrong tyres. The red and white machine came into view at the very same corner where Hamilton himself had been overtaken three laps before.

'IS THAT GLOCK?' thundered Martin Brundle in the commentary box. It was, and Hamilton's torture was at an end. He was elevated back to fifth place as he easily passed Timo Glock's car. Felipe Massa's gallant drive to come first went unrewarded; Lewis Hamilton was the new world champion, with the title changing hands inside the final mile of the championship. It was Hamilton's first title, and at the time of writing Ferrari's last ...

Some 16 years later, a day of frenzied media speculation was settled by two lines: 'Scuderia Ferrari is pleased to announce that Lewis Hamilton will be joining the team in 2025, on a multi-year contract.' Hamilton had added six more titles in the intervening years, and Ferrari wanted his next to be with them. When you've secured one of the biggest F1 driver transfers in history, you don't have to embellish the hype in the press release. It wasn't quite as short as Michael Jordan's: 'I'm back' statement after he rejoined the Chicago Bulls, but the brevity told the story. Seven-time F1 world champion Lewis Hamilton was moving to Ferrari for the start of the 2025 season. It was a move reminiscent of the journey made by all-time greats Michael Schumacher and Juan Manuel Fangio in previous decades.

Ferrari has a history of choosing current world champions. In 1956, the team hired one of the best drivers of all time, the aforementioned Juan Manuel Fangio, for a single season, where he won his fourth of five world titles. Fangio was a happy mercenary – he was the best and simply went to whoever had the fastest car. In contrast, Michael Schumacher is the defining example of a world champion driver moving to Ferrari. He left Benetton after winning two World Championships and joined the Scuderia in 1996. The move was not without risk; the last time Ferrari had won a Drivers' Championship was with Jody Scheckter in 1979. The team had seriously floundered in the early 1990s, but this provided Michael with a fantastic opportunity. He was able to dictate terms, both financial and operational, to ultimately create the most successful team in the sport.

Schumacher brought key figures he trusted from Benetton: Ross Brawn as technical director and Rory Byrne as chief designer. This legacy-defining dream team transformed the fortunes of Ferrari, and Michael went on to win a further five driver titles, breaking Fangio's long-standing record. Unlike Schumacher, Hamilton would have none of his old guard from Mercedes with him, but he did have a connection with Ferrari Team Principal Fred Vasseur that dated to his 2006 GP2 season, where he arguably had some of the greatest and most aggressive races of his career.

On the day of the announcement, there were many at the Mercedes team factory openly mocking the rumours. Hamilton leaving seemed unthinkable, but the year before he'd only been offered a 'one plus one' contract, with opt-out clauses at the one-year marker, and it was widely reported that he was looking for a three-year deal. Hamilton had also been considering the competitiveness of the Mercedes car. During 2022 and 2023, Mercedes had slipped in performance against Red Bull after the ground effect technical rule changes, and Hamilton had publicly spoken against the team ignoring his input on design fixes.

It's not unprecedented for the most titled driver on the grid to move to Ferrari, but it is unusual. In what Hamilton described as 'one of the hardest decisions I have ever had to make', he left the Mercedes team that he had raced with since 2013. Mercedes would replace Hamilton with a young rookie from Formula Two: Kimi Antonelli. CEO Toto Wolff appeared completely certain of Antonelli's early F1 promotion; the young driver had an impressive early racing career, having won both the Italian and German Formula Four titles, plus the FRECA Championship (formerly Formula Renault). In key moments, he has shown remarkable skill, including at Zandvoort, where he went from eighth to the lead in three laps. Having displayed such incredible touch and control, Mercedes had decided to move Kimi straight to Formula Two in 2024, skipping Formula Three in a highly unusual step for any driver. Perhaps driving the speed of the promotion were events back in 2014; Wolff has always seemed irked by missing out on a young Max Verstappen.

As Hamilton said farewell to Mercedes in Abu Dhabi in 2024, Ferrari were resurgent. The Italian team finished just 14 points off the championship-winning total set by McLaren. Bullishly, Ferrari stated that its 2025 car would be 95 per cent new, while most of the grid would rely on updated 2024 cars. It was a clear attempt to end their longest ever title drought, which now stretched to 17 years.

At the time of writing, Hamilton has endured a mixed start behind the wheel at Formula One's most famous team. The highlight being a brilliant sprint pole and sprint victory in Shanghai, a circuit Hamilton has won on for McLaren, Mercedes and Ferrari in his storied F1 career.

If he can succeed with Ferrari, it could provide one of Formula One's greatest stories – but if it doesn't all go to plan, while disappointing, it will still be the fulfilment of every go-karter's dream. The battle to win with Ferrari is one of sport's defining challenges, and as these pages have shown, the allure of driving for Ferrari in F1 is a story as old as the championship itself.

Picture Credits

The publishers would like to thank the following sources for their kind permission to reproduce the pictures in this book.

Plate section 1 photographs in order of appearance:

1) Keystone/Hulton Archive/Getty Images, 2) Sutton Motorsports/ZUMA Press/Alamy Stock Photo, 3) Bernard Cahier/Getty Images, 4) Bernard Cahier/Getty Images, 5) Associated Press/Alamy Stock Photo, 6) GP Library/Universal Images Group via Getty Image, 7) Bernard Cahier/Getty Images, 8) Sutton Motorsports/ZUMA Press/Alamy Stock Photo, 9) AllsportUK/Getty Images, 10) Sergio del Grande/Mondadori Portfolio/Mondadori via Getty Images, 11) Keystone Press/Alamy Stock Photo, 12-13) Bernard Cahier/Getty Images, 14) GP Library Limited/Alamy Stock Photo, 15-18) Sutton Motorsports/ZUMA Press, 19) Sutton Motorsports/ZUMA Press/Alamy Stock Photo

Plate section 2 photographs in order of appearance:

1) Paul-Henri Cahier/Getty Images, 2) Andreas Rentz/Bongarts/Getty Images, 3) Emmanuel Dunand/AFP via Getty Images, 4) Andreas Rentz/Bongarts/Getty Images, 5) Patrik Stollarz/AFP via Getty Images, 6) Formula 1/Formula Motorsport Limited via Getty Images, 7) Darren Heath/Getty Images, 8) Bertrand Guay/AFP via Getty Images, 9) Jasper Juinen/Getty Images, 10) Clive Mason/Getty Images, 11) Sutton Motorsports/ZUMA Press/Alamy Stock Photo, 12-13) Clive Mason/Getty Images, 14) Darren Heath/Getty Images, 15) Mark Thompson/Getty Images, 16) DPPI Media/Alamy Stock Photo, 17) Lars Baron/Getty Images, 18) Joe Portlock - Formula 1/Formula 1 via Getty Images, 19) Mark Thompson/Getty Images, 20) APA-PictureDesk/Alamy Stock Photo

Every effort has been made to acknowledge correctly and contact the source and/or copyright holder of each picture, and the publisher apologises for any unintentional errors or omissions, which will be corrected in future editions of this book.

Index

A
Alesi, Giovanni 'Jean' 153–6, 208
Alfa Romeo team and cars 13, 20, 21, 30, 51, 127
Alonso, Fernando 171, 216, 219, 222, 223, 224, 237–40, 244, 254–5, 261
Alpha Tauri team and cars 295
Alpine team and cars 103, 292, 310
Amon, Chris 67, 68, 69
Andretti, Mario 63, 67, 68, 69, 86, 98–9, 111–13, 130, 237
Antonelli, Kimi 276, 314
Arnoux, René 104–5, 118, 121
Arrows team and cars 128, 187, 188–91
ATS team and cars 122–3, 127
Australian Grand Prix (1986) 140–44

B
Balestre, Jean-Marie 21, 126, 127, 128, 148–9, 150, 152
bargeboards controversy, Ferrari 201–2
Barnard, John 115–18, 188
Barrichello, Rubens 108, 109, 168–9, 199, 207–9, 213, 214–17
Benetton team 140, 148, 160–62, 163, 165, 170, 173–6, 192, 194, 197, 207, 294, 313
Berger, Gerhard 140, 146
Bianchi, Jules 82, 308, 309
BMW teams and cars 74, 181, 205, 266
  Sauber team and cars 241–2, 246, 249, 250
Bottas, Valtteri 215, 266, 285, 298, 299, 307
Brabham, Jack 15–17, 46, 68, 72, 143
Brabham team and cars 19–20, 61, 68–9, 71–3, 88–9, 93, 136
fan car 111–14
Brawn GP team and cars 235, 251–2, 253, 257
Brawn, Ross 130, 132–3, 202, 208–9, 214, 215, 235, 249–52, 258–9, 314
Briatore, Flavio 160–61, 227, 232
Bridgestone tyres 189, 222, 226, 228–9, 254–6
BRM 27, 41–2, 49, 221
Brown, Zak 290–91
Brundle, Martin 25, 109, 167, 198
Burns, Richard 110
Button, Jenson 203–5, 219, 223, 231, 235, 248, 251, 254–5

C
carbon-fibre car, John Barnard's 115–18
Chapman, Colin 20, 48–50, 52–5, 58–9, 60–63, 111, 126, 130, 134, 220–21
Clark, Jim 46, 50, 51, 54–5, 56–9, 220, 221
Collins, Peter 31, 34, 136
Constructors' Championships 29–33, 52, 54, 62–3, 69
Cooper team and cars 17, 36, 34–6, 72
cost cap introduced (2021), F1 289–90, 291–2
Costin, Mike 49, 51, 53
Cosworth DFV engine, Ford 48–51, 55, 79, 117
Coulthard, David 9, 132, 133, 181, 190, 193, 196–7, 198, 207, 208, 226, 229, 234, 300

D
DeLorean, John 52, 63
Dennis, Ron 17, 71–5, 115–18, 133, 148, 162, 180, 202, 207, 224, 237–40
Depailler, Patrick 85, 86, 99
Diniz, Pedro 197, 208
Drive To Survive (Netflix docudrama) 286–8, 296
Duckworth, Keith 49, 50, 51

E
Ecclestone, Bernie 17, 18–21, 61, 70, 98, 106–7, 108, 111, 113, 114, 127, 135–6, 163, 170, 175, 228, 232, 256, 269–70, 286
Eddie Jordan Racing 157–9, 160–61, 162

F
F1 Academy 89–90
Fangio, Juan Manuel 14, 27, 35, 39–40, 47, 272, 312–13
Farina, Giuseppe 'Nino' 14
Ferrari, Enzo 26–8, 94, 100–101, 119, 121–2, 141, 145, 218, 221, 274
Ferrari team and cars 21, 26–8, 29, 30, 31–2, 34–8, 49, 50, 51, 65, 68, 80, 92, 93–5, 97–8, 100, 104–5, 117, 131, 132–3, 140–41, 146, 154, 155–6, 196, 198–9, 201–2, 208–9, 221, 229, 244, 250–51, 253, 254, 258, 261, 264, 274, 280, 281, 285, 287, 290, 291, 298, 300
  Charles Leclerc 310–311
  Lewis Hamilton joins 307, 312–15
  Michael Schumacher 176–8, 186, 189, 190, 192, 193–5, 196, 200–201, 202, 207, 211–12, 213–17, 218–19, 222, 229, 237, 313–14
  new tyre rule (2005) 222, 224, 228, 229
  Prost and Senna in Japan Grand Prix (1990) 150–52
  team order farce Austrian Grand Prix (2002) 213–16

Valentino Rossi 218–20
Villeneuve and Pironi fallout and tragedy 119–24
FIA (Fédération Internationale de l'Automobile) 13, 20, 21, 30, 48, 70, 126, 148–9, 152, 170–71, 195, 202, 207, 219, 224, 225, 226, 228, 235, 238, 252, 269, 294, 296, 302–3, 305–6, 307
Fisichella, Giancarlo 198, 207
Fittipaldi, Emerson 32, 93
Fittipaldi team and cars 129–30
Ford 58, 78, 165, 199
of Britain 49–51
Formula Ford 69, 77, 167
Formula One Constructors' Association (FOCA) 20–21, 113, 127
Formula One World Constructors' Championship 29–33, 52, 54, 62–3, 69, 75, 80, 113, 129, 131, 132, 137, 144, 186, 252, 258, 265, 266, 272, 292, 307, 315
Formula One World Drivers' Championship 14, 29, 32–3, 50, 52, 54, 75, 80, 99–100, 113, 124, 129, 131, 132, 133, 136, 137, 168, 173, 221, 247, 258, 264, 265, 266, 272, 283, 304, 307, 312–13
Formula Renault 231–2
Formula Three 67, 69, 74, 77–8, 115, 167–8, 181–2, 204, 231, 232, 275, 308, 314
Formula Two 19, 26–7, 35, 50, 55, 57, 58, 69, 73–4, 78–9, 115, 117, 136, 182, 204, 233, 309–10, 314
Frankenheimer, John 44–7
Frentzen, Heinz-Harald 24, 176–7, 184, 186, 187, 190–91, 196–7, 198, 208

G
Gachot, Bertrand 157–8
Gardner, Derek 84–5, 86
Giacomelli, Bruno 127, 128
Goodyear tyres 85, 86, 143, 189, 190

Gordon Bennett Cup 13
GP2 232–3, 237, 276
Grand Prix Drivers' Association (GDPA) 126, 171
Grosjean, Romain 293–6
Grouille, Nat 286–7

H
Haas team and cars 296, 310
Lola team and cars 130
Häkkinen, Mika 24, 32, 109, 132, 181, 190, 192, 193–4, 196–8, 199, 201, 202, 207–8, 274
greatest overtake of all time – Belgian Grand Prix (2000) 210–212
Hamilton, Lewis 28, 32–3, 171, 180–83, 233, 237, 238–40, 242–3, 246, 254–6, 270–72, 280–81, 284–5, 297–301, 302–5, 306, 310
joins Ferrari (2025) 307, 312–15
joins Mercedes (2013) 257–60
Haug, Norbert 208
Hawthorn, Mike 31, 36, 37–8
Hayes, Walter 49–50
Head, Patrick 32, 131, 132, 135, 137, 139, 140, 143, 144, 181, 185, 266, 267, 268
Hercules Aerospace 116–17, 118
Hesketh Racing team and cars 77–80, 303
Hesketh, Thomas Alexander Fermor-Hesketh, Lord 76, 77–80
Hill, Damon 23, 106, 132, 155–6, 157, 163, 173–6, 184–7, 188–91, 197, 284
Hill, Graham 42, 46, 50, 57, 58, 60, 73, 74, 115, 221
Hill team and cars 89, 115
Honda engines 144, 146
Honda Formula One team and cars 205, 217, 219, 235, 248–51
Horner, Christian 228, 234–5, 262–3, 266, 299, 306

Horsley, Anthony 'Bubbles' 76, 77–9, 80
Howard, Ron 47
Hulkenberg, Nico 258, 310
Hulme, Denny 68, 69, 79
Hunt, James 23, 25, 47, 66, 76–80, 92, 95–6, 97–8, 119
Japanese Grand Prix (1976) 99–100

I
Indianapolis 500 14, 30, 51, 52, 85
IndyCar 14, 69, 115, 130, 176
Irvine, Eddie 196, 198, 199, 201, 202, 217

J
Japanese Grand Prix (1976), first-ever 98–101
Jordan, Eddie 157–9, 160–61, 197
Jordan Racing team and cars 157–9, 160–61, 187, 196, 198, 208, 209, 214, 229, 230
Junqueira, Bruno 204–5, 231

K
kidnap of Juan Manuel Fangio 39–40
Kovalainen, Heikki 233, 245, 246
Kubica, Robert 241–4, 246, 251, 254
Kumpen, Sophie 273, 279
Kvyat, Daniil 274, 280, 295

L
Latifi, Nicholas 303–4
Lauda, Niki 27, 47, 70, 78, 80, 106, 112, 113, 150, 171, 242, 258–9, 260–61
driver's strike (1982) 125–8
drops out of Japanese Grand Prix 97–101
Nürburgring crash and recovery 91–6
Le Mans 24 Hours race 13, 51, 53, 82, 120, 221, 244, 274
Leclerc, Charles 125, 298, 299–300, 308–11

Leclerc, Herve 308–9, 310
Lewis-Evans, Stuart 18–19
Leyton House Racing 130–31
Lombardi, Maria Grazia 'Lella' 88–9
Lotus team and cars 19, 31, 48–9, 50, 52–5, 56–9, 60–63, 64–5, 85, 111–14, 115, 126–7, 130, 134, 141, 145, 168, 170, 220–21, 261, 271

M
McLaren, Bruce 32, 46–7, 75
McLaren Racing team and cars 29, 32–3, 50, 68, 69, 75, 79, 80, 82, 95, 97–8, 100, 112, 117, 132–3, 141–2, 154, 180–83, 187, 189, 190, 192–4, 195, 196–8, 199, 201, 202, 207–8, 214, 222–4, 226, 237, 250, 253, 291, 292, 300
  Ferrari and 'Spygate' 238, 240
  Hakkinen at the Belgian Grand Prix (2000) 210–212
  Lewis Hamilton 237–40, 254–6, 257–9
  Project 4/1 carbon-fibre car 115–18
  Senna and Prost in Japan Grand Prix (1989) 145–9
  Senna and Prost in Japan Grand Prix (1990) 150–52
  Senna at Donnington Park (1993) 163–6
  warring teammates – Alonso and Hamilton 237–40
McQueen, Steve 44–6, 47
Mansell, Nigel 23, 24, 131, 134, 135, 139, 140–44, 154, 155–6, 163, 175, 185
March Engineering team and cars 61, 67–70, 74, 77, 78–9, 89, 129
Marko, Helmut 263, 275, 276–7
Maserati 35–6, 39, 49, 88
Masi, Michael 302–3, 304, 306–7
Mass, Jochen 122, 126
Massa, Felipe 216, 219, 246, 266, 274

Mateschitz, Dietrich 234, 264, 276
Mayer, Teddy 20, 100, 130
Mercedes engines 250–51, 269–70
Mercedes factory employee protest 206–7, 208, 209
Mercedes team and cars 13, 83, 157, 182, 206–7, 208, 215, 253, 257, 266, 267, 269–72, 276, 279–81, 287, 290, 291, 297, 304–5, 310, 312–15
  Lewis Hamilton 257–60, 270–72, 279–81, 284–5, 297–301, 302–5, 306
  Nico Rosberg 270–72, 276, 279–81, 283–5
Mercedes young driver programme 158, 161
Michelin tyres 13, 226–30
Minardi team and cars 199, 228, 229, 230, 246
di Montezemolo, Luca 201, 219, 269
Montoya, Juan Pablo 203, 213, 224, 226, 266
Mosley, Max 20, 21, 67, 70, 77, 78, 79, 108–9, 152, 170–71, 202, 224, 228, 230, 240, 303
Moss, Stirling 26–8, 31, 34–8, 45–6, 54
Murray, Gordon 19, 111–14
Murray Walker, Graham 22–5, 65–6, 143, 147, 151, 176, 190, 194, 199, 207, 209

N
new tyre rule introduced (2005) 222–4, 225–30
Newey, Adrian 70, 129–33, 156, 177, 185, 186, 189, 192–3, 201–2, 234–6, 247, 266, 269
Norris, Lando 182–3, 300
Nürburgring European Grand Prix (1999) 196–9

O
Oatley, Neil 130, 132
Ocon, Esteban 275, 309

P
Perez, Sergio 256, 303, 307, 310
Peterson, Ronnie 62, 67, 69, 78, 93, 107
Piastri, Oscar 310
Piccinini, Marco 120
Piquet, Nelson 20, 117, 134, 135, 136, 139, 140, 141–3, 185
Pirelli tyres 243, 256, 261
Pironi, Didier 109, 119–25, 126, 128
Porsche team 88
Postlethwaite, Dr Harvey 79, 80, 129
Project 34 – six-wheeler car 84–7
Project Four Racing 74–5, 115–17
Prost, Alain 32, 117, 121, 123, 128, 131, 141–4, 145–9, 150–52, 155, 156, 163, 164–5, 168, 185, 204, 237, 285
Prost team and cars 189, 199, 208

R
Race of Champions 68–9, 79, 80, 233
Räikkönen, Kimi 222–4, 231, 261, 281–2, 285
Ratzenberger, Roland 108, 169, 171
Red Bull Racing team and cars 33, 133, 199, 226, 234–6, 247, 253, 254, 261–4, 276–7, 290, 291, 292, 297, 306–7, 310
  Max Verstappen 273–7, 279–82, 297–9, 301, 302–5, 307
  Toro Rosso team 219, 235, 245–7, 257, 273–6, 280, 281
  see also Toro Rosso
Renault engines 266
Renault team and cars 13, 21, 51, 102–5, 117–18, 120, 121, 219, 222, 227, 237, 241, 242, 254
Reutemann, Carlos 93–4, 95, 128
Ricciardo, Daniel 264, 276, 280, 281, 287

Rindt, Jochen 19, 46–7, 61–2, 68, 72
Roberts, Dr Ian 110, 294, 295–6
Rosberg, Keke 127, 137, 141–3, 233
Rosberg, Nico 233, 257, 270–72, 276, 279–81, 283–5
Rossi, Valentino 218–20
Rushen Green Racing 167

S
safety and medical care, F1 42–3, 81–3, 91–2, 106–10, 170–72, 224, 225–8, 294–6
safety cars, introduction of 81–3
Sainz, Carlos 281, 300, 310
Sauber team and cars 187, 197, 208, 223, 231, 271, 309–10 *see also under* BMW
Scheckter, Jody 79, 82, 85, 86, 121, 313
Schonberg, Johnny 15–16
Schumacher, Michael 23, 132, 156, 158–9, 160–62, 163, 170, 171, 173–9, 184, 186, 189, 190, 192, 193–5, 196, 200–201, 202, 207, 211–12, 213–17, 218–19, 222, 225, 229, 231, 233, 237, 313–14
Schumacher, Ralf 196–8, 213–14, 225, 266
Senna, Ayrton 23, 32, 108–9, 131–2, 141, 145–9, 150–52, 153, 154, 155, 156, 162–5, 209, 237, 242–3
death of (1994) 167–72
Servoz-Gavin, Johnny 67, 68
Sforza, Antonio Brivio 14
Siffert, Jo 67, 68, 69
Silverstone 14, 22–3
six-wheeler car — Project 34, Tyrrell 84–7
sponsorship 60, 64–6
sprint races, F1 297–8
Steiner, Guenther 287
Stewart Grand Prix team and cars 187, 199, 209
Stewart, Jackie 41–3, 46, 47, 57–8, 61, 67–9, 106, 199

Surtees, John 66, 218, 220–21
Surtees team and cars 65–6, 79, 99, 112, 221

T
Todt, Jean 133, 178, 202, 214, 216, 258, 269, 275, 309
Toro Rosso team *see under* Red Bull Racing
Toyota team and cars 225–6, 227, 241, 250
Trulli, Jarno 199, 208, 223, 227, 241
turbocharged engine, first 102–5
'26th of July Movement', Cuban rebels 39–40
Tyrrell, Ken 20, 84, 220
Tyrrell team and cars 51, 67–8, 69, 80, 82, 84–7, 112, 120, 153–4, 155

U
United States Grand Prix (2005) 225–30

V
Vanwall team 19, 31, 34–5, 37, 53–4
Vasseur, Fred 313
Verstappen, Jos 273, 275, 278–9, 294
Verstappen, Max 33, 195, 273–7, 278–80, 281–2, 297–9, 301, 302–5, 307, 315
Vettel, Sebastian 235, 236, 245–7, 250, 254–5, 261–4, 274, 276, 280, 281–2, 285, 310, 312
Villeneuve, Gilles 104–5, 117, 119–25, 127–8, 188–9, 191, 223
Villeneuve, Jacques 66, 156, 176–8, 185, 190, 241, 266, 275
virtual safety cars 81–2

W
Watkins, Professor Eric Sidney 'Sid' 106–10, 135–6, 137–8, 168–9, 170, 171
Watson, John 111–12, 117–18, 215

Webber, Mark 179, 223, 254–5, 261–4
Whiting, Charlie 226, 228, 302–3, 307
Whitmarsh, Martin 133, 181, 240
Williams, Claire 265–8
Williams, Frank 20, 32, 109, 132, 134–9, 153–5, 181, 184, 185, 186, 204, 231, 265–6, 267, 268
Williams, Ginny 134, 135–6, 137–9
Williams Grand Prix Engineering team and cars 29, 32, 51, 69, 112, 127, 128, 131–2, 134–9, 153–5, 163, 165, 173–8, 189, 190–91, 197, 198–9, 203–4, 213–14, 231, 233, 244, 265–8, 291, 292, 303–4
Australian Grand Prix (1986) 140–44
death of Ayrton Senna (1994) 168–72
Jenson Button wins contract shootout (2000) 203–5
sacking Damon Hill (1996) 184–7
Wolff, Susie 89
Wolff, Toto 266–7, 269, 275–6, 284, 313–14
women competitors, F1 88–90